FUNDING, POWE
COMMUNITY DEVEL

FUNDING, POWER AND COMMUNITY DEVELOPMENT

Edited by
Niamh McCrea and Fergal Finnegan

Rethinking
Community
Development

First published in Great Britain in 2019 by

Policy Press
University of Bristol
1-9 Old Park Hill
Bristol
BS2 8BB
UK
t: +44 (0)117 954 5940
pp-info@bristol.ac.uk
www.policypress.co.uk

North America office:
Policy Press
c/o The University of Chicago Press
1427 East 60th Street
Chicago, IL 60637, USA
t: +1 773 702 7700
f: +1 773-702-9756
sales@press.uchicago.edu
www.press.uchicago.edu

British Library Cataloguing in Publication Data
A catalogue record for this book is available from the British Library

Library of Congress Cataloging-in-Publication Data
A catalog record for this book has been requested

978-1-4473-3615-0 hardback
978-1-4473-3617-4 paperback
978-1-4473-3616-7 ePdf
978-1-4473-3618-1 ePub
978-1-4473-3619-8 Mobi

Cover design by Liam Roberts
Front cover image: Ian Martin
Printed and bound in Great Britain by CMP, Poole
Policy Press uses environmentally responsible print partners

Contents

Rethinking Community Development

Communities are a continuing focus of public policy and citizen action worldwide. The purposes and functions of work with communities of place, interest and identity vary between and within contexts and change over time. Nevertheless, community development – as both an occupation and as a democratic practice concerned with the demands and aspirations of people in communities – has been extraordinarily enduring.

This book series aims to provide a critical re-evaluation of community development in theory and practice, in the light of new challenges posed by the complex interplay of emancipatory, democratic, self-help and managerial imperatives in different parts of the world. Through a series of edited and authored volumes, *Rethinking Community Development* will draw together international, cross-generational and cross-disciplinary perspectives, using contextual specificity as a lens through which to explore the localised consequences of global processes. Each text in the series will:

- *promote critical thinking*, through examining the contradictory position of community development, including the tensions between policy imperatives and the interests and demands of communities.
- *include a range of international examples*, in order to explore the localised consequences of global processes.
- *include contributions from established and up-and-coming new voices*, from a range of geographical contexts.
- *offer topical and timely perspectives*, drawing on historical and theoretical resources in a generative and enlivening way.
- *inform and engage a new generation of practitioners*, bringing new and established voices together to stimulate diverse and innovative perspectives on community development.

If you have a broad or particular interest in community development that could be expanded into an authored or edited collection for this book series, contact:

Mae Shaw   Rosie R. Meade   Sarah Banks
mae.shaw@ed.ac.uk   r.meade@ucc.ie   s.j.banks@durham.ac.uk

Acknowledgements

We would like to thank all the contributors to the book for their hard work and commitment to the project. We are also grateful to the series editors, Mae Shaw, Rosie R. Meade and Sarah Banks for their encouragement. Thank you also to our peer reviewers for their very helpful and constructive comments. For assistance is securing contributors, we would like to thank Paddy Reilly, Collette O'Regan and Sue Kenny. We would also like to express our gratitude to Marie Moran, Mick Byrne and all our other colleagues in the critical political economy cluster at UCD. A heartfelt thank you too to Ramor Dagge, Alan Grossman and Sheila Long for their support for this project.

Fergal would particularly like to thank Paul Bowman, Oisín Gilmore and Aidan Regan for sharing material on financialisation. He also wishes to express his gratitude to his ever helpful and supportive colleagues in the Department of Adult and Community Education, Maynooth University. For intellectual and other forms of support and inspiration he wishes to thank Maya Finnegan, Ania Zajko, Mark Malone, Caoimhe Kerins and Fin Dwyer. Niamh would also like to thank John Baker for his many insights and ongoing support.

An earlier and shorter version of the material in Chapter Four by Gagyi and Ivancheva was published as 'The rise and fall of civil society in Central Europe' in M. Moskalewicz and Wojciech Przybylski (eds) *Understanding Central Europe* (Routledge 2018).

Some of the material in Chapter Ten by Thapa was published in 'Tewa – Doing the impossible, feminist action in Nepal: The founder's story' which is available at: www.oise.utoronto.ca/cwse/UserFiles/File/DoingTheImpossible.pdf.

Abbreviations

AKP	Adalet ve Kalkınma Partisi (Justice and Development Party)
ANC	African National Congress
BHPB	BHP Billiton
CBO	community-based organisation
CDFI	community development finance institutions
CHP	Cumhuriyet Halk Partisi (Republican People's Party)
COP	Community Organisers Programme
CSR	corporate social responsibility
DTK	Demokratik Toplum Kongresi (Democratic Society Congress)
EU	European Union
FIFO	fly-in, fly-out
GFW	Global Fund for Women
ICMM	International Council on Mining and Metals
ILO	International Labour Organization
IMF	International Monetary Fund
KCK	Koma Civaken Kurdistan (Union of Communities of Kurdistan)
M&E	monitoring and evaluation
MoU	memorandum of understanding
MST	Movimento dos Trabalhadores Rurais Sem Terra (Landless Workers' Movement)
MUIP	multi-user infrastructure package
NATO	North Atlantic Treaty Organization
NGO	non-governmental organisation
PKK	Partiya Karkerên Kurdistanê (Kurdistan Workers' Party)
RNO	Ravensthorpe Nickel Operation
SII	social impact investment
SSE	social and solidarity economy
TNC	transnational corporation
UN	United Nations
UNICEF	United Nations Children's Fund
UNIFEM	United Nations Development Fund for Women
USAID	United States Agency for International Development

Notes on contributors

Hélène Balazard is a French researcher in political science specialising in community organising in the UK and France. She is currently researching citizen empowerment and collective mobilisations against discriminations. After a postdoctoral position at the University of Lille 2 (CERAPS) and a visiting fellowship at Queen Mary University of London, she now holds a permanent position at the University of Lyon (ENTPE).

Lin Bender is CEO of the Helen Macpherson Smith Trust in Victoria, Australia. She began her career as a photographer and graphic designer, before establishing a number of social enterprises. A series of senior management roles in the not-for-profit sector followed, across operations and marketing to strategic business development, as well as CEO positions.

Fergal Finnegan became interested in issues of community development and equality through his work as a community educator in Dublin. He is now a lecturer at the Department of Adult and Community Education, Maynooth University where he is a co-director of the Doctorate in Higher and Adult Education programme. His research interests include social movements, popular education, biographical research, social class and equality and higher education.

Robert Fisher is professor and chair of Community Organizing, University of Connecticut, US. He is the author and co-author of numerous books on community organising, including *Let the people decide: Neighborhood organizing in America*, which was recently translated into Chinese, and *Contesting community: The limits and potential of local organizing*.

Ulrike Flader is lecturer in Anthropology and Cultural Research at the University of Bremen and founding member of DEMOS Research Centre for Peace, Democracy and Alternative Politics in Ankara. She holds a PhD from Manchester University and has worked in and on Turkey for many years. Her research centres on questions of citizenship, governmentality, political subjectivity, everyday resistance and social movements. Her most recent ethnographic work focuses on everyday resistance among the Kurdish population in Turkey.

Agnes Gagyi specialises in social movements, focusing on connections between politics and social movements in Central and Eastern Europe, and the social, economic and geopolitical aspects of the region's long-term world market integration. She is a researcher at the Department of Sociology and Work Science, University of Gothenburg, and member of the Budapest-based Working Group for Public Sociology 'Helyzet'.

Niamh Goggin has worked in social investment in the UK, Ireland and internationally since 1994. She was a member of the UK Alternative Commission on Social Investment and has researched the experience of charities in making and receiving social investments. Publications include *Charities and social investment: A research report for the Charity Commission in England and Wales* (IVAR, 2013).

Çetin Gürer is Philipp Schwartz Fellow of the Humboldt Foundation, currently working at the Centre for Labour and Politics at the University of Bremen. He studied Sociology and Political Science at the University of Hamburg and holds a PhD from the University of Ankara. He works on questions of minority rights and representation, specifically on territorial and non-territorial autonomy and the Kurdish Movement. He is author of *Democratic autonomy as a heterotopia of citizenship*, published in Turkish by Notabene in 2015.

Mariya Ivancheva is an anthropologist and sociologist. Her doctoral dissertation (CEU, 2013) explored ethnographically the development of the Bolivarian University of Venezuela. Since then she has worked as a postdoctoral research fellow on projects exploring housing in (post)socialist Sofia and Caracas (CAS, Sofia 2014), the casualisation of labour in post-crisis academia (UCD, 2014–17), and the impact of digital technologies and marketisation processes on inequalities in the South African and UK higher education sectors (University of Leeds 2017–18). Mariya has published widely on the legacy of socialist regimes, and the role of academic intellectuals and universities in processes of social change. She is a member of the editorial board of the web-portal for comments and analyses on Eastern Europe, 'LeftEast'.

Erica Kohl-Arenas currently serves as the faculty director of 'Imagining America: Artists and Scholars in Public Life', at the University of California, Davis, where she is also an associate professor in the Department of American Studies. Previously, she was an assistant professor at the Milano School of International Affairs, Management, and Urban Policy at The New School where she received university awards in Outstanding Achievements in Diversity and Social Justice Teaching and the Distinguished University Teacher Award. Kohl-Arenas is the author of *The self-help myth: How philanthropy fails to alleviate poverty* (2016) which investigates the relationship between private foundations and immigrant and farmworker organising. Prior to her graduate studies, Kohl-Arenas worked as a popular educator and community development practitioner in a variety of settings including urban public schools, immigrant not-for-profit organisations and rural communities in Appalachia, Scotland and Wales.

Sarasij Majumder is associate professor of Anthropology and Interdisciplinary Studies at the Department of Geography and Anthropology, Kennesaw State University. Born and raised in Calcutta, India, he received his PhD from Rutgers University. He previously worked as a consultant for a World Bank project on health among the urban poor in Delhi. His doctoral research focused on the politics of land acquisition in India. He was awarded an American Institute of Indian Studies fellowship and United States National Science Foundation Doctoral Improvement Grant for his doctoral research in West Bengal, India. He has published widely on this and related topics.

Japhet Makongo is a development consultant based in Tanzania. He began his career as a field extension officer in the Department of Livestock and Agriculture. Between 1990 and 1993 he worked on flood and irrigation projects, funded by the International Labour Organisation (ILO), then becoming a trainer in community and rural development at the Training for Community Development Centre in the Monduli district of the Arusha region in Tanzania. He has also worked for HakiElimu, a national advocacy organisation promoting equitable and quality education for all children in 2002.

Robyn Mayes is associate professor at the QUT Business School, Queensland University of Technology, Brisbane, Australia. Her interdisciplinary research draws on critical approaches in human/cultural and feminist geography, sociology and cultural studies to elucidate crucial contemporary intersections of (transnational) business and society. She has published widely on topics such as mobile/migrant labour, global production networks and corporate social responsibility, digital platforms and new social movements. This work is grounded through sustained critical attention to everyday experiences in local communities and workplaces, and through ongoing empirical work on the social and cultural impacts of the Australian mining industry.

Niamh McCrea is a lecturer at the Department of Humanities, Institute of Technology Carlow, Ireland where she teaches in the areas of youth work, community development and adult education, with a particular focus on equality studies. She previously worked, in a paid or voluntary capacity, in the field of development education, community education and youth work and has co-written a number of development education practice resources. She has researched and published in the area of community development and venture philanthropy, and inclusive youth work. She is a member of the editorial board of the *Community Development Journal*.

Natascha Mueller-Hirth is Lecturer in Sociology at Robert Gordon University in Aberdeen. Her research utilises qualitative, often ethnographic methodologies, to examine issues around peace, conflict, development and gender in South Africa and in Kenya. She has published on time and temporality in transitional societies, NGOs and civil society, the governance of development and corporate social responsibility. She is co-editor of *Time and temporality in transitional and post-conflict societies* (2018) and co-author of *The sociology of everyday life peacebuilding* (2018).

Brendan Murtagh is a reader in urban planning in the Natural and Built Environment at the Queen's University Belfast. He has researched and written widely on social economics, community development and urban regeneration including a recent book *Social economics and the solidarity city* (Routledge, 2019).

Debarati Sen is associate professor of Anthropology and Conflict Management at the Department of Geography and Anthropology, Kennesaw State University. Born in India, she holds a PhD from Rutgers University. Debarati is a dedicated advocate of women's voices in academe and beyond. Her research explores gendered mobilisations around development in rural India and she has published widely on this and other topics. Her publications include *Everyday sustainability: Gender justice and fair trade tea in Darjeeling* (SUNY Press, 2017).

Marcelo Lopes de Souza is professor of Socio-spatial Development and Political Ecology at the Department of Geography of the Federal University of Rio de Janeiro/UFRJ. He pioneered the study of spatiality and the social production of space from an 'autonomist' perspective (mainly inspired by the work of Cornelius Castoriadis) from as early as the 1980s. He has published 11 books and more than 100 papers and book chapters in different languages covering subjects such as spatial theory, popular participation in urban planning, social movement theory, urban 'utopias'/alternative visions, urban problems and urban political ecology. His books include *Mudar a cidade* (*Changing the city*, 2002, 11th edition 2016) and *A prisão e a ágora* (*The prison and the agora*, 2006).

Rita Thapa has over 30 years' experience as a feminist educator and community activist, initiating and supporting institutions for women's empowerment and for peace. In 1995 she founded Tewa, the Nepal Women's Fund. Rita also founded and led (2001–09) Nagarik Aawaz, an initiative for conflict transformation and peace-building in Nepal. In recognition of her work, Rita has named an Ashoka Fellow. She has extensive experience in building links among community, non-governmental, governmental and academic institutions. She served as a past board member and chair of the Global Fund for Women and the Urgent Action Fund, as well as on the board of the Global Fund for Community Foundations (GFCF) and the South Asian Women's Fund (SWAF). In 2005, she was included in the 1000 Women for Peace nomination for the Nobel Peace Prize.

ONE

Funding, power and community development: an introduction

Fergal Finnegan and Niamh McCrea

Introduction

Sourcing, managing and sustaining funding is a fundamental and usually pressing concern for community development workers. Many of the most important practical choices facing organisations revolve around funding. It is also a profoundly political topic – any discussion of funding immediately brings up questions of power and purpose, and forces us to examine how varying visions and agendas overlap or conflict. Yet, despite the absolute centrality of funding to community development, few of the recent books published on the topic have focused specifically on the community development field[1] (INCITE! Women of Color Against Violence, 2007; Choudry and Kapoor, 2013; Edwards and Hulme, 2013; Salamon, 2014; Morvaridi, 2015; Jung et al, 2016), and those that have, do not address the range of funding arrangements that govern contemporary practice globally (Martinez-Cosio and Rabinowitz Bussell, 2013). This book intends to fill this gap.

Moreover, as we elaborate on later, there are a number of broad international trends that make the critical scrutiny of funding particularly timely. Community organisations in diverse contexts are grappling with reconfigured states and diminished state resources. They are also negotiating new and complex ensembles of power as well as a multiplication of funding modalities. Against the backdrop of a deep crisis of democracy (Brown, 2015) and of staggering levels of economic inequality[2] (Sayer, 2015), it is crucial to consider how funding relationships, structures and processes contribute to or undermine the possibility of meaningful democratic community development.

Funding, power and community development brings together academics and practitioners,[3] from a range of contexts to explore the impacts, opportunities, contradictions and dilemmas associated with the resourcing of community development. The book is international in scope and includes contributions from the Indian subcontinent, the Middle East, Latin America, Europe, Africa, Australia and North America. The book's purpose is to share insights and stimulate debate on how funding, in its various forms, is shaping the theory and practice of community development; to examine how communities, community development workers, activists and funders manage the day-to-day realities of funding; and to analyse the interrelationship between funding and broader economic and political developments. The specific modes of funding addressed in the volume are: state funding (at a national and regional level); international grants and aid; corporate funding; and philanthropy, including foundations and community philanthropy. In addition, it explores hybrid funding models such as microfinance as well as the self-funding of communities and community-based movements.

In this introductory chapter, we set out some of the most important themes across the book and illustrate why funding offers a powerful lens through which to 'rethink' community development in the current historical conjuncture, a task in keeping with the aim of the series in which the book is included. In the first section, we unpack the term 'community development' a little more, with reference to the varied conceptualisations deployed across the book. In particular, we want to draw attention to the importance of the widely shared democratic 'ethic', and to the inherent complexity of community development as a set of processes that call for a historical and social-spatial analysis of power. We build on this in the subsequent section where we expand on the analytical, political and practice significance of funding. Finally, we highlight three major cross-cutting themes of the collection: new configurations of power and governance; the role of the state in relation to democracy; and the complex connections between community development and egalitarian social change.

Before proceeding, we wish to note that despite our commitment to the inclusion of diverse perspectives on a range of funding sources, there are gaps within the collection. Potentially fascinating avenues of inquiry such as funding by faith-based organisations (Beaumont, 2008), a detailed analysis of trade unions (Bisset, 2015) or the forms of development fostered by international institutions such as the World Bank, International Monetary Fund (IMF) or World Trade Organization (Gaynor, 2016) were not pursued due to restrictions of space.

Defining community development: fostering dialogue and debate

Historically, we know that the mobilisation of communities under the banner of community development has taken multiple forms and has been linked to both progressive and conservative political projects (Meade et al, 2016). Community development has been used in state and imperial projects of control and colonial 'modernisation' which have sought the integration, pacification and incorporation of subaltern communities. Nevertheless, in many contexts, community development initiatives have served as a seedbed for experiments in popular democracy and egalitarian change (see for example Freire, 1972; Tett, 2002). The editors of the present collection situate themselves firmly within this radical 'tradition', and are interested in identifying the political, economic and cultural conditions for fostering egalitarian forms of practice today. Community development, from this broadly Freirean perspective, is envisaged as a process of political formation and praxis whereby community members come together to identify and confront sources of oppression, and, through collective agency, articulate and develop a more expansive notion of freedom.

But as one might expect in a book which is part of a series dedicated to rethinking community development, we do not think it is useful simply to reassert the value of the radical tradition. After all, the modes of thinking and repertoires of action which have sustained emancipatory practice may no longer be appropriate or sufficient for meeting the challenges we face, not least in terms of securing and sustaining funding for projects. Rethinking community development requires, we believe, a friendly scepticism towards the claims made by various traditions, including 'our' own, and a willingness to resist romantic and tidy narratives of community empowerment (Amit and Rapport, 2002; Joseph, 2002; Newman and Clarke, 2016). We want the book to spark dialogue and debate about the various ways community development is conceptualised internationally. As editors, we have sought to include a wide range of views and to present outlying as well as mainstream perspectives in order to trouble established boundaries and assumptions. The contributors are a diverse group and include community development workers, activists and academics as well as activist-scholars and, in one case, a funder. In addition to community development, they draw on a variety of disciplines such as critical development studies, geography, heterodox economics, sociology, adult education, anthropology, urbanism and social movement studies. Their political orientations range from liberal egalitarian to radical libertarian and they employ diverse theoretical resources; community development is interrogated in the book through Gramscian, post-structuralist, Alinskyite, Freirean, feminist and postcolonial lenses.

As well as offering rich resources for rethinking community development, this multiperspectival approach helps capture the complex and multidimensional relationship between funding, power and community development. We have also sought to complement this with a variety of modes of presentation and registers. Accordingly, alongside a series of academic case studies, the book features two personal reflections on the politics and practicalities of sourcing, researching and teaching about funding (Kohl-Arenas, Chapter Two; Thapa, Chapter Ten), an interview chapter (Souza, Chapter Eight) and a dialogue between a community development worker and a funder (Bender and Makongo, Chapter Nine) which was specifically organised for this project.

In order to provide coherence across the book, contributors were asked to be explicit about how they understood community development in relation to their work, and the national, regional or political context in which it is situated. Consequently, as is to be expected, the reader will encounter multiple and even conflicting meanings given to community development across the collection. It is also worth underscoring that several of the contributors question the salience and/or value of the term altogether. For instance, community development carries little meaning in places such as Kurdistan (Flader and Gürer, Chapter Twelve). Further, even when the term is in circulation in non-Anglophone contexts, for instance in Latin America (Souza, Chapter Eight), it carries very different connotations than is typically the case in Ireland, the UK or the US. Interestingly, several authors highlight the influence of international and transnational agencies in the promotion of community development, for example in Nepal and Eastern and Central Europe (Thapa, Chapter Ten; Gagyi and Ivancheva, Chapter Four). This is not, however, a simple top-down process: while we can point to the existence of a broad international conception such as that sponsored by the United Nations (UN) and other such bodies, this is frequently renegotiated across borders, and between funder and recipient (Thapa, Chapter Ten; Bender and Makongo, Chapter Nine).

Nevertheless, despite these distinct differences, there are also a number of striking commonalities across the collection. First, regardless of wider debates on the meaning and nature of community development, all of the contributors are concerned to emphasise a *'bottom up' conception of democracy*. Nearly all the authors share a concern with how power circulates and is reinforced, challenged and altered on a 'local' level. Methodologically, this is explored in two very different ways. Most of the chapters draw primarily on ethnographic or first-person accounts to make sense of funding, power and community development. These chapters take an idiographic focus and use intensive, comparatively small-scale research as the route to wider structural analysis. The remaining chapters provide macrosociological perspectives but are nevertheless anchored in the same interest in the potential for local empowerment. Of course, while we can point to this widely shared normative worldview, perhaps sometimes even taken-for-granted 'democratic ethic', what this exactly means in theory and practice is tackled in diverse ways, a point to which we return later.

Second, every chapter takes up the *complex and highly mediated nature of community development*. Contributors variously describe it as a dynamic, discontinuous and uneven process which exists in dialectical relation with the activity of other communities and movements and which is embedded in wider social structures. Thus, we would argue for careful attention to the socio-spatial dimensions of community development through history. From this perspective, communities can be understood more correctly as complex, relational social entities which have 'depth', that is to say, they are layered, structured by both proximate and distant powers and mechanisms, which, due to the interplay of these powers, are constantly subject to emergence and change (Bhaskar, 1979).

Funding, power and community development

Community – and, by extension, community development – is produced relationally 'through interactions, from the immensity of the global to the intimately tiny' (Massey, 2005: 9). Crucially, funding is a key mechanism through which relationships of power are created and mediated across social space, on various scales and levels and through time. It connects communities, practitioners, the state, NGOs, corporations and other social institutions. Funding in this sense functions as a connective tissue within power configurations: it is not simply an *enabler* of community development, it is also *constitutive* of it (Meade, 2012; Mayes et al, 2014). For example, funding influences ideas and practices relating to organisational governance, management and expertise, and helps determine the parameters and perceived legitimacy of tactics and political goals. Through the interactions that it enables and defines, as the chapters in this volume indicate, the very meaning of development is adapted, negotiated, subtly changed and sometimes even emptied of its democratic potential altogether.

Furthermore, funding arrangements are profoundly linked with the positioning of community development 'in that contradictory space between being part of the problem and part of the possibility for democratic life' (Shaw, 2011: ii143). In a social context marked by deep and enduring inequalities of power and resources, public funding for 'the political activity of relatively powerless groups' may enhance the conditions for participatory democracy (Baker et al, 2004: 116; Fisher and Balazard, Chapter Seven). Donors and grantees may converge around social justice agendas (McCarthy, 2004; Murtagh and Goggin, Chapter Five; Bender and Makongo, Chapter Nine; Thapa, Chapter Ten), while private or foreign funders can play a role in enabling dissent towards unresponsive or repressive state regimes (Baoumi, 2016). Resources, in sum, can catalyse communities' agency, creativity, influence and reach (Alvarez, 2009; Bender and Makongo, Chapter Nine; Thapa, Chapter Ten). Moreover, perspectives on, and strategies for, the resourcing of community action can themselves be an expression of emancipatory praxis, inspiring experiments in radical philanthropy, prefigurative politics, and forms of community which challenge the commodifying and care-less logic of capitalism (Ostrander, 1995, Caffentzis and Federici, 2014; Souza, Chapter Eight; Thapa, Chapter Ten; Flader and Gürer, Chapter Twelve). On the other hand, however, funding can also draw projects into relationships, structures and processes that compromise democratic accountability (Horvath and Powell, 2016; Mayes, Chapter Six), displace popular participation (Feldman, 2003; Mueller-Hirth, Chapter Three) or perpetuate structural inequalities (Kothari, 2005; Kohl-Arenas, Chapter Two; Mueller-Hirth, Chapter Three; Gagyi and Ivancheva, Chapter Four; Souza, Chapter Eight; Sen and Majumder, Chapter Eleven).

Finally, and critically, changes within the world of funding since the turn of the millennium are raising new questions and bringing new inflections to older debates around the role of state and market, the meaning and desirability of professionalism, the contours of self-help and the possibilities for empowerment. There are many continuities: the state unquestionably remains a key sponsor of community activities in many contexts (Chile, 2006; Chen and Ku, 2017), as do interstate and transnational bodies such as the European Union (EU) and the UN. Other well-established sources such as philanthropy, faith-based organisations and social enterprises continue to be features of the community development scene across many jurisdictions (Beaumont, 2008; Sahakian and Dunand, 2015; Pill, 2017). 'Autonomous' sources of funding from social movement organisations and neighbourhood associations as well as political parties and trade unions, remain important. There has, however, been a growth in, and diversification of, the people, institutions and organisational configurations involved in the resourcing of community development globally, as well as shifts in *how* established funding sources disseminate their resources. We have seen, for example, a proliferation of corporate, foundation and community philanthropy (Jung et al, 2016) – including giving by poor or indigenous people (Wilkinson-Maposa et al, 2005) and a rise in social-media driven tools such as crowdsourcing (Amtzis, 2014). There is also evidence that money is increasingly emanating from – and producing – hybrid models of organisation that blur the categories of public and private (Newman and Clarke, 2009). This is linked to developments within so-called 'new' philanthropy and social finance and to the multiplication of governance arrangements involving collaboration between state and non-state actors, a theme we take up in more detail in the next section.

The key themes of the book

While we have endeavoured to ensure diverse perspectives on funding, it is also evident that community development workers, activists and researchers are confronting similar issues across different contexts. Three interrelated themes are particularly prominent:

1. The growing significance of governance in funding community development.
2. The changing role of the state and the impact this has had on grassroots democracy.
3. The most effective way to effect egalitarian social change in the contemporary context of community development.

Contributors' discussions of these themes indicate that the issues raised in relation to governance, the state and egalitarian social change cannot be easily or simply resolved. They highlight contradictions, raise questions and suggest enduring dilemmas in the theory and practice of community development. Below we offer some framing remarks in relation to each of these themes before outlining how they are addressed in the book. The significance of these themes is also reflected in the organisational structure of the volume: chapters within each section of the book reflect with particular clarity questions relating to governance, the state and possibilities for emancipation respectively.

New configurations of power and governance

As suggested earlier, community development involves understanding how a given local context is being shaped on various levels and scales by multiple processes. We live in a period of startling changes in politics, technology and culture. Modern capitalism has created a global space of flows – of commodities, money and people but also of ideas, practices and images – and the increased velocity and changing rhythm of these flows has altered how power works on a global scale (Sum and Jessop, 2013; Harvey, 2014; Berardi, 2015). In a single generation we have seen a remarkable rise in the power of transnational corporations (TNCs), in the influence wielded by transnational bodies such as the World Bank and the IMF and, perhaps most significantly, the emergence of 'financialised' capitalism which 'prioritises making money out of money' (Sayer, 2015: 37). The consequences of these developments are significant. The rise of TNCs – global bodies wedded to a neoliberal agenda and financialisation – are directly linked to the redistribution of wealth upward and to the erosion of democracy since the 1990s (Sayer, 2015). As Soederberg (2014) points out, this neoliberal turn can be directly linked to corrosive policies of 'financial inclusion', in which poor communities are drawn into financial markets – and debt – through the provision of 'affordable' financial products and services.

The concentration of wealth and power and the emergence of new financial instruments and practices also partly underpin the previously noted *complexification* of contemporary community development practice. Funding often operates within and through these new configurations of power, in the form of 'new' philanthropy, social finance, corporate social responsibility (CSR), and partnerships of various kinds between state, market and community organisations. 'New' philanthropy refers to a model of giving that emphasises collaboration between government and business, the transformative potential of technology- and market-based solutions and the direct and active involvement of philanthropists in the process of social change (Edwards, 2015). Many forms of social finance are associated with the 'new' philanthropy trend. Social finance is a broad and heterogeneous field that ranges from cooperatively run social enterprises to philanthrocapitalist tools, such as 'pay-for-success' financing, which seek both progressive social outcomes as well as financial returns (Salamon, 2014). Perhaps the most familiar forms of social finance in the community development field are microcredit which has, since its popularisation in the 1990s, assumed a central place in poverty alleviation strategies in the Global South (Chari-Wagh, 2009), and earlier models of community-oriented financial institutions such as credit unions and development banks (Richter, 2014).

The rise of financialised capitalism and the emergence of new forms of 'extra-territorial' power has also reconfigured the role of the state, such that, as Nancy Fraser (2007) outlines, the nation state – so long the dominant frame for discussions of justice and democracy – has been significantly decentred. States have increasingly adopted a 'partnering' or 'enabling' role, whereby they mobilise the resources and ideas of business, social entrepreneurs, communities, philanthropy and other sectors in pursuit of social goals (Fyfe, 2005; Kim, 2016).

It is important not to overstate the novelty of developments in private giving or state welfare provision – the application of business acumen to charity or the intertwining of state and philanthropy are by no means unprecedented (McGoey, 2014; Edwards, 2015; Jung et al, 2016). What does seem novel in contemporary arrangements, however, is the complexity and range of cross-sectoral collaborations (Salamon, 2014; Jung et al, 2016), the degree of policy influence enjoyed by philanthropists and NGOs (Ball, 2012; Lang, 2013) and the extent to which funding strategies emphasise 'the power of factors that are internal to the market' (Edwards, 2015: 35). A number of chapters in the volume address these themes, illustrating that contemporary governance arrangements are leading to new discourses, standards and practices for describing, directing and measuring community development (Kohl-Arenas, Chapter Two; Mueller-Hirth, Chapter Three; Murtagh and Goggin, Chapter Five; Bender and Makongo, Chapter Nine; Sen and Majumder, Chapter Eleven).

Two chapters explore, from different perspectives, the growing importance of social finance. Sen and Majumder's nuanced account in Chapter Eleven of microcredit programmes among rural women in Darjeeling, India, underscores with particular force the importance of context-specific analyses of 'global' processes. The women's ambivalence to these state-initiated, NGO-administered credit programmes is clear: they enjoyed some of the new economic freedoms which accrued, but critiqued the narrow focus of the 'empowerment' on offer, as they carried the burden of debt repayment and of managing household and community tensions. Murtagh and Goggin (Chapter Five) discuss social finance as part of the Social and Solidarity Economy and, drawing on case studies from Bangladesh and Mondragon in the Basque country in the Spanish state, argue that, despite the risk of incorporation into 'market cultures and outcomes' and the inevitable integration with capital circuits, strategic, value-driven investment can play a role in developing alternative economic relationships and in addressing key social needs.

The involvement of TNCs in community development projects is considered by Mayes (Chapter Six) in her research on the CSR practices of a mining company in Ravensthorpe, Australia. Here, it is suggested that significant levels of corporate funding led to short-term, top-down and highly uneven forms of community and development aligned with the company's business interest. Strategies of governance are also a core concern of Mueller-Hirth's work (Chapter Three) on NGOs in South Africa. Here, the repositioning of NGOs as service-delivery organisations involved in multisectoral partnerships with state, corporations and international donors has led to the 'technicisation' of practice, as professional roles are increasingly bound up with the managerialist imperatives of tendering and auditing. In the process, South African NGOs have morphed into a form of 'proxy public', translating community needs and actions into solutions for funders, rather than participating in the messy politics of deliberation and dissent. Kohl-Arenas describes similar processes of neoliberalisation and 'technicisation' in the entrepreneurial, 'self-help' strategies of foundation-funded development projects that sidestep important questions about power and capital and foreclose more radical alternatives.

The repositioning of private funders from enablers of citizen action to 'partners' in the development process (see Edwards, 2015) features in the discussions between Lin Bender and Japhet Makongo (Chapter Nine). Makongo, a community development worker in Tanzania, outlines how funders there typically take the lead on development projects, inviting proposals from organisations to implement initiatives developed by the donor itself. This leads him to ask 'what if the communities were the ones who were putting up calls for proposals?' However, the work of the Helen Macpherson Smith Trust in Victoria, Australia described by its CEO, Lin Bender, illustrates that not all foundations work according to investment logics or insist on funder-imposed metrics (see also Thapa's positive assessment of international Women's Funds, Chapter Ten). The chapter highlights this donor's firm commitment to funding community-led projects and the often delicate negotiation of values and goals involved in building relationships between funders and recipients. In doing so, it demonstrates the potentially pivotal role played by individual workers on both 'sides' of the funding relationships in steering programmes in progressive directions, a point also discussed by Kohl-Arenas (Chapter Two).

Community development, the state and grassroots democracy

As already noted, the state remains an important node in these wider configurations of power and one that deserves to be explored in its own right in relation to the theme of funding, power and democracy. As Jones and Jessop (2010: 1119) argue, 'States comprise historically variable ensembles of technologies and practices that produce, naturalize, and manage part of terrestrial space as a relatively bounded container within which political power is exercised to achieve various, more or less well integrated, policy objectives'. Historically, a great deal of community development has been directly dependent on state power and has assumed the state as the major interlocutor and/or opponent in analyses of funding (for example, CDP, 1981; Mayo, 1997; Kim, 2016). While the strong interest in 'questions of state' in this book echoes earlier debates on the state in the 1970s and 1980s, they do so with the important difference that, since then, we have seen the complete unravelling of social democracy, the hollowing out of the state's welfare functions and the adoption of market 'solutions' to social problems in the global north (Wacquant, 2009).

Gagyi and Ivancheva (Chapter Four) take up the theme of the hollowed-out state. They describe how, since the 1980s, and in a process partly driven by the dynamics of foreign funding, a discourse of 'civil society' has become the 'normative model' for defining community activism in East-Central Europe. However, they argue that the term is far from neutral and has served to shore up market-friendly strategies of development. Interestingly, therefore, while the rollback of the state in this case is linked primarily to neoliberal policies, it is also secondarily attributed to the activity of grassroots democratic movements who promoted a notion of 'civil society' against the state.

This is a problem addressed too by Fisher and Balazard (Chapter Seven) who contend that we need to now reconsider left-wing critiques of state funding. Based on US history and recent initiatives in the UK, they suggest that practitioners should view the state both as a 'site of struggle' and as potential funder of democratic community development. This, they believe, is a more stable and transparent source of funding than foundations – the most important source of funding in the US. On the other hand, the inherent tendency of the state to 'defang' and co-opt radical potential is taken up by Souza (Chapter Eight) who, in a wide-ranging assessment of the possibilities for emancipation in Latin America, argues for a social movement–based form of community development that maintains a strategic distance from the state, an institution that he regards as, ultimately, 'liberticidal'. In a very different context, Thapa's account (Chapter Ten) of building a community-based women's fund in Nepal highlights how 'self-help' approaches to funding take on a particular power and urgency in situations where the state has failed to provide for the social protection of its citizens, where development is highly dependent on bureaucratic foreign aid and where most formal NGOs are aligned with one or other of the political parties.

Trying to manage the conflicts between the state's role in the management of people's needs and demands while also supporting capital accumulation are at the heart of the policy changes Mueller-Hirth (Chapter Three) discusses in post-Apartheid South Africa. There, the state embraced neoliberal policies but also passed laws with egalitarian objectives, thereby creating a very specific form of neoliberal governance which is characterised by tensions and contradictions.

The regulatory power of the state in relation to TNCs is addressed by Mayes (Chapter Six), whose research on mining companies demonstrates that a change in government in Australia had major consequences for how infrastructural funding for communities was approached. The state remains an important player in directing development processes but, nevertheless, in detailing the sudden withdrawal of a large mining company from the Ravensthorpe region due to global market volatility in commodity prices, the chapter also points to the deterritorialisation of capital and the limits of state power.

Perhaps the most novel exploration of the state role's in community development is offered by Flader and Gürer (Chapter Twelve) who describe an attempt to think beyond the boundaried nation state to invent entirely new political structures of coordination and direction altogether. What is envisaged is a complete remaking of the state by building up from municipalities in Kurdistan. Embedding power at a local level is seen as the first step to grassroots democracy, and offers one response to both the limits of nation states as 'imagined communities' and the deterritorialisation of power and democratic 'void' in contemporary capitalism.

Community development and strategies for egalitarian social change

The concerns over state and governance are, of course, linked to varying political visions of community development. Asking 'What is to be done?', exploring what is possible in a certain context to equalise power relations, and encountering the tension between what is and what might be, is the source of some of the most enduring dilemmas within the field. As noted earlier, all contributors are committed to the extension of democratic practice at a community level but what this precisely means depends on how this is situated within a broader structural analysis and how political possibilities are imagined and conceived. Using different foci, the collection explores the role and agency of community development workers and activists, funders and related intermediaries as well as educators and researchers. The selection of chapters in the third section of the book illustrates how these various roles impact on the way funding is approached and discussed.

One important axis of differentiation across the book as a whole is how *collective agency* is envisaged. The contributors explore the role of social movements, NGOs, community development organisations, communities 'themselves', community organisers and the state. Given the complex configurations of power discussed earlier, it is obvious that alliances and networks are crucial and no author suggests that community development can occur in splendid isolation. But it is interesting to note how the primary collective agent of democratic practice is conceptualised and where the major points of opposition and conflict are located. Within a significant proportion of the chapters, there is a marked interest in social movements as collective agents (Kohl-Arenas, Chapter Two; Gagyi and Ivancheva, Chapter Four; Fisher and Balazard, Chapter Seven; Souza, Chapter Eight; Flader and Gürer, Chapter Twelve). However, the extent to which movements should rely on established organisers or on their own autonomous power is a point of historical contention. Other contributors see movements as important (Thapa, Chapter Ten) but see existing communities linked to NGOs and international organisations as the primary locus of change (see also Bender and Makongo, Chapter Nine).

The political imaginaries that emerge across the book can also be differentiated by the extent to which authors link democratic community development to the possibility of a different social system altogether and how this is underpinned by different timescales and rhythms of change. For some this is seen as a proximate possibility based on ongoing militant activity (Souza, Chapter Eight; Flader and Gürer, Chapter Twelve). For Thapa (Chapter Ten) it is the slow building of the new in 'the shell of the old' that counts in Nepal, as feminists build alternatives quietly and even surreptitiously. Others discuss progressive social change as a forestalled project (Gagyi and Ivancheva, Chapter Four, Kohl-Arenas, Chapter Two), which needs to be rethought and renewed especially in the face of the growth of the nationalist right in the US and Eastern Europe. Other authors argue in their context for strategic intervention or incremental improvement (Murtagh and Goggin, Chapter Five; Bender and Makongo, Chapter Nine).

It is noteworthy that the chapters that discuss very dramatic transformations of social institutions link this to the reinvention of democracy. Just as significantly, it appears that some of the most advanced forms of democratic experiment at a community level are taking place at the 'margins' of global power structures among the indigenous, the poor and the stateless.

Of course, these different perspectives can be readily linked to historical debates about the pace and aim of social change. But there are two chapters that suggest that we need to be careful in how we establish the threshold on what is deemed political and where possibilities for emancipatory community action lie. Sen and Majumder (Chapter Eleven) focus on forms of agency which, while not explicitly political, are nevertheless crucial to understanding gender inequalities in rural Darjeeling. From a different perspective, Murtagh and Goggin (Chapter Five) accept that 'the expansion of social finance is critical to neoliberal rollout tactics' but caution against one-dimensional analyses which negate its progressive possibilities or which apply 'a pure, but ultimately unattainable, ethical vision for the [community] sector.'

Finally, it is important to emphasise again, even though this may be obvious, that political visions are never pure and always contextual. Contemporary forms of governance mean that apparently contradictory traditions and logics are more likely to be entangled, enabling the *coexistence* of co-option and resistance within the same organisation, programme or funding relationship (Sharma, 2006; Kohl-Arenas, Chapter Two; Murtagh and Goggin, Chapter Five; Fisher and Balazard, Chapter Seven; Sen and Majumder, Chapter Eleven). It is also clear that careful attention to the mode, duration, intensity and extent of egalitarian community development in a specific context is important. It is entirely possible to identify moments of conscious agency and even emancipatory action that are folded into processes which are, in the medium term, profoundly disempowering (see Mueller-Hirth, Chapter Three; Sen and Majumder, Chapter Eleven).

Conclusion

The collection explores the meanings of community, the contested purpose of community development and the complexities of funding and power from a wide variety of angles. In this introductory chapter, we have framed community development as a process in which local, regional, national and global structures and agents interact. We have also foregrounded funding as a 'connective tissue' within these relationships of power. But how precisely the global and local intersect, how flows between places within social space disturb and embed social relations, and how this is facilitated by various actors, is a matter for intellectual and empirical investigation. Thus in 'rethinking community development' through the prism of funding, we want to make a case for critical theorising that is capable of discerning patterns in social relations and identifying structures behind phenomena, without erasing the particularities of local contexts. We believe the value of an international collection comprising diverse perspectives and contexts around a single broad theme is to illustrate the impossibility of claiming that there is one way to approach democratic community development, or that there is a 'recipe' for funding these processes. Indeed, all the funding modalities analysed in the book – from autonomous cooperatives, to foundations, social finance, state and EU sources – have been shown to have unintended consequences; they may beget weak compromises that do little to advance democratic forms of community development, or fail altogether. We think acknowledging and working through this complexity and diversity is a crucial part of rethinking theory and praxis. Contradictions, tension and dilemmas are generative. Accordingly, what we have set out to do in this chapter is to synthesise the enduring dilemmas explored by our contributors in order to offer a departure point for further debate. In highlighting and interrogating the claims and tactics of community organisations, professionals, activists, the state and corporations with regard to funding; in exploring how governance structures and questions of state are being negotiated; and in examining how agency is being deployed, we seek to support community development practitioners to think critically about their work, encouraging them to question funding as a self-evident 'good', but to also be open to new possibilities and alliances in the struggle for a more egalitarian world.

Notes

[1.] That noted, implicitly or explicitly, questions regarding how community development is resourced, and with what effects, have long underpinned key debates within the field pertaining to such issues as community development's relationship with the state, the impact of professionalisation, the possibilities for social transformation, the meaning of development and the politics of aid (CDP, 1981; Ferguson, 1990; Shaw, 2011).

2. Globally, seven out of ten people live in countries where economic inequality has increased in the last 30 years and where 46% of the world's wealth is owned by just 1% (Sayer, 2015: 7). According to Oxfam (2017: 2), 'the incomes of the poorest 10% of people increased by less than $3 a year between 1988 and 2011, while the incomes of the richest 1% increased 182 times as much'.

3. In this chapter, we use the term 'practitioner' in a general sense to refer to community development workers, community-based social movement activists and those who work for funding organisations. We use the term 'community development worker' to refer to those working for community development organisations in either a paid or voluntary capacity. We also use the term 'activist' to refer to those engaged with community-based social movements. We recognise that the distinction between 'activist', 'community development worker' (and, arguably, in some cases, funder) is in many cases an artificial one. However, we have maintained it to accommodate those who self-identify more as 'activists' and for those operating in contexts where the term 'community development' carries limited currency.

References

Alvarez, S.E. (2009) 'Beyond NGOization? Reflections from Latin America', *Development*, 52(2): 175–84.

Amit, V. and Rapport, N. (2002) *The trouble with community: Anthropological reflections on movement, identity and collectivity*, London: Pluto Press.

Amtzis, R. (2014) 'Crowdsourcing from the ground up: How a new generation of Nepali nonprofits uses social media to successfully promote its initiatives', *Journal of Creative Communications*, 9(2): 127–46.

Baker, J., Lynch, K., Cantillon, S. and Walsh, J. (2004) *Equality from theory to action*, Basingstoke: Palgrave Macmillan.

Ball, S. (2012) *Global Education Inc.: New policy networks and the neo-liberal imaginary*, Abingdon: Routledge.

Baoumi, H. (2016) 'Local funding is not always the answer', *Open Democracy*, 27 June, www.opendemocracy.net/openglobalrights/hussein-baoumi/local-funding-is-not-always-answer.

Beaumont, J. (2008) 'Faith action on urban social issues', *Urban Studies*, 45(10): 2019–34.

Berardi, B. (2015) *Heroes: Mass murder and suicide*, London: Verso.

Bhaskar, R. (1979) *The possibility of naturalism: A philosophical critique of the contemporary human sciences*, Atlantic Highlands, NJ: Humanities Press.

Bisset, J. (2015) 'Defiance and hope: Austerity and the community sector in the Republic of Ireland', in C. Coulter and A. Nagle (eds) *Ireland under austerity: Neoliberal crisis, neoliberal solutions*, Manchester: Manchester University Press, pp 171–91.

Brown, W. (2015) *Undoing the demos: Neoliberalism's stealth revolution*, New York: Zone Books.

Caffentzis, G. and Federici, S. (2014) 'Commons against and beyond capitalism', *Community Development Journal*, 49(s1): i92–i105.

CDP (1981) *The costs of industrial change*, Newcastle Upon Tyne: CDP Publications.

Chari-Wagh, A. (2009) 'Raising citizenship rights for women through microcredit programmes: MASUM, Maharashtra, India', *Community Development Journal*, 44(3): 403–14.

Chen, Y. and Ku, Y. (2017) 'Community practice at a crossroad: the approaches and challenges in Taiwan', *Community Development Journal*, 52(1): 76–91.

Chile, L. (2006) 'The historical context of community development in Aotearoa New Zealand', *Community Development Journal*, 41(4): 407–25.

Choudry, A. and Kapoor, D. (eds) (2013) *NGOization: Complicity, contradictions and prospects*, London: Zed Books.

Edwards, M. (2015) 'From love to money: Can philanthropy ever foster social transformation?' in B. Morvaridi (ed) *New Philanthropy and social justice: Debating the conceptual and policy discourse*, Bristol: Policy Press, pp 33–45.

Edwards, M. and Hulme, D. (eds) (2013) *NGOs, states and donors: Too close for comfort?* (2nd edn), Basingstoke: Palgrave Macmillan.

Feldman, S. (2003) 'Paradoxes of institutionalisation: The depoliticisation of Bangladeshi NGOs', *Development in Practice*, 13(1): 5–26.

Ferguson, J. (1990) *The anti-politics machine: Development, depoliticization, and bureaucratic power in Lesotho*, Cambridge: Cambridge University Press.

Fraser, N. (2007) 'Transnationalizing the public sphere: On the legitimacy and efficacy of public opinion in a post-Westphalian world', *Theory, Culture and Society*, 24(4): 7–30.

Freire, P. (1972) *Pedagogy of the oppressed*, Harmondsworth: Penguin.

Fyfe, N.R. (2005) 'Making space for "neo-communitarianism"? The third sector, state and civil society in the UK', *Antipode*, 37(3): 536–57.

Gaynor, N. (2015) 'The politics of democracy and the global institutions: Lessons and challenges for community development', in R.R. Meade, M. Shaw and S. Banks (eds) *Politics, power and community development*, Bristol: Policy Press, pp 179–95.

Harvey, D. (2014) *Seventeen contradictions and the end of capitalism*, London: Profile.

Horvath, A. and Powell, W.W. (2016) 'Contributory or disruptive: Do new forms of philanthropy erode democracy?', in R. Reich, C. Cordelli and L. Bernholz (eds) *Philanthropy in democratic societies: History, institutions, values*, Chicago: University of Chicago Press, pp 87–122.

INCITE! Women of Color Against Violence (eds) (2007) *The revolution will not be funded: Beyond the non-profit industrial complex*, Cambridge, MA: INCITE! and South End Press Collective.

Jones, M. and Jessop, B. (2010) 'Thinking state/space incompossibly', *Antipode*, 42(5): 1119–49.

Joseph, M. (2002) *Against the romance of community*, Minneapolis: University of Minnesota Press.

Jung, T., Phillips, S.D. and Harrow, J. (eds) (2016) *The Routledge companion to philanthropy*, Abingdon: Routledge.

Kim, S. (2016) 'Silent counteractions of community organizations in a welfare partnership: A case study of South Korean workfare agencies', *Community Development Journal*, 51(1): 95–113.

Kothari, U. (2005) 'Authority and expertise: The professionalisation of international development and the ordering of dissent', *Antipode*, 37(3): 425–46.

Lang, S. (2013) *NGOs, civil society and the public sphere*, Cambridge: Cambridge University Press.

Martinez-Cosio, M. and Rabinowitz Bussell, M. (2013) *Catalysts for change: Twenty-first century philanthropy and community development*, Abingdon: Routledge.

Massey, D. (2005) *For space*, London: Sage.

Mayes, R., McDonald, P. and Pini, B. (2014) ' "Our" community: Corporate social responsibility, neoliberalisation, and mining industry community engagement in rural Australia', *Environment and Planning A*, 46(2): 398–413.

Mayo, M. (1997) 'Partnerships for regeneration and community development: Some opportunities, challenges and constraints', *Critical Social Policy*, 17(3): 3–26.

McCarthy, D. (2004) 'Environmental justice grantmaking: Elites and activists collaborate to transform philanthropy', *Sociological Inquiry*, 74(2): 250–70.

McGoey, L. (2014) 'The philanthropic state: Market–state hybrids in the philanthrocapitalist turn', *Third World Quarterly*, 35(1): 109–25.

Meade, R.R. (2012) 'Government and community development in Ireland: The contested subjects of professionalism and expertise', *Antipode*, 44(3): 889–910.

Meade, R.R., Shaw, S. and Banks, S. (2016) 'Politics, power and community development: An introductory essay', in R.R. Meade, M. Shaw and S. Banks (eds) *Politics, power and community development*, Bristol: Policy Press, pp 1–27.

Morvaridi, B. (ed) (2015) *New philanthropy and social justice: Debating the conceptual and policy discourse*, Bristol: Policy Press.

Newman, J. and Clarke, J. (2009) *Publics, politics and power: Remaking the public in public services*, London: Sage.

Newman, J. and Clarke, J. (2016) 'The politics of deploying community', in R.R. Meade, M. Shaw and S. Banks (eds) *Politics, power and community development*, Bristol: Policy Press, pp 31–46.

Ostrander, S.A. (1995) *Social movement philanthropy at the Haymarket People's Fund*, Philadelphia, PA: Temple University Press.

Oxfam (2017) *An economy for the 99%*, Oxfam briefing paper, Oxford: Oxfam International, www.oxfam.org/sites/www.oxfam.org/files/file_attachments/bp-economy-for-99-percent-160117-en.pdf.

Pill, M.C. (2017) 'Embedding in the city? Locating civil society in the philanthropy of place, *Community Development Journal*, ahead of print, https://doi.org/10.1093/cdj/bsx020.

Richter, L. (2014) 'Capital aggregators', in L.M. Salamon (ed.) *New frontiers of philanthropy: A guide to the new tools and actors reshaping global philanthropy and social investing*, Oxford: Oxford University Press, pp 91–120.

Sahakian, M.D. and Dunand, C. (2015) 'The social and solidarity economy towards greater "sustainability": Learning across contexts and cultures, from Geneva to Manila', *Community Development Journal*, 50(3): 403–17.

Salamon, L.M. (ed) (2014) *New frontiers of philanthropy: A guide to the new tools and actors reshaping global philanthropy and social investing*, Oxford: Oxford University Press.

Sayer, A. (2015) *Why we can't afford the rich*, Bristol: Policy Press.

Sharma, A. (2006) 'Crossbreeding institutions, breeding struggle: Women's empowerment, neoliberal governmentality, and state (re) formation in India', *Cultural Anthropology*, 21(1): 61–95.

Shaw, M. (2011) 'Stuck in the middle? Community development, community engagement and the dangerous business of learning for democracy', *Community Development Journal*, 46(s2): ii128–ii46.

Soederberg, S. (2014) *Debtfare states and the poverty industry: Money, discipline and the surplus population*, Abingdon: Routledge.

Sum, N. and Jessop, B. (2013) *Towards cultural political economy: Putting culture in its place in political economy*, Cheltenham: Edward Elgar.

Tett, L. (2002) *Community education, lifelong learning and social inclusion*, Edinburgh: Dunedin Academic Press.

Wacquant, L.J.D. (2009) *Punishing the poor: The neoliberal government of social insecurity*, Durham, NC: Duke University Press.

Wilkinson-Maposa, S., Fowler, A., Oliver-Evans, C. and Mulenga, C.F.N. (2005) *The poor philanthropist: How and why the poor help each other*, Cape Town: University of Cape Town.

PART 1

New configurations of power and governance

Critical issues in philanthropy: power, paradox, possibility and the private foundation

Erica Kohl-Arenas

Introduction

This chapter is an attempt to take stock in a time of change: it is a reflection on what I have learnt about the politics of philanthropic funding from my community organising experience, and through empirical research and teaching. I propose that this sort of holistic, open biographical reflection is necessary in a moment of such intense political transition. It is important to discuss in a clear way how we move between theory and practice in handling ambiguities and dilemmas of funding. Given the rise of inequality and the resurgence of right-wing politics in the US and elsewhere, many scholars may refrain from critiquing liberal philanthropy. I argue that when faced with complex historical contexts it is important to remain aware of how even the most seemingly progressive philanthropic frameworks can promote common-sense narratives that reinscribe systems of power and control.

I moved to Ivanhoe, Virginia, in 1989 to live and work with Maxine Waller, a charismatic woman caught up in the struggle to save her deindustrialising coal-mining town. Alerted to the proposed sale of Ivanhoe's industrial land, Maxine, the wife of a former coal miner, launched a campaign to prevent the sale. She initially hoped that, if saved, the town might attract new industry. Raised in the culture of a company town, many miners believe that the land would be sold because they did not work hard enough, that 'better' workers attracted big coal to move elsewhere. Despite their original doubts, a cadre of local women joined Maxine, prevented the sale of the land, and embarked on an educational and organising campaign to plan for the redevelopment of Ivanhoe.

I was changed by this brilliant, rebellious woman and by a community that pulled together. As a participant in Ivanhoe's people's economics classes, I saw locals begin to understand the global economy and their place in the world around them, becoming active participants in planning for a future they shared. Coal miners and their wives studied and received high school diplomas, a group of women organised feminist Bible studies classes, microenterprises were formed, an oral history book was published, and local theatre productions retold the story of Ivanhoe as one of jubilee and renewal. The Ivanhoe Civic League was incorporated to identify future community development problems and plans. All of these things happened on the townspeople's own terms.

Living and working in Ivanhoe made me passionate about adult education and the potential of grassroots community development that is directed by poor people and not defined by outside agencies, institutions or funding requirements. Since Ivanhoe, I have not come across a community project so self-directed, so willing to take risks and, most of all, so unconcerned with the constant chase for private foundation funding. Through my work as a community development practitioner during the 1990s and early 2000s and in subsequent doctoral research, I became increasingly critical of programmes that espouse 'grassroots' or 'participatory' approaches to social change yet are led by elite institutions fearful of taking on structural inequalities.

Despite the co-optation, professionalisation and bureaucratisation of community development and social movements, I remain committed to the participatory practices that so changed my life in Appalachia. As a result, the tensions and contradictions that emerge when grassroots organisers, leaders, and not-for-profit staff members engage with large-scale philanthropic and development initiatives have become a thread that runs through my research (Kohl-Arenas, 2016). It is also a central theme in my teaching. Creating opportunities for students to learn how to navigate these tensions through experiential partnerships with community-based institutions in New York City has become a central part of my work.

In 2017 I launched a course specifically focused on philanthropy – 'Critical issues in philanthropy: Power, paradox, possibility and the private foundation'. This graduate seminar aimed to engage professional management, policy and international development students in a critical investigation of relationships of power in philanthropic initiatives to address poverty and inequality. Given that my students and I are practitioner-scholars, the course was also designed to explore spaces of possibility and risk that not-for-profit professionals negotiate when brokering relationships with donors. Drawing on my own research and inspired by several new books from an emerging cohort of critical philanthropy scholars, I was eager to use ethnography, cultural studies and journalistic research materials with students more accustomed to management 'best practices' and techniques.

The week before classes were to commence in January 2017, something shifted. Despite my magical (delusional) thinking that this day would not come, Donald J. Trump was inaugurated as the 45th President of the United States of America. Suddenly, my critique of mainstream funders like the Ford Foundation and the Rockefeller Foundation, and of smaller progressive funders including the Rosenberg Foundation and Field Foundation as complicit in watering down the radical agendas of the US social movements of the 1960s felt petty. Should we spend a semester analysing the compromised politics of liberal philanthropy while the US President receives counsel from the Heritage Foundation, a right-wing think-tank committed to the destruction of the welfare state? Instead of assigning ethnographies of failed community development initiatives, should I assign the groundbreaking *Axis of ideology: Conservative foundations and public policy* (Krehely et al, 2004)? Or the exposé on the Koch brothers, *Dark money: The hidden history of the billionaires behind the rise of the radical right* (Mayer, 2016)? And what of the not-for-profit organisations who will need every penny of liberal philanthropic support they can find as they react to the 'rolling thunder' of executive orders targeted at poor people, immigrants, refugees, transgender people, women and children? Was it really the right time to hold the Left's feet to the fire?

Then, I was reminded by a colleague that times of political turbulence and crisis are the critical moments when social movement leaders and not-for-profit professionals risk accepting private funding that alters organising agendas and introduces accountability structures that orient 'upwards' to elite donors and not the people these movements initially aimed to serve. I decided to teach the class as planned. Although studies of right-wing philanthropy are desperately needed, we would instead ask, 'What risks do current and emergent social movements and grassroots community development initiatives take when partnering with mainstream private foundations during politically turbulent times?'

To proceed, I first draw on my research on farmworkers' movements in California to outline the approach to studying philanthropy and social change which informed the 'Critical issues in philanthropy' course. I then review a selection of recent literature on philanthropy used to spark critical discussion among the professional not-for-profit management, urban policy and international development students who took the course. I close with conclusions about the importance of studying and teaching philanthropy within the context of the rise of right-wing politics and white supremacy in the United States.

The self-help myth: philanthropy and social change

My research explores the relationship between private philanthropy and grassroots community development and social movements working to address regional poverty and inequality. The critical questions that drive my research concern historical and contemporary patterns of professionalisation, institutionalisation, bureaucratisation and political co-optation that occur when social movements form relationships with large-scale philanthropic initiatives. In recent years, these trends have become of central concern to a growing interdisciplinary body of research across American poverty and social movement studies, critical development theory, and the more traditional not-for-profit and philanthropy field.

Since the rapid growth of the privately funded not-for-profit sector in the United States during the 1980s and 1990s, which corresponded with increasing inequality resulting from neoliberal reforms, scholars have presented accounts of private foundations as unaccountable institutions that use wealth generated through exploitation of both labour and the environment, to fund palliative programmes that pave the way for continued capitalist development and structural inequality (Roelofs, 2003; INCITE! Women of Color Against Violence, 2007). Most recently, critical development and philanthropy scholars critique the 'philanthrocapitalist' turn where charitable institutions seek new profits through private-sector investments in major social policy arenas including global health, agriculture, education and disaster relief (Arena, 2012; Morvaridi, 2012; Adams, 2013; McGoey, 2015).

The findings of this growing body of critical philanthropy scholarship overlaps with what I have discovered through my research on foundation investments in California's Central Valley. Here, it is clear that seemingly benevolent programme frameworks, such as self-help housing development and immigrant civic participation, can weaken and redirect efforts to confront long-standing abuses of agricultural fieldworkers and discrimination against undocumented immigrants. Private philanthropy does not always follow or promote clear-cut capitalist agendas. Instead of always enacting top-down 'philanthrocapitalist' plans, foundation involvement in poor people's social movements and community development is often a piecemeal process where not-for-profit and philanthropic professionals negotiate, translate and adapt the more confrontational strategies of grassroots organisations to fit idealised 'theories of change' agreeable to mainstream publics and to the institutions in which they work. In my book (Kohl-Arenas, 2016), I show how foundation and organisational staff struggle to address migrant poverty in California's Central Valley, simultaneously one of the wealthiest agricultural production regions in the world and home to the poorest Californians. Compromises between foundation staff and social movement leaders, such as Cesar Chavez of the farmworkers' movement, and modern-day farmworker and immigrant organisers, in the end produce non-threatening, individualised frameworks of poverty alleviation that make poor people responsible for alleviating their own suffering and ensure that critique of or confrontation with industry is avoided.

Within these funding agreements and institutional arrangements, a key contradiction of 'self-help' philanthropy is revealed. Because asking poor people to help themselves can contain radically different purposes for the different stakeholders involved (from changing behaviour in a family to organising a boycott), such programmes sometimes activate and even politicise the people engaged. Yet, that politicisation eventually upsets funders who find this politics threatening. The aspirations of grassroots organisations are typically derailed by grant agreements and reporting duties that proscribe firm limits and make demands on the time, energy and ideology of newly professionalised staff. For example, a recent $50 million foundation initiative to improve conditions in Central Valley agricultural communities sought to identify where growers and workers can collaborate on regional development issues. Despite worsening conditions and increasing insecurity for undocumented farmworkers, and in keeping with the now hegemonic 'double-bottom-line development' trend in poverty alleviation, which proposes that which is good for capital is good for the poor, this initiative avoided challenges to the growers' economic interests. Operating under this model, community organisers who were initially inspired to address rising rates of pesticide poisoning and financial and sexual abuse in the fields were required to busy themselves with professional development, local 'asset mapping' and building consensus with diverse stakeholders. Despite the sincere hopes of the lead foundation programme officer to improve conditions for farmworkers, by the end of the five-year initiative structural issues inherent in the farm labour system had not been addressed.

Sometimes grassroots or social movement actors make small gains through their own negotiations and brokered relationships. More often consensus politics generates consent which favours dominant groups.

Antonio Gramsci's (1971) understanding of hegemony is particularly useful in this context. Cultural hegemony can be understood as a system of ideological power managed through a set of world views, such as double bottom-line or trickle-down development, imposed on poor and oppressed people. As a central part of his theory of cultural hegemony, Gramsci used the term *common sense* to represent the world views propagated by the dominant bourgeois culture to serve as the commonly held values of all. When successful, people in the working class identify their own good with the good of the bourgeoisie, which helps to maintain the status quo rather than catalyse revolution.

Through my research I found that hegemonic framings are not blindly received and immediately embodied; rather, they are constantly negotiated and contested. Beyond clear-cut examples of top-down capitalist imperialism and market agendas (which can be found in much of the new literature on philanthrocapitalism), a Gramscian understanding of hegemony requires that we pay attention to brokering processes and the 'strategic articulations' formed in what Gramsci calls a 'war of position' between divergent social actors. For example, in the critical philanthropy research the idea of 'service provision' is often understood as hegemonic, representing a decline in anti-capitalist social movement organising. Despite the historical accuracy of this observation, the experiences of the California farmworker movement demonstrate that 'service provision' is also an active space of contestation. In the case of the farmworker movement, the 'service-centre' model was strategically rearticulated as funders and Cesar Chavez negotiated the terms of collaboration. For Chavez and other movement leaders, building community-service institutions was originally a long-term strategy for radical economic independence, pride and movement building based on collective ownership, mutual aid and cultural self-love. Archival correspondence between Chavez and the Field Foundation revealed that philanthropic investors were attracted to the movement's service-centre model because of its potential to build institutions governed by diverse regional stakeholders. Yet through the founding of not-for-profit farmworker service institutions, funders privileged direct social services and education while excluding questions of unionisation, strikes, worker cooperatives, and the conflictual praxis that originally inspired broad-based farmworkers' mobilisation. Through negotiations with movement leaders and the eventual founding of the not-for-profit National Farm Worker Service Center in 1966, several foundations came to support the social-service tradition while 'disarticulating' the radical aspects of the approach and 'rearticulating' it within the apolitical not-for-profit model. Not unitary or controlling by definition, a counterhegemonic idea is reinscribed on hegemonic terms through the process of negotiating with powerful stakeholders such as foundation programme officers. Thus, never completely foreclosed, privately funded social movements are often, as Piven and Cloward propose in their classic book *Poor people's movements* (1978), both constituted by, and in resistance against, bureaucratic institutional structures.

On a broader scale, Cesar Chavez contributed to the farmworker movement's acceptance of foundation grants to incorporate not-for-profit organisations and to its strategic alignment with the American War on Poverty, both of which he and his allies initially thought to be rigid, unaccountable, elite forms of social change (Kohl-Arenas, 2016). The decision to accept foundation funding and incorporate not-for-profit institutions in the last years of the 1960s was partially in line with Chavez's vision to build the self-sustaining farmworker 'mutual aid' institutions mentioned above, and directly enabled the movement to attract a diversity of resources, catapulting the United Farm Workers onto the national stage. Yet, the not-for-profit institutions formed also presented a politically constrained space of retreat from field organising when the movement faced serious challenges such as violence against strikers on the picket lines, political repression and surveillance from the state, and competition with the more moderate Teamsters union.

Unlike much of the critical philanthropy scholarship, however, my research and classroom discussions often consider how certain framings, positions, identities and interests are never fixed or complete but rather grow contingently – and often strategically – in the course of struggle. In this sense, programmes funded by foundations may control grantees at one moment, yet they may also contain elements of alternatives to the dominant framework they represent, and they may be understood and used differently across a diverse range of organisations and networks at different historical moments. Specific attention is drawn to the role of not-for-profit professionals and non-state actors engaged in poverty-alleviation projects. Reliance on foundation funding alters the very nature of social change. Distracted and bogged down by negotiating relationships with donors and professional management and partnership requirements, short-term foundation-funded programmes replace the day-to-day engagement, listening, relationship building and strategising required for movement building. While an emerging body of research from critical development, American poverty and not-for-profit/philanthropy scholarship pays attention to trends in the professionalisation and institutionalisation of grassroots projects, few study the practitioners themselves and the specific roles that they play on a daily basis.

Teaching critical philanthropy: the scholar-practitioner standpoint

'Critical issues in philanthropy: Power, paradox, possibility and the private foundation' was designed as an advanced-level graduate seminar to examine popular debates and new academic scholarship on the politics of private philanthropy. Through a critical review of media and research and through discussion we explored the following questions:

- If philanthropy is broadly understood as the mobilisation of private assets for public benefit, then how is this public benefit assured and by whom?
- In their focus on inequality, many foundations seek to promote broader social change, yet foundations often require short-term measureable impact when social change is a slow, non-linear and uneven process. How might foundations support long-term movement building in our current political-economic moment?
- And, what are the specific limits they face as institutions created by private wealth generated in capitalist markets that produce inequality?

We began the semester reading critical philanthropy bloggers and chapters from the now widely read *The revolution will not be funded: Beyond the non-profit industrial complex* (INCITE! Women of Color Against Violence, 2007). In this collection of essays, scholars and activists document the emergence over the mid- to late-20th century of a set of entrenched symbiotic relationships between the state and private funders – the 'non-profit industrial complex' (NPIC). They show how the NPIC monitors and controls social justice organisations, redirects activist energies into professionalised behaviours and encourages social movements to model, rather than challenge, corporate practices. At the broad scale, these studies show how private foundations use public money and tax breaks to engage in ameliorative activities that mask exploitative capitalist relations.

While not all students agreed with the analysis of these authors, everyone appreciated the detailed history of 'ideas' and institutional transformations promoted through a network of private and state actors. For the first time, many students (including a social worker, a domestic violence counsellor, a foundation staff person, a restaurant professional, a South American slum dweller legal advocate, a Spanish socialist community organiser and several not-for-profit development officers) saw their own experiences with professionalised funding cultures and frameworks mapped onto a powerful and troubling historical context.

We then studied the ways in which *The revolution will not be funded* builds on a tradition of Gramscian scholarship that suggests that the 'Big Three' foundations (Carnegie, Rockefeller and Ford) are central to maintaining Western capitalist imperialism in educational systems and foreign policy (Arnove, 1980; Berman, 1983; Roelofs, 2003; Parmar, 2012). These studies show how capitalist control is not only maintained through direct force or economic systems of production but through cultural hegemony bound to ideas of 'common sense' (Gramsci, 1971).

In a time of financial insecurity, rising rents, college debt and heightened consciousness of inequality inspired by scholarship (Piketty, 2014) and by movements such as Occupy Wall Street, we now, more than ever, understand how capitalism produces inequality. Yet, in the US, we still often embrace the myth that a poor person can only improve their conditions by changing their own behaviour (O'Connor, 2001). This 'self-help myth' was promoted by private foundations and, alongside the neoliberal policies initiated in the 1980s, has contributed to and legitimised economic inequality (Reich, 2007). Discussing how foundations engage in a politics of 'common sense', the tropes of self-help and entrepreneurship resonated with my millennial students. Revealing the contradictions embedded within common-sense framings, my students could grasp the generative causes of poverty, but only a few could imagine poverty-alleviation approaches that do not ask poor people to fix their own problems or create individualistic entrepreneurial solutions.

Other discussions about the contradictions within 'common sense' philanthropic framings came from readings about how the Bill and Melinda Gates Foundation and the Rockefeller Foundation, widely congratulated for addressing pressing food-security problems in sub-Saharan Africa, are promoting dependency on genetically modified crops and enacting new forms of land privatisation through partnerships with Cargill and Monsanto (Morvaridi, 2012; McGoey, 2015). While the Gates' and Rockefeller's philanthrocapitalist approach was eye-opening to most students, they were well aware of how foundation investments in US public school reform have advanced privatisation, 'choice' and competitive approaches that build market opportunities for private educational service providers while failing to improve outcomes for poor students (Barkan, 2012; Tomkins-Stange, 2016). As a class, we were most struck by the groundbreaking ethnographic studies in settings such as post-Katrina New Orleans, where disaster recovery aid was pitched and commonly understood as charitable but then quickly revealed as a for-profit endeavour that produces new soul-crushing debt structures for victims of natural disaster (Arena, 2012; Adams, 2013).

Though there is a growing body of scholarship on philanthropic power, there is little focus on the specific negotiations of foundation professionals who attempt to ally with grassroots social movements. This was the space of enquiry of most concern to my professional students. One reading that the participants found useful in this context was the study by Ostrander et al (2005) of social movement philanthropy, which does allude to the role of foundation staff as they collaborate with grassroots grantees. Through a series of case studies of progressive grant-making institutions (the Crossroads Fund, the Haymarket People's Fund and the Chicago Initiative), the authors claim that there is a great deal of professional negotiation at play. One of their most insightful findings is that many foundation professionals come from social movement and grassroots organisations and have ideological and political commitments of their own, prior to getting a job with a foundation. As Ostrander states, much of the research on philanthropy and social change ignores the '[c]omplex roles held by progressive members of the foundation community,' who, 'while not always successful, … did actively represent grantees and served as important potential allies to social movement organizations' (Ostrander et al, 2005: 280).

While Ostrander et al stand out in their attention to the professional negotiations involved in funding grassroots organisations and movements, the analysis leaves several questions unanswered. First, the study features three of the most progressive, or radical, funders in the United States. My students asked, 'What might these negotiations look like for professional allies of grassroots poor people's organisations who work in large mainstream foundations and who report to wealthy boards? Do the compromises they make when brokering between grassroots organisations and large mainstream foundations have significant "co-optive" effects?' We brought our own experiences into the classroom in order to better understand the role of not-for-profit staff and relationships with funding professionals. We studied and debated the relationships that have developed between The Movement for Black Lives and the Ford Foundation and other major donors. We looked at social movement-aligned funding networks such as Solidaire, Resource Generation and IDEX/A Thousand Currents. We decided that theorising cultural domination without investigating the conflicted professionals, the battles over frames and ideas, and the potential political opportunities revealed, only answers a limited range of questions.

Sharing data from my recent research on the political negotiations of individual foundation programme officers who aim to address structural inequality through their large mainstream foundations (Kohl-Arenas, 2017), we discussed some of the tensions experienced by these conflicted philanthropic managers. Through the lens of Erving Goffman's *Presentation of self in everyday life* (1959), this study reveals how the micropractices, roles and received scripts associated with professional 'grantor–grantee' relationships, reproduce institutional structures of power. While foundation programme officers broker political opportunity for grassroots organisations, they more commonly generate consent. We discussed the less pessimistic ideas of poverty scholar Ananya Roy who suggests that development professionals can enact an ethic of 'doubleness' where complicity in the project of empire building can be transformed into subversion (Roy, 2005). Similarly, a recent 'practitioner-scholar' book, *Feminists in development organizations* (Eyben and Turquet, 2013), explores the 'feminist bureaucrats' who transform their own institutions from the inside out, while negotiating the risks of co-opting grassroots movements. We ended the semester with similarly uplifting stories from philanthropic practitioners who are working with grassroots leaders around the globe to support community-driven social change (Lentfer and Cothran, 2017).

Conclusions

In class, I introduce the idea of philanthropy as twice-stolen wealth (Gilmore, 2007). Wealth is stolen once by industries that create profit on low-wage or unpaid labour and/or exploitation of the environment. The second steal occurs through charitable tax deductions that place this wealth in privately managed philanthropic endowments rather than public programmes. In the US, annual charitable tax deductions alone cost the Treasury nearly US$36 billion in forgone income tax. This is more than the federal government spends on the entire TANIF (Temporary Assistance for Needy Families) programme (Reich, 2007). Thus, foundation endowments can be understood as the untaxed, unaccountable and undemocratic spending of surplus wealth – in other words, a plutocracy (see Callahan, 2017). I then ask my students to consider 'philanthrocapitalism' as a form of thrice-stolen wealth. As McGoey (2015) argues, it used to be somewhat shameful to claim to make money on charitable contributions, but now many are comfortable with the idea of 'doing well while doing good'. The third steal represents efforts to make money by investing the twice-stolen wealth in new markets – or what has been called 'capitalism saving capitalism from capitalism'.

Let us return to the question of whether it is useful to study and teach a critique of liberal and mainstream philanthropy during a political resurgence of right-wing, conservative, anti-state politics and white supremacist movements. My answer is yes and no. No, there is no point in critiquing mainstream philanthropy when we need every penny and every ally to stand up against hate, racism and fearmongering politics. There is also little point in becoming so consumed with the second and third stealing of wealth (modern-day philanthropy and philanthrocapitalism) if we forget to pay attention to the enduring presence of the first steal, economic systems that produce poverty and inequality.

On the other hand, yes, we must pay attention to the role of philanthropy in creating common-sense narratives that contribute to individualist solutions to collective structural problems. A book we read in class which speaks to this theme was Willoughby-Herard's *Waste of a white skin* (2015). In the days after the 2017 US Presidential inauguration, this book read as eerily relevant to our times. Analysing the global race project and US–South Africa historical connections forged through the Carnegie Foundation-funded *Poor white study* and the nascent system of Apartheid, Willoughby-Herard shows how histories of white nationalism, segregationist philanthropy and global racial politics repeatedly rediscover the white poor to suture over racial regimes. Concealed in the debate over white poverty in the *Poor white study* was an overriding anxiety that white South Africans would organise and collaborate with Africans who had been mobilised by urban activists in the black radical tradition (Willoughby-Herard, 2015).

It is difficult not to see similar patterns playing out in our current time, where media pundits and politicians draw attention to angry and disillusioned poor and 'working class' whites, while crafting stigmatising narratives of black and brown immigrants. The discourses and practices driven by the Carnegie-funded *Poor white study* emboldened a white separatist class ready to advocate for the Apartheid state. I learned from Willoughby-Herard's text that the lead social worker of the study, Marie Elizabeth Rothmann, was also funded to travel to Appalachia during the 1960s to study white poverty and white and black relations in order to develop scientific justification for categorising 'deserving' white citizens. Willoughby-Herard's study brilliantly reveals the political-state-economic violence done to white communities as pawns in the anti-Black project, a violence I witnessed first-hand during my time working in Ivanhoe, VA. Without diminishing the urgency to act directly against any forms of racism, I also agree with Willoughby-Herard's conclusion that when we think about whiteness as loss and misery rather than privilege *alone*, we can more carefully analyse systems and patterns of intra-white violence that are at the root, alongside anti-black violence, of white supremacist power.

It is clear that philanthropy plays a role in promoting common-sense narratives that can either reinscribe systems of power, or align with and catalyse the struggles of oppressed people. In this context, critical philanthropy studies are more important than ever. Future scholars may reveal the complicated ways in which private donors support current social movements that fight for economic equality and racial justice, and would be wise to look out for false narratives that neglect intersectional and interracial analysis and strategy. And if we care about poverty and inequality, we must also pay close attention to philanthropic initiatives and 'theories of change' that blindly promote corporate market strategies and tropes of competition and individualism that, in the end, produce poverty for many and steal profit for a few future wealthy philanthropists.

References

Adams, V. (2013) *Markets of sorrow, labors of faith: New Orleans in the wake of Katrina*, Durham, NC: Duke University Press.

Arena, J. (2012) *Driven from New Orleans: How nonprofits betray public housing and promote privatization*, Minneapolis, MN: University of Minnesota Press.

Arnove, R. (ed) (1980) *Philanthropy and cultural imperialism*, Boston, MA: G.K. Hall.

Barkan, J. (2012) 'Hired guns on Astroturf: How to buy and sell school reform', *Dissent*, 59(2): 49–57.

Berman, E.H. (1983) *The ideology of philanthropy: The influence of the Carnegie, Ford, and Rockefeller Foundations on American foreign policy*, Albany, NY: State University of New York Press.

Callahan, D. (2017) *The givers: Wealth, power and philanthropy in a new Gilded Age*, New York: Knopf.

Eyben, R. and Turquet L. (eds) (2013) *Feminists in development organizations: Change from the margins*, Rugby: Practical Action Publishing.

Gilmore, R.W. (2007) 'In the shadow of the shadow state', in INCITE! Women of Color Against Violence (eds) *The revolution will not be funded: Beyond the non-profit industrial complex*, Cambridge, MA: INCITE! and South End Press Collective, pp 41–52.

Goffman, E. (1959) *The presentation of self in everyday life*, New York: Anchor Press.

Gramsci, A. (1971) *Selections from the prison notebooks of Antonio Gramsci*, ed Q. Hoare and G.N. Smith, New York: International Publishers Co.

INCITE! Women of Color Against Violence (eds) (2007) *The revolution will not be funded: Beyond the non-profit industrial complex*, Cambridge, MA: INCITE! and South End Press Collective.

Kohl-Arenas, E. (2016) *The self-help myth: How philanthropy fails to alleviate poverty*, Oakland, CA: University of California Press.

Kohl-Arenas, E. (2017) 'The presentation of self in philanthropic life: The political negotiations of the foundation program officer', *Antipode*, 49(3): 677–700.

Krehely, J., House, M. and Kernan, E. (2004) *Axis of ideology: Conservative foundations and public policy*, Washington, DC: National Committee for Responsive Philanthropy, www.ncrp.org/wp-content/uploads/2016/11/AxisofIdeology.pdf.

Lentfer, J. and Cothran, T. (eds) (2017) *Smart risks: How small grants are helping to solve some of the world's biggest problems*, London: Practical Action Publishing.

Mayer, J. (2016) *Dark money: The hidden history of the billionaires behind the rise of the radical right*, New York: Doubleday.

McGoey, L. (2015) *No such thing as a free gift: The Gates Foundation and the price of philanthropy*, London: Verso Press.

Morvaridi, B. (2012) 'Capitalist philanthropy and hegemonic partnerships', *Third World Quarterly*, 33(7): 1191–210.

O'Connor, A. (2001) *Poverty knowledge: Social science, social policy and the poor in twentieth-century U.S. history*, Princeton, NJ: Princeton University Press.

Ostrander, S., Silver, I. and McCarthy, D. (2005) 'Mobilizing money strategically: Opportunities for grantees to be active agents in social movement philanthropy', in D.R. Faber and D. McCarthy (eds) *Foundations for social change: Critical perspectives on philanthropy and popular movements*, Lanham, MD: Rowman & Littlefield, pp 271–90.

Parmar, I. (2012) *Foundations and the American century: The Ford, Carnegie, and Rockefeller Foundations in the rise of American power*, New York: Columbia University Press.

Piketty, T. (2014) *Capital in the twenty-first century*, Cambridge, MA: Harvard University Press.

Piven, F.F. and Cloward, R. (1978) *Poor people's movements: Why they succeed, how they fail*, New York: Vintage Books.

Reich, R.B. (2007) *Supercapitalism: The transformation of business, democracy, and everyday life*, New York: Alfred A. Knopf.

Roelofs, J. (2003) *Foundations and public policy: The mask of pluralism*, Albany, NY: State University of New York Press.

Roy, A. (2005) 'Praxis in the time of empire', *Planning Theory*, 5(1): 7–29.

Tompkins-Stange, M. (2016) *Policy Patrons: Philanthropy, education reform, and the politics of influence*, Cambridge, MA: Harvard Education Press.

Willoughby-Herard, T. (2015) *Waste of a white skin: The Carnegie Corporation and the racial logic of white vulnerability*, Berkeley, CA: University of California Press.

THREE

"Walking the tightrope": the funding of South African NGOs and the governance of community development

Natascha Mueller-Hirth

Introduction

This chapter examines the role of intermediary NGOs in community development in post-Apartheid South Africa, specifically exploring how these organisations have been shaped by changing funding modalities. The South African not-for-profit sector is very large and diverse, encompassing a great variety of organisations that differ in size, scope, activities, political orientation and location. Habib's (2003) typology remains useful in making sense of post-Apartheid civil society, which he argues is made up of three blocs: 'formal' NGOs, 'survivalist' community-based organisations (CBOs) and social movements. CBOs, which numerically dominate civil society, are concentrated in areas of service delivery at a local level and might therefore be seen as more involved in community development; Habib (2003: 236) terms them 'survivalist' because 'they enable poor and marginalized communities to simply survive against the daily ravages of neo-liberalism'. However, this chapter focuses on the role in community development of the formal, or intermediary, NGOs, arguing that they are important sites in which to observe the dynamics and dilemmas of funding.[1] Describing such organisations as intermediary directs attention to their location between various types of authority (such as the state and corporations) and citizens or communities; to their organisational structure (they are structurally equipped to benefit from state, donor and corporate funding); as well as to the types of activities they undertake (such as capacity building, research, lobbying, advocacy and training) (Mueller-Hirth, 2012). It is important to note that these intermediary NGOs clearly do not represent communities, although the two are often conflated. However, in many cases this is a role they have been assigned because government, international donors and the private sector rely on NGOs to channel their funds to communities. This renders their role in community development particularly significant.

In this chapter, community development is understood as essentially contested, enabling empowering and less empowering practices and policies to emerge from, and for, communities. Importantly, the chapter resists a vertical understanding of power in which communities or civil society 'at the bottom' are contrasted with the state 'at the top'. Rather, communities are elements in the transnational and multiscalar governance of development; community development is also a discourse that corporations, NGOs and the state all employ to gain legitimacy. The following section summarises the socio-historical developments that have enabled NGOs to become such significant actors in community development. The chapter will then examine partnerships as a specific neoliberal mode of funding that has shaped the role of NGOs in community development. It is argued that partnerships provide a context within which shared values, practices and techniques appropriate to particular, often neoliberal, forms of community development, can be developed in NGOs. Partnerships link intermediary NGOs with corporations, the state and communities and are shown to enable claims of legitimacy, build consensus through homogenisation, and necessitate particular auditing techniques and capabilities.[2]

The socio-historical context of South Africa's NGO sector

Since the democratic transition in 1994, a number of trends have shaped the contours of community development, in particular the move from adversarial to more collaborative relationships with the state, the experience of funding crises and the emergence of fairly extensive corporate responsibility policies. During the Apartheid era, the state worked in mutually beneficially relationships with white civic organisations, whereas progressive anti-Apartheid organisations provided a 'shadow' welfare system to the majority of the population neglected by the regime. Foreign governments and international donor agencies channelled funds through these civil society organisations to fight Apartheid. The negotiated settlement had an enormous impact on state–civil society interactions: NGOs were shifting from an 'oppositional mode' to a 'developmental mode' and became increasingly involved in policy development, training, networking and implementation of service-delivery programmes. As former civic leaders began integrating into the state bureaucracy and into the business sector, organisational capacity and expertise in not-for-profit organisations was depleted. NGOs and the state institutions were now seen as partners in the nation-building project, leading in some cases to codependent relationships with the ruling ANC party and to certain NGOs growing distant from communities. It also led to 'biographical alignment' between the NGO and state sectors: for instance, networks of former comrades in the struggle for freedom are evident in the composition of many NGOs' governing boards (Mueller-Hirth, 2010). The integration of many NGOs into state and corporate structures can be understood as a desire to contribute to the shaping of progressive policies in the newly democratising South Africa. But by the late 1990s the NGO sector found itself sidelined and unable to challenge the government in a meaningful way over new inequalities that began to emerge due to its neoliberal turn.

A crisis in funding after 1994 led to many, particularly oppositional or critical, NGOs closing, and eventually to the professionalisation of those that remained. International funders now supported the democratically elected South African government directly through bilateral agreements, thereby reducing the resources available for NGOs. The reclassification of South Africa as a middle-income economy by the World Bank meant a further reduction in international donor funding. Those NGOs that survived found that they needed to reposition themselves as service-delivery organisations, carrying out contract work for the government, or undertaking corporate social responsibility (CSR) projects for the corporate sector. The state accordingly provides the majority of funding to the NGO sector. This extract from an interview with the director of an education NGO illustrates these changing modalities:

> 'We were forced onto the market and had to become self-sufficient. [We] really walked the dusty streets of Pretoria from embassy to embassy and went to various big companies trying to beg money and tried to get tenders, I mean we were pretty bad at that in those days. Now we are pretty good, now we churn out those tenders like we are a factory. A tender factory.'

Accordingly, the state provides the majority of funding to the NGO sector, effectively outsourcing services it does not have the capacity to deliver. The funding crisis and demise of the traditional donor funding model then effectively created NGOs increasingly characterised by multisectoral linkages and professionalisation. Among the complex resource-mobilisation and sustainability strategies that NGOs now needed to employ, multisectoral partnerships were the most significant. Newer NGOs that have emerged since the early 2000s have become accustomed to these modalities and incorporated them into their organisational form. Many NGO staff described what might be called the 'partnership mode' in contrast to an older NGO model that was deemed inflexible, unsustainable and outmoded. Some interviewees explicitly distanced themselves from organisations they perceived as not versatile enough to adapt to the changing rules: "A lot of the NGOs are still working with the pre-'94 mindset, people and strategies. And that is where they're not much advancing"; or "those poor NGOs, they spend most of their time trying to find where next year's money's coming from, or next month's".

The contemporary partnership logic mirrors Post-Washington Consensus global developmental priorities. The Post-Washington Consensus had identified the state and institutions as important in the efficient functioning of markets and understands the importance of governing through consensus building (Craig and Porter, 2006). In South Africa, the partnership approach to community development issues had initially been particularly characteristic of donor responses to projects concerned with HIV/AIDS and education, but now applies to funding areas across the board. International donors are keenly supporting development projects that integrate voluntary, private and public sector efforts. Government also emphasises the need for development collaboration through partnerships at all levels, evident in the recent South African National Development Plan and the 2011 Basic Education Accord, a partnership agreement between government, businesses, trade unions, NGOs and community organisations.

A further influence on community development has been the rising importance of the private sector. Businesses in South Africa have been forced to adopt socially responsible policies that are more advanced than those in many of the richer economies, partly due to Black Economic Empowerment (BEE) legislation. BEE involves affirmative action policies adopted by the post-Apartheid government to give historically disadvantaged groups economic opportunities. Any South African company's performance is rated on a number of BEE scorecards, with companies collecting points for CSR activities. Unlike in other countries and despite its non-voluntary character, CSR in South Africa has a strong emphasis on community development and poverty alleviation (Mueller-Hirth, 2016). Importantly for the concerns of this chapter, most corporations channel their social investment through NGOs and CBOs in order to reach beneficiaries and communities: CSR spending in 2015 was estimated to be about R8.1 billion (£360.33 million), of which 52% went to NGOs (Trialogue, 2015).

However, it has been South Africa's rapid adoption of a set of neoliberal policies after the transition that has most significantly impacted NGOs and their role within community development. Moreover, the changes already outlined – funding crises and the expanding role for businesses in development – are themselves associated with the adoption of free-market models in global and South African development. Community development in South Africa can be described as neoliberal in three important senses that are explored later, they are: the creation of new inequalities and new developmental challenges; the impact of neoliberalism on funding modes, especially partnerships; and the effects on organisational activities, especially managerial techniques and impact measurement.

South Africa is one of the most unequal countries in the world, and developmental needs are great: over half of South African children live in poverty; 20% of people live in extreme poverty; and just under 25% of people live without formal housing (Statistics SA, 2012).[3] Unemployment stood at 26.6% in July 2016, with youth unemployment at 53.7% (Statistics SA, 2016).[4] These inequalities are in part legacies of uneven development under colonialism and Apartheid, but are also the product of the adoption of neoliberal macroeconomic policies since 1994 (Marais, 2011). Trade liberalisation, export-oriented manufacturing, privatisation of state enterprises, wage control and increasing 'flexibility' in the labour market were supposed to foster higher economic growth and attract more private capital investment. Large numbers of organised workers were made redundant, casualised or forced into the informal economy and the commodification of basic services had disastrous effects for the poor (Hart, 2014).

At the same time, since 1994 the government has undertaken a range of initiatives that are developmental and pro-poor, for example social grants and housing (Ferguson, 2010). In this analysis, neoliberalism is understood as encompassing a range of projects on multiple scales (supranational, national and local) that are concerned with expanding and universalising free-market social relations, but that play out in locally specific ways in different places (Ong, 2006). As Hart (2008: 680) argues, writing about South Africa, 'the challenge … is coming to grips with how identifiably neo-liberal projects and practices operate on terrains that always exceed them', that is to say, articulations of nationalism, development, community and so on are multiple projects and move in many different directions. In South Africa, a neoliberal ideology is differentially articulated with other political projects such as African nationalism and the developmental state.

This chapter draws from a larger multisited ethnographic study that explored transformations in South African NGOs in the post-Apartheid era and highlighted that auditing and partnerships are increasingly core activities of NGOs that impact on their logic of operation and their location in wider civil society (Mueller-Hirth, 2010, 2012). This approach differs from studies of NGO accountability or effectiveness, instead focusing on NGOs in order to analyse modes of governance and power relations in development.

Multisectoral partnerships, NGOs and community development

Despite considerable differences among them, all of the NGOs in this study had working relationships with a range of different actors as well as with traditional donors. In interviews, NGO staff described what are in practice highly varied and often normative relationships as 'partnerships'. This was reflected in companies' documents as well as in data gathered through observation in the field, where reference to partners denoted anything from NGOs to CBOs, governments and companies, and comprised a range of activities such as funding, capacity-building technical assistance, sharing information or managing projects jointly. NGO professionals, despite their use of this partnership language, often appeared deeply uncomfortable with their corporate relationships and their contracts with governments. This is arguably because of the persistent claim by most NGOs that they retained their independent, critical voice despite their role as service delivery on behalf of their funding 'partners'. These multiple roles gave rise to dilemmas that were acutely felt by NGO practitioners:

> 'We continue to do independent research with money raised from donors, and this often put us in a situation where we were critical of Government and sometimes they get sensitive about criticism. So one has to walk a tightrope, and I think we have been doing this for a long time and we are still standing on the rope, maybe we are still sitting on the fence.'

Drawing on older ideals of participatory development that originated in the 1970s and sought to encapsulate an ideal of cooperation and capacity building between equal partners, partnerships are based on the argument that contemporary complex developmental challenges cannot be solved by one sector alone. Their proponents highlight that they allow for the participation of a range of actors, increase social learning and reduce NGOs' dependence on traditional donors (Banks et al, 2015). Conversely, a range of critical scholars have argued that the rhetoric of participation and integration often serves to conceal the operation of powerful interests within communities and that it is deliberately employed to mask continuous unequal power relations in development (Baaz, 2005; Miraftab, 2004). The contention in this chapter is that partnerships encourage the sharing of values, practices and techniques appropriate to particular, often neoliberal, forms of community development. As such, they can be empowering or restrictive: the partnership mode gave some NGOs in this study relative autonomy and independence in relation to funding, while its multiple commitments and intensified reporting demands had negative impacts for many others. Three main outcomes of this partnership mode are examined here: legitimacy and access to communities; consensus building and homogenisation; and the circulation of auditing techniques.

Securing legitimacy

The partnership mode in community development is a way for various partners to gain legitimacy. For the South African government for instance, it offers the opportunity to include potentially adversarial actors, such as oppositional NGOs, and create a consensus on the direction of policy. Moreover, both the Mbeki and Zuma administrations have seen explicit attempts to rein in critics, including human-rights NGOs and others that have aligned themselves with social movements. For corporations, the need to win legitimacy with communities in order not to lose their so-called 'social licence to operate'. This has been one of the main motivations for direct involvement in development issues (Idemudia, 2014) and has been further encouraged by South Africa's BEE legislation. This is significant for the present discussion of NGOs' role in community development because corporations usually do not engage these communities directly, but rather through partner NGOs.

Importantly, the partnership mode holds the promise of increasing legitimacy for NGOs, too. For example, NGOs strategically used partnerships with the provincial or national government to increase their legitimacy with international donors or corporations, which they in turn use to leverage new partnerships. For example, one of the NGOs in this study received funding for some of its HIV education programmes from provincial health departments whereas its Gauteng project was supported by a mining corporation that supported their work as part of the CSR strategy. The North West Province project employed yet another funding model using budget support from the Dutch government. As one informant put it: "It becomes a little more complex than simply going to the funder looking for money directly. Sometimes it's about creating relationships that leverage and leverage and leverage to the point where we can actually get access to funds." Conversely, professionals at progressive human-rights NGOs reported difficulties in accessing funding because of their activist and sometimes critical stance towards either the South African government or the corporate sector.

Many organisations in this study also strategically used the language of partnership to describe their relationships with CBOs in order to gain and enhance credibility with their corporate or government donor-partners. This is because community development discourses clearly envisage particular ideal-typical roles and functions for NGOs. In interviews with CSR professionals, NGOs' most frequently cited "comparative advantages" were service delivery, capacity building of smaller CBOs and their ability to deliver at local level due to their power to mobilise communities and reach the grassroots. CSR discourse, moreover, frequently assumes that the objectives of NGOs and communities are congruent and that NGOs are able to represent the interests of communities. This conflation of CBOs with highly formalised NGOs is not coincidental but reflects the language, policies and concern with civil society of global institutions, which in turn has been integral to the neoliberalisation of development over the past decades (Banks et al, 2015). This makes it paramount for more formalised NGOs to demonstrate proximity to communities. The very concept of 'community' in development discourse is of course deeply problematic: its identification and discursive construction by various actors frequently provides 'moral legitimation' to corporate or governmental authority and helps to underwrite their position of power (Rajak, 2011: 47). In order to sustain the claim of their comparative advantage towards donors, NGO staff frequently evoked a common 'we as civil society organisations' frame, which sought to assert that they, and the CBOs they work with, are one and the same. This was sometimes done by NGO workers referring to their own pasts as activists or to their credentials as grassroots practitioners: "someone like me who comes from the purest background"; "some of my closest buddies are from hardcore social movement backgrounds"; or "I have always worked at a grassroots level" are just some examples of this invocation of commonality and authenticity from interviews.

This claim is not backed up by this research: all intermediary NGOs were urban, formalised and distant from marginalised or rural communities. In order to reach such communities, NGOs themselves must partner with CBOs. In practice, rather than being able to represent the interests of communities or grassroots organisations, NGOs are more likely to act as an intermediary between government or corporates and local communities, translating community needs and issues into a manageable solution for a corporation. For example, NGOs collected and translated narratives and qualitative data into formats that suited corporate reporting. They might also translate the language people use in relation to their development needs into one that is seen as more suitable to government or corporate needs by "tidying up" reports. The following quote from an interview with an NGO worker illustrates this at times uncomfortable positioning:

> 'We can travel, we can take the language, we can make that crossover into the board room easily and now we are putting our foot into the shanty town shack and the other foot in the boardroom and kind of creating a bridge in that way which is quite a subtle thing but it is has added a lot of value to [our] brand. That you can talk the boardroom speak and then they are learning more and more about meaningful development speak, too.'

Overall, it was notable how NGOs were themselves reproducing donor understanding of their roles, despite their awareness of critiques against these perceived advantages. Claims of proximity to communities served to attribute legitimacy both to NGOs and to state- or donor-run projects.

Building consensus

Partnerships are emblematic of a global development project that sees cooperation and harmonisation as the most effective way to ensure broad-based growth, while further extending the reach of the market into social areas (Craig and Porter, 2006). This is particularly relevant in the South African context where consensus building resonates with the nation-building project and cross-sectoral collaboration is portrayed as necessary for the greater good of the nation. For example, patriotism was a key theme both in NGO practitioner narratives and in CSR staff's portrayal of their involvement in community development. Most respondents related their involvement in community development to their identities and responsibilities as South Africans and citizens in an emerging young democracy. Their motivation as development professionals was cited as wanting to "contribute to the future of South Africa" or to "to contribute to the bigger picture". Time and again, the idea was expressed that collaboration between the sectors is the only way to tackle developmental challenges of the magnitude that South Africa is facing. "The point is to try to get together and do whatever we can to make sure that it is in the interest of the greater good", as one NGO director put it. This notion of a greater good resonates with the normative claims generally made on behalf of partnerships, such as inclusiveness, participation, building broad-based support and sharing the goals of development. Interviewees often evoked an apparently self-evident and unproblematic commonality, as in this narrative by an NGO manager in Johannesburg: "I firmly believe partnerships in South Africa are so important and working so well because there is no arrogance ... We'll reach a common understanding to make sure that we implement what is good for the country."

It is suggested here that this understanding of partnerships as a development modality is deeply rooted in the state–civil society relations after the negotiated settlement. As already indicated, the emphasis on being partners in a shared national project, frequently cast in terms of social cohesion and reconciliation, was an important discursive building block of the initial post-Apartheid years and has significantly impacted on the funding models and value orientations of today's NGOs. However, the appeal to a not-quite-defined notion of the "greater good" or "common understanding" can also be problematic if it implies that non-adherence means being unpatriotic, or if it serves to marginalise alternative visions of development and change. This again highlights that partnerships are always also an opportunity for government and corporations to bring adversarial groups into the nation-building project, turning 'potential civil society critics into consensual governing partners' (Craig and Porter, 2006: 79).

The rise of auditing culture

At the organisational level, calls for greater NGO accountability, transformations in public management and increasing funding scarcity have combined to lead to the growth of monitoring and evaluation

(M&E) and impact assessment. New Public Management, the philosophy guiding neoliberal public sector reform, has impacted on every kind of organisation, forcing them to 'organize their activities as if they were little businesses' (Rose, 1999: 152). M&E and quality assurance mechanisms – what Dean (1999) terms 'technologies of performance' – are clearly not limited to South African community development but constitute a large part of (funded) NGO activity globally. Impact assessment has produced a wide range of indicators, instruments and methods, and M&E were negotiated in different ways by individual NGOs (see Mueller-Hirth, 2012).

Despite their heterogeneity, measurement and reporting were core activities of all of the NGOs in this study. Moreover, in order to secure future funding, NGOs must show that they are able to apply a range of auditing techniques, which crucially requires specific skills and capacities that do not fall into the core expertise of many NGOs. These include quantitative-analytical and statistical skills, epidemiological expertise and econometrics expertise, but also linguistic abilities, as the director of a human-rights NGO highlighted:

'For me it's fine, I've got a postgraduate degree, I've got a lot of experience … But if you are a relatively young NGO, and you are in an area where your focus is addressing social work or something, you're expected to read EU-ese documents, which are not written in plain English. If English is a second or third language for you, you're gonna have major problems.'

These various requirements for new forms of expertise have the potential to shape NGOs' organisational cultures and forms. Because target-oriented development favours particular ways of measuring the success of a project, modifies organisational structures and impacts on the types of activities or services provided, NGOs are transformed in line with neoliberal regimes of government. The demands for efficiency and transparency of financial management necessitate organisational restructuring and the acquisition of financial skills. M&E practices require certain organisational conditions that favour and indeed produce highly organised and professionalised types of NGOs (Mueller-Hirth, 2012). Here however, the focus is particularly on the relationship between the partnership mode and the increasing demands for impact assessment.

First, partnerships as a preferred development mode necessitate multiple levels of accountability, and multiple ways of counting and evaluating. Different partners have different M&E requirements and the prevalence of multisectoral funding demands organisational and methodological flexibility. Partnerships in fact require heightened monitoring capacity due to a range of accountability demands by different partners. For example, international donors such as USAID or the European Union frequently required high-level impact data to feed into results-based management or logical analysis frameworks. Large Northern NGOs who occasionally funded some of the organisations in this study required a mixture of M&E methodologies, including participatory techniques such as community surveys. Corporate partners needed qualitative and often visual data that could feed into CSR documentation for shareholders, staff and the public, and quantitative tracking information, although some corporations have also developed their own M&E tools that they want NGOs to be able to use. These varying demands are putting increasing strains on NGOs. Improved skills in terms of standardised M&E are in turn considered indicators of improved capacity by partners.

Second, audit culture affects NGOs' relationships with other CBOs. Once a formalised NGO has entered into funding and monitoring regimes, it becomes harder to work with less formalised CBOs. This is because CBOs are not structurally equipped to prove results-based management or adhere to complicated reporting systems. As one NGO director put it, "we only work with the ones who do have a photocopying machine, who can account for all the money and so on". Where relationships with CBOs exist, NGOs often play the role of 'translator': for example, participatory processes may be used to design or evaluate programmes but NGO staff repackage the stakeholder process in more quantitative terms to meet the demands of their funders. Here, the interface between partnerships and auditing becomes apparent: they are mutually dependent in that auditing practices are attached to the funding flows and intersectoral networks that connect actors in community development partnerships. Within these power relations intermediary NGOs become the 'experts' that circulate particular ways of thinking about, practising and monitoring community development programmes.

Relatedly, the partnership mode positions NGOs in relation to social movements and wider popular struggles. NGOs are far less likely to be able to support progressive (but not professionalised) actors in civil society, such as social movements that challenge the effects of neoliberal development. This can be especially problematic when communities want to challenge corporate practices in relation to working conditions or the environment. While NGOs may see themselves as aligned with the values of social movements, the extent to which they are able to support movements materially is clearly dependent on their own funding modalities. For example, staff at progressive NGOs revealed in interviews that their donors had expressed concerns about support of social movements and had indicated that funding could be withdrawn.

Conclusion

This chapter has explored development funding dynamics in South Africa, specifically examining how changing funding modalities have shaped intermediary NGOs as key actors in community development processes. It has argued that a new NGO model – shaped in South Africa by Post-Washington neoliberalism but also by the country's post-conflict nation-building project – can be characterised by the ability to maintain partnerships, act flexibly and demonstrate fluency in auditing techniques.

Partnership is a ubiquitous, ambiguous and polymorphous concept that is shaping how many NGOs think and act. Being involved in these increasingly complex partnerships and funding arrangements – with international donors, the state, corporations and CBOs – meant that the NGOs in this research found themselves in the difficult position of simultaneously acting as governing partner, community representative and critical civil society voice. NGOs seemed to be caught in the middle, claiming alignment with civil society organisations that resist corporate and government policies while needing to access corporate monies and government funds for survival. It is this paradox that renders claims of legitimacy so central for NGO staff. As this chapter demonstrated, legitimacy and authenticity was often asserted through claims to organisational independence, the personal pedigree and social movement experience of members or by deploying the idea of civil society.

The image of "walking the tightrope" that was used by the NGO director cited earlier captures NGOs' relationship to broader civil society, government and corporations well. The tightrope is also a useful metaphor for the pressures they face by having to balance the requirements of their diverse partners, their distinct ways of working and their partners' differing M&E needs. Partnerships linked to specific modes of funding pose significant dilemmas for intermediary NGOs in terms of their roles and identities. But partnerships and their associated technologies such as M&E also empowered some NGOs, whose strategic adoption of particular technologies and vocabularies gave them considerable influence. Intermediary NGOs supposedly bridge the gulf between a shack and a global corporation's boardroom, as one of the informants cited earlier put it, but intermediary NGOs are often structurally unable to progressively engage with the grievances of many communities. As translators, they come to speak for, rather than with, those who may be able to bring about progressive change, further shrinking the space for marginalised groups and voices in community development. This is particularly alarming given the inequalities and developmental challenges facing South Africa.

Notes

[1.] Primary data informing this paper was gathered in two periods of fieldwork (February 2007 to March 2009 and February to March 2011) through semi-structured interviews with over 40 NGO practitioners and corporate social responsibility (CSR) professionals, observation research with two additional NGOs, and documentary analysis of relevant development policy texts and organisational outputs. The author is extremely grateful to all participants for sharing their time, expertise and insights.

[2.] An important caveat: the South African NGO sector – even within the narrower focus of this chapter on intermediary NGOs – is highly differentiated, with the partnership rhetoric being employed with different effects and outcomes. The length and scope of this chapter necessarily only allows a snapshot of this varied terrain, but the intention here is to chart how a particular mode of funding and governing of community development – partnerships – has shaped organisational modes and values of the studied NGOs.

[3.] These data are drawn from the most recent census, held in 2011 (Statistics SA, 2012).

[4.] The figure of actually unemployed people is considerably higher: in South Africa the unemployment rate measures the number of people actively looking for a job, but does not include those who have given up looking for work.

References

Baaz, M.E. (2005) *The paternalism of partnership: A postcolonial reading of identity in development aid*, London: Zed Books.

Banks, N., Hulme, D. and Edwards, M. (2015) 'NGOs, states, and donors revisited: Still too close for comfort?', *World Development*, 66(2): 707–18.

Craig, D. and Porter, D. (2006) *Development beyond neoliberalism? Governance, poverty reduction and political economy*, Abingdon: Routledge.

Dean, M. (1999) *Governmentality: Power and rule in modern society*, London: Sage.

Ferguson, J. (2010) 'The uses of neoliberalism', *Antipode*, 41(s1): 166–84.

Habib, A. (2003) 'State–civil society relations in post-Apartheid South Africa', in J. Daniel, A. Habib and R. Southall (eds) *State of the nation: South Africa 2003–2004*, Cape Town: Human Sciences Research Council, pp 227–41.

Hart, G. (2008) 'The provocations of neoliberalism: Contesting the nation and liberation after Apartheid', *Antipode*, 40(4): 678–705.

Hart, G. (2014) *Rethinking the South African crisis: Nationalism, populism, hegemony*, Athens, GA: University of Georgia Press.

Idemudia, U. (2014) 'Corporate social responsibility and development in Africa: Issues and possibilities', *Geography Compass*, 8(7): 421–35.

Marais, H. (2011) *South Africa pushed to the limit: The political economy of change*, London: Zed Books.

Miraftab, F. (2004) 'Public–private partnerships: The Trojan horse of neoliberal development?', *Journal of Planning Education and Research*, 24(1): 89–101.

Mueller-Hirth, N. (2010) 'Freedom betrayed: NGOs and the challenges of neoliberal development in the post-Apartheid era', doctoral dissertation, Goldsmiths College, University of London.

Mueller-Hirth, N. (2012) 'If you don't count, you don't count: Monitoring and evaluation in South African NGOs', *Development and Change*, 43(3): 649–70.

Mueller-Hirth, N. (2016) 'Corporate social responsibility and development in South Africa: Socio-economic contexts and contemporary issues', in S. Vertigans, S.O. Idowu and R. Schmidpeter (eds) *Corporate social responsibility in sub-Saharan Africa: Sustainable development in its embryonic form*, London: Springer, pp 51–68.

Ong, A. (2006) *Neoliberalism as exception: Mutations in citizenship and sovereignty*, London: Duke University Press.

Rajak, D. (2011) *In good company: An anatomy of corporate social responsibility*, Stanford, CA: Stanford University Press.

Rose, N. (1999) *Powers of freedom: Framing political thought*, Cambridge: Cambridge University Press.

Statistics South Africa (2012) *Census 2011*, Pretoria: Statistics South Africa.

Statistics South Africa (2016) *Quarterly labour force survey* (2nd Quarter 2016), Pretoria: Statistics South Africa.

Trialogue (2015) *The Trialogue 2015 handbook* (18th edn), Cape Town: Trialogue.

FOUR

The reinvention of 'civil society': transnational conceptions of development in East-Central Europe

Agnes Gagyi and Mariya Ivancheva

If we take the United Nations' definition of community development as a 'process where community members come together to take collective action and generate solutions to common problems' (United Nations, 2010), East-Central Europe has a rich and ongoing history of such initiatives that have played a decisive role in the build-up of 'modern' institutions throughout the region (Stokes, 1986). Thus, East-Central Europe offers rich ground for reflection on how modernity and community development are understood in relation to each other. Yet it should be noted that community development as a specific term has limited currency in East-Central Europe. In fact, it has been a discourse of 'civil society' rather than 'community development' that has been dominant in the region in making sense of social change from the bottom up. This chapter explores how the notion of 'civil society' in East-Central Europe, and the discursive and organisational practices attached to the term, have been deployed in politics and how this has affected how local development and empowerment are conceived and funded. In this respect, struggles over the meaning and practice of 'civil society' activism in the region, speak to long-standing debates within the community development field relating to the role of state and market; the status, function and relevance of professionalised organisations within communities; the relationship between political and economic freedoms; and the possibilities for meaningful transnational solidarity.

The specific way of framing community action and democracy in a given context matters a great deal. We will argue that far from being a transparent term for self-organisation at a local and then, cumulatively, at a national level, the notion of civil society is burdened with complex transnational historical baggage. Its emergence and use as a paradigmatic concept for denoting civic activism and self-organisation happened within a specific historical process – the so-called democratic transitions – in which local institutions, organisations and movements were expected to serve the reintegration of the region into global markets. Against this backdrop, we analyse civil society as an ideologically loaded notion, the historical construction of which was marked by the dominant epistemic and geopolitical hierarchies of the post-socialist period. Our analysis brings attention to the importance of macrohistorical struggles in the formation and understanding of community action, and to the role of foreign, philanthropic and movement funding in shaping the content and contours of these struggles.

In the first section of the chapter, we highlight the fact that although large sections of the populations participated in mass protests before the regime change, only a tiny intellectual elite capitalised on the framing of this activity as the work of 'civil society'(Piotrowski, 2009). In this period a good deal of the visibility of this group and their activism within transnational networks was dependent on foreign sponsorship (Petrescu, 2013). Civil society – a term associated with the *specific* organising practices of this time – became the buzzword of the democratic transition (Ivancheva, 2011). Yet, in practical terms it inherited two tendencies characteristic of late socialist East–West 'dialogue'. First, it was based on a perceived asymmetry in levels of social progress; the 'backward' East was supposed to catch up with the 'developed' West. Second, it was dominated by an elite- and donor-driven model of organising: one which later assumed a neoliberal logic that represented the state as evil and championed the free market. In the second section we focus on the way these two tendencies were transmuted in the post-1989 context. In spite of institutionalised efforts to encourage participation in community initiatives through NGOs – funded primarily through foreign donors – these did not become part of everyday life and practice for the majority of people. Most NGO activities did not tackle the major social issues thrown up by transition (Ivancheva, 2015) – political alienation and polarisation, as well as economic deprivation and insecurity for a large portion of the population (Dale, 2011). Forms of political action that did not conform to the model of NGO-led civil society were denounced as 'uncivil' (Kopecký and Mudde, 2003), that is, as not ripe for, or deserving of, democracy. In the third section we narrate a second smaller post-socialist wave of hopes for 'civil society', linked to the alter-globalisation movement in the 2000s which also sustained discourses of inferiority and 'failure' of the East (Gagyi, 2013). We conclude by pointing to the present-day repercussions of this process.

The re-emergence of 'civil society' in the last decades of the Cold War

The concept of civil society which has its roots in Enlightenment political theory re-emerged as a 'keyword' in the dialogue between Eastern European dissidents and Western intellectuals and activists during the last decades of state socialism, after the Prague Spring in 1968. Informed by a socialist-era dissident opposition between state and society, it spread into the public and academic discourse after 1989 as a normative model for describing political mass participation and socioeconomic development.

Dissident self-organisation and the content of smuggled samizdat writings under repressive state-socialist regimes were central to the development of this concept of 'civil society'. But the theory was not just developed by East-Central European dissidents. After the violent Soviet suppression of the Hungarian Revolution and the Prague Spring, and martial law against the Polish Solidarity movement, Western critical intellectuals became disillusioned with 'really existing socialism'. Venturing behind the Iron Curtain, some started seeking cooperation with anti-authoritarian dissidents (Keane, 1988; Kaldor et al, 1989). This cooperation sought to address urgent issues such as nuclear disarmament, human rights and environmental protection. It also expressed profound disillusionment with welfare capitalism and the Western imperialist wars in the developing world (Ivancheva, 2011). A number of these Western *peaceniks* attempted to engage activists from 'the other Europe' in their global concerns. Yet, their language of nuclear doomsday and economic austerity was met with reticence by most dissidents whose main concern was lack of freedom (Fehér and Heller, 1987; Tismaneanu, 1990; Burke, 2004). Nevertheless, a dialogue was built out of a shared interest in reclaiming solidarity, extending democratic participation, and enhancing personal autonomy within overly bureaucratised socialist and liberal polities (Cohen and Arato, 1992).

With civic activism regarded as central to the gradual collapse of state socialism, the fame of some (mostly male) dissident intellectuals from East-Central Europe like Adam Michnik, György Konrád, János Kis, Václav Benda and Václav Havel spread to the West. Western publication of their writings throughout the 1980s allowed for these few voices to overshadow those of less high-profile women or men in the movement (Falk, 2003). Their work, however, was often less popular in their own country than in the West (Petrescu, 2013), where they were praised for developing what became known as 'Eastern European civil society': the bottom-up civic initiatives against state surveillance, repression and the denial of human rights and civil liberties of which the Czechoslovak Charter 77 is a particularly famous example. The attendant retheorisation of civil society (Keane, 1988; Kaldor, 1991; Cohen and Arato, 1992; Tamás, 1994) piqued widespread academic interest and increased the influence of intellectuals in the region. By the late 1980s, civil society had become a central 'currency' in East–West intellectual dialogue (Ivancheva, 2011). Yet, while Western publications often championed one dissident voice as representative of a variety of positions on the ground, civil society was conceived differently by prominent dissident individuals: 'anti-politics' (Konrád), 'independent life of society' or 'life in truth' (Havel), 'parallel polis' and 'second culture' (Benda), or 'new evolutionism' (Michnik). These conceptions reflected different views on appropriate tactics vis-à-vis the state, respectively non-engagement, lobbying or taking state power (Renwick, 2006). Different aspects of the ideal were emphasised by authors writing from different ideological positions in the Western academic literature (see for example, Rau, 1987; Cohen and Arato, 1992; Murthy, 1999; Outhwaite and Ray, 2005).

How does this relate to questions of funding? The majority of prominent dissidents were humanistic intellectuals, who were either civil servants or people placed in precarious, underpaid low-skilled jobs as ideological punishment. By the 1980s many were receiving funding under informal arrangements or through academic institutions, publishing houses, grants and international peace awards/scholarships (Wedel, 2001). These forms of funding and recognition did not so much valorise grassroots activity, but rather enhanced a particular intellectual's eminence within certain networks based on their visibility in the West (Petrescu, 2013). It was also contingent on their ability to voice the 'truth' to audiences especially West of the Iron Curtain: here, 'truth' was constructed as an intellectual and moral value in and of itself, the relevance of which was not defined by its acceptance by or accountability to any constituency beyond small circles of like-minded friends, but by the perceived authenticity of the intellectual who expressed it (Körösényi, 2000). In this hierarchy of 'life in truth', political freedom was seen as an ultimate value and dissidents used their international networks to raise awareness and attract funding. Economic security in society more widely, on the contrary, was not seen as meaningful or related to human dignity. Once the euphoria of the 'revolutions' of 1989 was over, the anticipated success of 'civil society' never materialised.

We think there are two noteworthy problems with the way civil society came to be understood in this period. First, it masked the relationship between market and civil society and/or it normalised the 'market' as the most natural expression of human freedom (Ivancheva, 2011). Second, grassroots organising practices under state socialism, retrospectively branded 'civil society', were characterised as Western democracy finally taking root in less developed Eastern ground. The emergence of civil society signified East-Central Europe's 'evolution' within a framework of global relations in which the backward East needed to meet the standards of the advanced West (Melegh, 2006). Community action was construed as part of civil society in a nascent democracy.

Civil society in the aftermath of 1989

After 1989 the dissident ideal of civil society lingered on as an anticipated utopia that never arrived. Clinging to the East-Central European transition as the 'end of history' and victory of the advanced capitalist West over the 'backward' socialist East (Fukuyama, 2006), civil society initiatives functioned in an economic context where neoliberal policies were becoming dominant. Former humanistic intellectuals and dissidents often managed – more or less successfully – to translate their skills into consultancy, as members of think tanks and in other jobs funded through aid from foreign governments, and through US and European private foundations (Wedel, 2001). Ideologically this funding structure aimed to circumvent dependency on the socialist state and public funding, often seen as corrupt and detrimental to the free market. In this way it became linked to a liberal anti-statist narrative which demanded the 'trimming' of the corrupt public service and shrinking of the state (Mikuš, 2016). The Euro-Atlantic integration of the region was accompanied by the global promotion of an East-Central European ideal of civic activism (Kaldor, 2003), framed as independent from relations of political and economic power. The geopolitical commitment to civil society was in this way aligned with strategic and economic goals of Western governments and businesses. By the early 1990s, programmes that aimed to 'build civil society' through humanitarian assistance were replaced with programmes aimed at introducing market institutions that would replace the social function of the state in order to fit a more competitive model of free-market society (Axford, 2005; Vetta, 2012). These programmes were highly bureaucratic and used a short-term project logic that undermined attempts at sustainable social intervention and social change. The admission into the EU and NATO of many East-Central states between 1999 and 2004 led to economic austerity, tighter fiscal policies, deregulation and massive privatisation of public assets, increasing labour market flexibility and internationalisation of the economy (Dale, 2011).

Although marginal, critical evaluations of civil society did gain some purchase after 1989, though most were written in English and targeted academic audiences. These ranged from pointed critiques of the term itself (Kennedy, 1992) to attempts to redeem valuable aspects of the idea (Kaldor, 2003) to apologias for post-socialist societies' 'betrayal' of civil society's putative democratic potential (Tismaneanu, 1999). Former proponents of civil society expressed growing disillusionment with the failure of East-Central European societies to live up to their ideals, denouncing the political passivity of local populations as a burdensome legacy of socialism (Felkai, 1997; Tismaneanu, 1999). Their disillusionment was not a response to the dire conditions of local populations but with what they saw as locally specific failures to 'modernise'.

In the 1990s, sponsored by international foundations and philanthropists such as George Soros, a booming NGO scene was mobilised to implement a free-market society (Wedel, 2001; Kalb, 2002) and this led to a critique of the post-1989 'NGOisation' of civil society in East-Central Europe (Kalb, 2002; Howard, 2003; Mendelson and Glenn, 2002). With the 'integration' of the former socialist periphery of Europe into the Euro-Atlantic core through NATO and the EU, donors' priorities shifted. Following the accession of countries into the EU in 2004, US foundations withdrew from the region. Most NGO funding now came from the EU and was distributed through national governments (Ivancheva, 2015). The financial survival of NGOs increasingly depended on activists mobilising their pre-existing networks, which were typically linked to the liberal elite and which extended into the state administration where funding decisions were made (Vetta, 2012; Ivancheva, 2015). In the redistribution of already scarce resources, university-educated professionals utilised their cultural capital, their ability to speak the language of policy, and their personal and professional links to those working within the state to leverage influence and funding (Ivancheva, 2015). Some organisations managed to solidify their relation with the state; some were directly involved in state building through capacity training of government personnel in schools, prisons, ministries and local administration (Vetta, 2012). When the expected growth of civil society activity did not extend beyond a small circle of NGOs, this did not lead to any reconsideration of what meaningful civic engagement might involve in post-socialist contexts. Instead, they denounced the non-active segments of the democratic constituency they were seeking to build, framing their own mobilisation failures as the fault of post-socialist social reflexes (Gagyi, 2013). Hit hard by post-2008 funding cuts, the instability of the cyclical project culture, and the attendant increase in precariousness among NGO professionals (Mikuš, 2016), members of these circles joined the post-2010 protest wave. With few exceptions, they did not frame this as the local effects of a global capitalist crisis. Instead, liberals blamed the 'backward' development of Eastern capitalism and the persistence of 'communist', that is, oligarchic *nomenklatura*, networks in power (Ivancheva, 2013; Gagyi, 2015).

At the same time, new instances of popular mobilisation, such as community organisations supporting local agricultural producers, environmentalism or housing movements increasingly mixed economic and ethnonationalist claims. Similar claims were evident in trade union activities (Buzogány, 2011; Halmai, 2011). The fact that NGO activists overlooked the economic arguments of the participants of such mobilisations, implicitly framing them as 'un-civil', further solidified the latter's alienation and their political identification with tropes of national loss and pride deployed by the populist right (Ost, 2006; Kalb and Halmai, 2011). Groups articulating economic grievances increasingly depicted civil society activists espousing Western liberal values as national traitors (Mikuš, 2015). NGOs were regarded as 'secretive, manipulative, ineffective, nepotistic ... an "NGO mafia" who reward each other with trips, computers, and other benefits' (Sampson, 2002: 29), or they were viewed as foreign sell-outs (Mikuš, 2016). When right-wing populist leaders like Hungary's Viktor Orbán today propagate anti-NGO policies to 'defend the nation' against the intrusion of Western interests, their words resonate because of the legacy of decades of elitist NGO discourse which has sought Western-type democratisation, and which has downplayed negative local experiences in the post-1989 period.

A global civil society? The alter-globalisation movement in East-Central European

Of course, the use of the term 'civil society' is not limited to the nation state. With the rise of the alter-globalisation movement, the term 'global civil society' also gained prominence (Kaldor, 2003; Della Porta and Tarrow, 2005). Around the late 1990s, political liberals and left activists started to speak about an autonomous civil society as a counterpower to economic globalisation (for example, Salamon et al, 1999). Critics, pointed out that civil society, in particular as manifested in the growth of NGOs globally, was not 'autonomous', but was often providing social services vacated or outsourced by states under neoliberal governance (Axford, 1996). In East-Central Europe this idea of global civil society also re-entrenched East–West divisions; treating more advanced Western movements as their models, East-Central European activists often saw their local contexts as inferior, and dismissed their complex historical formation, embracing 'universally valid' (Western) activist norms (Gagyi, 2013).

According to the movement's ideology, newly emerging movements were to be equal participants in a global activist network. Yet the practice of these groups was determined by their peripheral position in the international movement infrastructure (Gagyi, 2013). As new, small and weak movement groups in East-Central Europe joined the European alter-globalisation movement, the East–West relations within the movement were asymmetric. Western groups had much better access to funding and ideological resources. Generous donations and logistical support came with a degree of control over the direction and framing of joint actions. Even when the challenges of post-socialist contexts were raised, they never became part of the common action agenda within the Eastern enlargement of the European Social Forum (the European chapter of the World Social Forum, which sought to provide a space for dialogue across the alter-globalist movement). Efforts by East-Central European activists to problematise the applicability of Western tactics in post-socialist contexts (like marches under red flags) were rendered irrelevant. East-Central European groups often felt they needed to emulate Western forms of organising and action repertoires in order to prove their position as equals (Gagyi, 2013). The framework of an autonomous, horizontal 'global civil society' seemed to free Eastern political activism from the inferiority complex of post-socialist 'catch up'. Yet it also obfuscated these activists' own position and the relevance of their politics within their societies. 'Autonomous' islands of Western-style alter-globalist activism frequently came to function as local copies of political practice that was not adapted to post-socialist contexts (Gagyi, 2013). When confronted with the fact that activist tactics successful in Western contexts did not bear fruit in post-socialist environments, alter-globalist activists tended to dismiss local societies as 'backward' (Gagyi, 2013). Interestingly, when a discussion emerged on whether East–West funding and epistemic asymmetries enabled or constrained socially relevant progressive activism in the region, it came to be known as the 'co-optation debate' (see Císař, 2010). While one side of the debate emphasised foreign-funding dependence of local actors, the other side maintained that crucial functions of civic activity could only be maintained with that help. In these respects, while the sources of funding were different in autonomist Marxist and anarchist networks who were critical of neoliberal globalisation, they often reproduced a similar dynamic to the NGO culture they criticised.

When a radical right-wing anti-globalism emerged in the region, under the trope of 'national loss', it emphasised the value of local context over the global market (Kalb and Halmai, 2011). While left alter-globalisation activism was ignored by NGO and think-tank elites, right-wing anti-globalism was 'honoured' and arguably nurtured by the moral outrage it caused among the liberals who still dominated public discourse in the late 2000s. In such circles this was attributed to the failures of the local contexts to live up to Western modernity, and was regarded as the nascent resurrection of 1930s' fascism. Yet, narratives of 'civil society' or its 'global' version fall short of explaining the dynamic of the East-Central European alter-globalisation movement or that of its 'evil twin' – the anti-globalist extreme right (Gagyi, 2015). As long as these scholarly paradigms follow normative assumptions of modernisation based on Western historical models, the region is bound to appear as an 'anomaly' in a hierarchical, developmental narrative of democratisation. As right-wing populism, both in terms of ideological frame and as an active element of popular mobilisation, becomes one of the main political challenges of the present, revisiting East-Central European democratisation and the forms of community mobilisation left out of the 'civil society' lens is timelier than ever.

Conclusion

The chapter dealt with the transnational construct of 'civil society', the idea and institutional practice that dominated formal approaches to community empowerment and self-organisation during and after the 1989 regime change. We argued that this universalising normative concept was applied to East-Central Europe in the context of post-socialist transformation, but that the concept of civil society is analytically unfit to address issues of democratic inclusion or community mobilisation. While micro- and meso-level details in the overall funding model of civil society in each period are important, with this chapter we argue that these developments can only be explained vis-à-vis the overall macro level context of the Eastern European 'transitions'.

As a tool for democratic participation during the post-1989 transitions, civil society did not include the burning questions of economic democracy. As a tool of empirical analysis, it has been impaired by overgeneralisation: small intellectual circles have projected the 'ideal' of Western-type democracy on society. When East-Central European societies failed to meet that projected ideal, it was they who were deemed faulty, not the descriptive capacity of the term. It encouraged moralising and pejorative descriptions of local populations as somehow lacking. To challenge this approach, a reflection on the complex evolution of the transnational history of the concept of civil society is more urgent than ever, in three complementary directions. First, it needs to be interpreted vis-à-vis the positions of those who reinvented the concept and brought it into view. Findings from the scant research on the role of intellectuals and civil society activists in the process of regime change and transition can be used to recontextualise the civil society idea within broader social and political relations (for example, Eyal et al, 2000; Falk, 2003; Vetta, 2009; Mikuš, 2015). Second, academic and political discussions of East–West cooperation need to shake off the normative 'democratisation' and 'civil society' frameworks. It needs to be reassessed with regard to the actual limitations that global capitalism poses to transnational political activism, for example, dynamics of funding, communication apparatuses of geopolitical powers, and changing geographies of social tensions. Third, we need to reconstruct the historical experience and contemporary reality of Eastern Europe within collective debates around the current global economic crisis. New perspectives beyond the simplistic East–West divide need to engage discussion of persistent global hierarchies. We should discuss community initiatives and transnational cooperation not in terms of their conformity, or otherwise, to prescriptions of Western modernity, but according to their capacity to intervene in a meaningful way in local and global struggles against rising poverty, insecurity and violent conflicts.

This has clear relevance to debates over how emancipatory community development might be imagined in the context of Central-Eastern Europe. This is even more urgent given the quick advancement of the far-right in the region and across the world. By adopting an anti-globalisation rhetoric that substitutes the inferiority imposed by the pro-Western liberal framework of 'catching up' with ethnonational pride, the far-right has gained electoral ground. In a sad irony, East-Central Europe for once preceded similar developments in the West. With the rise of the Popular Front, the Austrian People's Party or the victories of Brexit and Donald Trump, the West is now 'catching up' with the East. Yet, instead of using the historical experiences in the region to understand what went wrong with the neoliberal Euro-Atlantic integration of the region, a quarter of a century after 1989, and despite the recession, insecurity and poverty that the transition to a market economy has brought across the world, liberal and centrist parties continue to entertain these frameworks even at risk of perpetual electoral loss. A globally comparative reconceptualisation of what popular politics and self-organisation means in East-Central Europe is necessary if we wish to understand how present-day mobilisations relate to local conditions and global processes. Research into and engagement with local realities on the ground is the only route to explore possible political alliances and work towards the institutionalisation of protest movements into alternative political practices.

References

Axford, B. (1996) *The global system: Economics, politics and culture*, Cambridge: Polity Press.

Axford, B. (2005) 'Critical globalization studies and a network perspective on global civil society', in R.P. Appelbaum and W.I. Robinson (eds) *Critical globalization studies*, New York: Routledge.

Burke, P.D.M. (2004) 'A transcontinental movement of citizens? Strategic debates in the 1980s Western peace movement', in G.-R. Horn and P. Kenney (eds) *Transnational moments of change: Europe 1945, 1968, 1989*, Oxford: Rowman & Littlefield, pp 189–206.

Buzogány, Á. (2011) 'Stairway to heaven or highway to hell? Ambivalent Europeanisation and civil society in Central and Eastern Europe', in H. Kouki and E. Romanos (eds) *Protest beyond borders: Contentious politics in Europe since 1945*, New York: Berghahn Books, pp 69–85.

Císař, O. (2010) 'Externally sponsored contention: The channelling of environmental movement organisations in the Czech Republic after the fall of Communism', *Environmental Politics*, 19(5): 736–55.

Cohen, J.L. and Arato, A. (1992) *Civil society and political theory*, Cambridge, MA: MIT Press.

Dale, G. (ed) (2011) *First the transition, then the crash: Eastern Europe in the 2000s*, London: Pluto Press.

Della Porta, D. and Tarrow, S.G. (eds) (2005) *Transnational protest and global activism: People, passions, and power*, Lanham, MD: Rowman and Littlefield.

Eyal, G., Szelényi, I. and Townsley, E. (2000) *Making capitalism without capitalists: Class formation and elite struggles in post-communist Central Europe*, London: Verso.

Falk, B.J. (2003) *The dilemmas of dissidence in East-Central Europe: Citizen intellectuals and philosopher kings*, Budapest: Central European University Press.

Fehér, F. and Heller, Á. (1987) *Eastern left, Western left: Totalitarianism, freedom and democracy*, Cambridge: Polity Press.

Felkai, G. (1997) 'Két társadalomelméleti illúzió széttörése a jelenkori magyar közgondolkodáson', *Szociológiai Figyelő*, 1(1): 100–24.

Fukuyama, F. (2006) *The end of history and the last man*, New York: Free Press.

Gagyi, A. (2013) 'The shifting meaning of "autonomy" in the East European diffusion of the alter-globalisation movement: Hungarian and Romanian experiences', in C. Flesher Fominaya and L. Cox (eds) *Understanding European movements: New social movements, global justice struggles, anti-austerity protest*, Abingdon: Routledge, pp 143–57.

Gagyi, A. (2015) 'Why don't East European movements address inequalities the way Western European movements do? A review essay on the availability of movement-relevant research', *Interface: A Journal for and About Social Movements*, 7(2): 15–26.

Halmai, G. (2011) '(Dis)possessed by the spectre of socialism: Nationalist mobilisation in "transitional" Hungary', in D. Kalb and G. Halmai (eds) *Headlines of nation, subtexts of class: Working-class populism and the return of the repressed in neoliberal Europe*, New York: Berghahn Books, pp 113–41.

Howard, M.M. (2003) *The weakness of civil society in post-Communist Europe*, Cambridge: Cambridge University Press.

Ivancheva, M. (2011) 'The role of dissident-intellectuals in the formation of civil society in (post)communist East-Central Europe', in H. Kouki and E. Romanos (eds) *Protest beyond borders: Contentious politics in Europe since 1945*, New York: Berghahn Books, pp 177–87.

Ivancheva, M. (2013) 'The Bulgarian wave of protests, 2012–2013', *CritCom*, 7 October, Center for European Studies, Columbia University, http://councilforeuropeanstudies.org/critcom/the-bulgarian-wave-of-protests-2012-2013.

Ivancheva, M. (2015) ' "The spirit of the law": Mobilizing and/or professionalizing the women's movement in post-socialist Bulgaria', in A. Krizsán (ed) *Mobilizing for policy change: Women's movements in Central and Eastern European – domestic violence policy struggles*, Budapest: CPS Books, Central European University, pp 45–84.

Kalb, D. (2002) 'Afterword: Globalism and post-socialist prospects', in C.M. Hann (ed) *Postsocialism: Ideals, ideologies, and practices in Eurasia*, London: Routledge, pp 317–34.

Kalb, D. and Halmai, G. (eds) (2011) *Headlines of nation, subtexts of class: Working-class populism and the return of the repressed in neoliberal Europe*, New York: Berghahn Books.

Kaldor, M. (2003) 'The idea of global civil society', *International Affairs*, 79(3): 583–93.

Kaldor, M. (ed) (1991) *Europe from below: An East–West dialogue*, London: Verso.

Kaldor, M., Holden, G. and Falk, R.A. (eds) (1989) *The new detente: Rethinking East–West relations*, London: Verso.

Keane, J. (ed) (1988) *Civil society and the state: New European perspectives*, London: Verso.

Kennedy, M.D. (1992) 'The intelligentsia in the constitution of civil societies and post-communist regimes in Hungary and Poland', *Theory and Society*, 21(1): 29–76.

Kopecký, P. and Mudde, C. (eds) (2003) *Uncivil society? Contentious politics in post-communist Europe*, London: Routledge.

Körösényi, A. (2000) *Értelmiség, politikaigondolkodáséskormányzat*, Budapest: Osiris.

Melegh, A. (2006) *On the East–West slope: Globalization, nationalism, racism and discourses on Eastern Europe*, Budapest: CEU Press.

Mendelson, S.E. and Glenn, J.K. (eds) (2002) *The power and limits of NGOs: A critical look at building democracy in Eastern Europe and Eurasia*, New York: Columbia University Press.

Mikuš, M. (2015) 'Indigenizing "civil society" in Serbia: What local fund-raising reveals about class and trust', *Focaal*, 71(1): 43–56.

Mikuš, M. (2016) 'The justice of neoliberalism: Moral ideology and redistributive politics of public-sector retrenchment in Serbia', *Social Anthropology*, 24(2): 211–27.

Murthy, V. (1999) 'Leftist mourning: Civil society and political practice in Hegel and Marx', *Rethinking Marxism*, 11(3): 36–55.

Ost, D. (2006) *The defeat of solidarity: Anger and politics in postcommunist Europe*, Ithaca, NY: Cornell University Press.

Outhwaite, W. and Ray L.J. (2005) *Social theory and postcommunism*, Malden, MA: Blackwell.

Petrescu, C. (2013) '"Free conversations in an occupied country": Cultural transfer, social networking and political dissent in Romanian Tamizdat', in F. Kind-Kovács and J. Labov (eds) *Samizdat, Tamizdat and beyond: Transnational media during and after socialism*, Oxford: Berghahn, pp 107–36.

Piotrowski, G. (2009) 'Civil society, un-civil society and the social movements', *Interface: A Journal for and About Social Movements*, 1(2): 166–89.

Rau, Z. (1987) 'Some thoughts on civil society in Eastern Europe and the Lockean contractarian approach', *Political Studies*, 35(4): 573–92.

Renwick, A. (2006) 'Anti-political or just anti-communist? Varieties of dissidence in East-Central Europe, and their implications for the development of political society', *East European Politics and Societies*, 20(2): 286–318.

Salamon, L.M., Anheier, H.K., List, R., Toepler, S. and Sokolowski, S.W. (1999) *Global civil society: Dimensions of the nonprofit sector*, Baltimore, MD: The Johns Hopkins Center for Civil Society Studies WP.

Sampson, S. (2002) 'Weak states, uncivil societies and thousands of NGOs: Benevolent colonialism in the Balkans', in S. Resic and B. Törnquist-Plewa (eds) *The Balkans in focus: Cultural boundaries in Europe*, Lund: Nordic Academic Press, pp 27–44.

Stokes, G. (1986) 'The social origins of East European politics', *East European Politics and Societies*, 1(1): 30–74.

Tamás, G.M. (1994) 'A disquisition of civil society', *Social Research*, 61(2): 205–22.

Tismaneanu, V. (1990) *In search of civil society: Independent peace movements in the Soviet bloc*, New York: Routledge.

Tismaneanu, V. (ed) (1999) *The revolutions of 1989: Rewriting histories*, London: Routledge.

United Nations (2010) *Community development*, https://unterm.un.org/UNTERM/Display/Record/UNHQ/NA/bead44b0-ac66-48f8-86b1-ff78c6c334da.

Vetta, T. (2009) 'Revived nationalism versus European democracy: Class and "identity dilemmas" in contemporary Serbia', *Focaal*, 55(1): 74–89.

Vetta, T. (2012) 'NGOs and the state: Clash or class? Circulating elites of "good governance" in Serbia', in B. Petric (ed) *Democracy at large: NGOs, political foundations, think tanks and international organizations*, New York: Palgrave Macmillan, pp 169–90.

Wedel, J.R. (2001) *Collision and collusion: The strange case of Western aid to Eastern Europe*, London: St. Martin's Press.

FIVE

Social finance and community development: exploring egalitarian possibilities

Brendan Murtagh and Niamh Goggin

Introduction

The last three decades have seen a considerable global expansion of social finance providers, products, legal formats and intermediaries (OECD, 2015). Put simply, social finance involves investment and lending to community businesses and charities to achieve social, environmental and financial returns (Benedikter, 2011). A range of governments have established new community finance organisations, fiscal instruments (in the form of tax relief) and technical assistance programmes to enable and extend the social enterprise market. For critics, this is repositioning the community and voluntary sector around a neoliberal politics that privileges marketisation, state rollback and the disciplining of community groups to adopt more commercial modes of self-reliant working (Wheeler, 2017). This chapter argues that the expansion of social finance is critical to neoliberal rollout tactics but that it is also necessary and useful for community development approaches that respond to the needs of the excluded. Here, we are concerned with the relationship between community development and economic regeneration highlighting the importance of the ownership of assets and critically, finance, to support the social and solidarity economy (SSE).

Social economics and solidarity finance are fraught with definitional difficulties (Moore et al, 2014). In this chapter, we focus on the SSE, which is characterised by: community organisations that trade goods and services for profit but whose surpluses are used for social benefit; cooperative forms of ownership rather than shareholder interest; and governance rules that share a commitment to redistribution and ethical ends (Defourny and Nyssens, 2010; Utting et al, 2014). The chapter argues that social finance, as a support to the SSE, is a necessary component of local economic development, institution building and the development of skills and knowledge across the community and voluntary sectors. McFarlane (2011) draws on the work of Latour to show that neoliberalism is worked through a set of assembled relations that include institutions, resources, networks, actors (political and civic), decision-making routines, laws and knowledge producers. In turn, he argues that resistance is shaped by assembling countermoves, which to be effective, need to engage with the everyday realities of economic development and especially finance. In this spirit, this chapter advances social finance as a potential 'countermovement'. It sets social finance in the context of the relationship between money and capitalist markets, before briefly describing the development of a range of services, products and intermediaries, nationally as well as globally. This is followed by a review of issues related to demand and supply, and two case studies of progressive social finance initiatives. To conclude, the implications of social finance for community development are set out.

Finance, the market and the 'double movement'

For Karl Polanyi (2001), finance, along with land and labour, is at the heart of the crises of modern markets, economic instability and even global conflict. Writing at the end of the Second World War, he drew attention to the disembedding tactics of capital, that is, its attempt to separate the market economy from non-economic actors, laws, regulations and social relations. Neoliberalism has attempted to do just this and to redefine the market as an independent and self-regulating system and as the most efficient (and even fairest) mechanism for distributing private and public goods (Peck, 2013). This process is, in part, shaped by the way in which land, labour and finance have been treated as what Polanyi calls 'fictitious commodities'. These 'factors of production' are essential for making goods and services and cannot, Polanyi claims, be treated as commodities to be valorised and bought and sold in their own right. Attempts to disembed economics in this way creates an inevitable 'double movement' in which society attempts to protect itself against the intensification of pure market logic (Block and Somers, 2014). Here, he details how dehumanising labour, exploiting nature and the inherent instabilities created by financialisation also shape possibilities to mobilise around alternatives – the double movement.

How, in Polanyi's terms, can society re-embed the market? Ferguson (2015) is critical of radical movements for avoiding, rather than directly engaging, the modalities of the market. The point, he argues, is to change it by identifying when and where the market operates and in particular, how it typically privileges individualism over the commons and profit over social benefit. As noted earlier, McFarlane (2011) sees resistance as the practice of assembling institutions, networks, skills, projects and resources capable of both encountering and working through alternatives to neoliberalism. In this sense, working with the realities of money, contracts, business models and surplus is envisaged as a possible basis for a politics of resistance (Margarian, 2017).

Developments in social finance

The social impact investment (SII) field has expanded rapidly in response to: 'a growing interest by individuals and investors in tackling social issues at the local, national and global level. ... Governments are seeking more effective ways to address these growing challenges and are recognising that private sector models can provide innovative approaches' (OECD, 2015: 11).

These arguments featured strongly in the G8 Social Impact Investment Forum in London in 2013, the subsequent launch of the Social Impact Investment Taskforce and the OECD *Overview Paper* published a year later (Wilson, 2014). This sees SII as 'the provision of finance for organisations with the explicit expectations of a measurable social as well as a financial return' (OECD, 2015: 18). But this covers a broad spectrum of products and purposes from responsible investments that simply mitigate risky environmental practices, to impact-only funds that address social challenges but which cannot guarantee a financial return for investors. The United Nations Research Institute for Social Development (UNRISD) definition is less restrictive and involves the concept of 'solidarity' to distinguish the explicit egalitarian qualities and purposes of social finance:

> Exchange and financial mechanisms based on collective self-organization through which people manage their resources according to principles of solidarity, autonomy, trust and mutual aid. Social and Solidarity Finance (SSF) encompasses ethical banking, financial cooperatives, community development banks, solidarity microfinance, crypto and complementary currencies, community based savings schemes (such as rotating savings and credit associations, RACS), participatory budgeting, crowd funding, social impact bonds and forms of solidarity impact investing. (UNRISD, 2016: 1)

These funds do not prioritise financial returns but aim to integrate surpluses within the social and/or environmental objectives of the organisations they support. Figure 5.1 identifies the range of actors, networks and trading relationships that comprise an increasingly complex assemblage. On the demand side, there are organisations that both seek impact investment and returns (increasingly governments) and those who need capital, including community development organisations diversifying income streams or forming as social enterprises (Benedikter, 2011). The sources and channels of capital have also diversified with a range of intermediaries, social banks, crowd-funding platforms (such as community shares) and community development finance institutions (CDFIs) offering a variety of loans, bonds and equity investments.

The use of social finance thus varies from asset-locked charities, to impact-driven, for-profit organisations seeking some form of social return. Nicholls (2010) sees this lack of definition as a barrier to growth, not least because it undermines its credibility to asset managers, governments and the mix of beneficiary interests. These differences also create a tension within community development as each is driven by a distinct set of rationalities and business models. Nicholls (2010: 75) sees these expressed in three social investment logics:

> First, it can focus on generating only social and environmental returns, for example through government spending or support for social movements. Second, it can generate 'pure' financial returns to capital in an analogous way to conventional investing ... [and third] ... blended value creation that combines both an attention to financial return and a focus on social/environmental outputs and outcomes.

Table 5.1 shows that each of these logics range between a distinctive set of means-ended rationalities to more value-based orientations and approaches. In between, a systemic rationality combines utilitarian and mission-driven practices to generate a mix of social, economic and environmental returns. The table shows that the first logic is about means-end profit maximisation reflected in commercial green energy sectors but also in a range of socially responsible investments as well as venture philanthropy, where high net worth investors seek social impact as well as some form of financial return. The second broad category reflects investor approaches that aim to balance means-ends and value-driven rationalities. Again, it is differentiated between socially responsible investment for profit; direct investment in social enterprises encouraged by new legal formats such as community

Figure 5.1: The structure of social impact investment

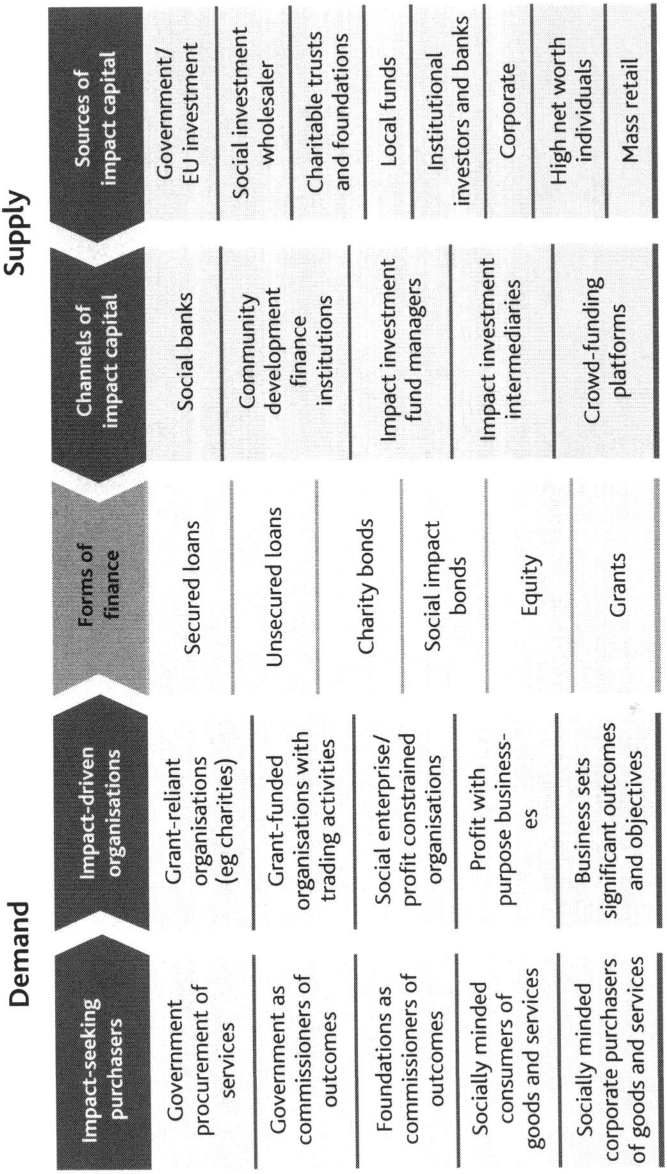

Demand

Impact-seeking purchasers	Impact-driven organisations	Forms of finance	Channels of impact capital	Sources of impact capital
Government procurement of services	Grant-reliant organisations (eg charities)	Secured loans	Social banks	Government/EU investment
Government as commissioners of outcomes	Grant-funded organisations with trading activities	Unsecured loans	Community development finance institutions	Social investment wholesaler
Foundations as commissioners of outcomes	Social enterprise/profit constrained organisations	Charity bonds		Charitable trusts and foundations
		Social impact bonds	Impact investment fund managers	Local funds
Socially minded consumers of goods and services	Profit with purpose businesses	Equity	Impact investment intermediaries	Institutional investors and banks
				Corporate
Socially minded corporate purchasers of goods and services	Business sets significant outcomes and objectives	Grants	Crowd-funding platforms	High net worth individuals
				Mass retail

Supply

Source: SIIT, 2014: 3

Table 5.1: Social investment matrix

Investor rationality	Investor logic			Type of investor	Capital created
	Financial	Blended	Social/ environmental		
Means– ends driven	Clean energy investment	Socially responsible investment	Venture philanthropy	Profit maximising individuals and institutions, venture philanthropists	£900 bn
Systemic	Impact investment	Social enterprise investment	Government investment	Social investors, social venture capitalists, government	£17 bn
Value driven	Philanthropy	Mutual investment/ Mission-related investments	Social change investment	Charitable trusts, philanthropists, cooperatives, community development finance institutions, members of social movements	£3.6 tn

Source: based on Nicholls, 2010, tables 1 and 2, pp 88–9

interest companies; and new forms of public sector funding such as social impact bonds, which aim to use private investment to tackle a range of complex social problems. The third type places a much stronger emphasis on social returns, often with limited or no expectation of financial returns and includes: traditional forms of philanthropy; mission-related investments that blend social and economic returns; and more radical instruments designed to achieve longer-term, systemic social change. Nicholls shows that each of these sectors has grown significantly in monetary terms but, despite the assumption that market logics are driving the SSE and a new culture of community development, value-driven investment is still the largest in terms of capital flows at £3.6 trillion in 2011.

Social finance investment logics: implications for community development

This diversity of social finance logics, norms and modes of working is striking. Each of the investor logics presents a different set of scenarios for community development and how it might evolve in relation to changing public sector and private markets. On the one hand, community sector involvement with financial investment carries risks. For instance, Trudeau (2012) argues that social finance is being used to support the third sector to develop services outside government as an alternative, low cost 'shadow state'. Similarly, Edwards (2010) warns about the way in which community organisations are invited to use contractual metrics that shift their understanding of impact to economic rather than social outcomes. Roy (2012: 39) also criticises the 'financialization of development' and the circulatory capacity of 'centres of calculation' such as the World Bank and USAID to transfer best practice from Northern finance regimes to the Global South. On the other hand, social finance investment has also been shown to lead to progressive outcomes. Roy (2012), for example, acknowledges that microfinance schemes have supported significant pro-poor, gender inclusive and equality objectives. Here, Moore et al (2014) see social enterprise investment focusing on accelerating growth in small-scale, break-even, start-up businesses that can address a range of social, economic and environmental problems. An alternative scenario is more politically radical by suggesting that social investment can institutionalise value-driven rationalities and then bring them into mainstream capital markets. 'This scenario would generate systemic change across all investment via radical and disruptive action seeking a broader or deeper transformation of society marked by more explicitly political, critical and counter-cultural orientations' (Nicholls, 2010: 92). Nicholls argues that the rise of ethical consumption, a concern about climate change and banking failures could drive a double movement that seeks to re-embed economics in a wider set of egalitarian concerns. But, as Ferguson (2015) makes clear, this needs to be *made* and involves the assembly of institutions, rules and resources, which are inevitably entangled with market finance to push back financialisation in favour of more socially inclusive outcomes.

The social and solidarity economy and the demand for social finance

Part of the challenge for social finance is the lack of viable commercial projects created by community development organisations that can access and pay back loans. Baker and Goggin (2016) point out that most charities are small, that they face distinctive skills and resource obstacles to the use of social finance and that demand for this type of funding remains weak, despite falling grant income. Their study showed that the segmentation of the market highlights the need for a more sophisticated range of products given the size, stage of development and asset base of larger community businesses. Social investment is thus increasingly shaped by the needs of larger, well-secured charities capable of delivering public sector contracts, rather than the challenges of small and medium-sized enterprises. At this level, community organisations are not likely to be prime providers as local authorities shift from grants to contracts and they often find themselves at the end of a long supply chain (Baker and Goggin, 2016). The delay in receipted payments compared with up-front grants has created cash flow problems and a demand for working capital which, given the comparatively small amounts involved, short lending periods and comparatively high transaction costs, lenders are reluctant to supply. Smaller charities and community development organisations have thus seen an increase in demand for *patient capital*, which involves blended loans and grants, technical support, lower than market rate returns and significantly longer (and renegotiable) repayment periods than private sector loans (Thorlby, 2011).

Iona et al (2011) emphasise the need to stimulate demand for finance by building awareness, marketing products and developing a preliminary understanding of the grant–loan relationship to help charities to become investment ready. The need for community development organisations to improve their financial literacy and ability to scale up or replicate successful business models has created new thinking about community development skills, knowledge and learning frameworks. For example, Maas and Grieco (2017) called for training to focus on the technical use of social finance, on how to prevent mission drift and on how to account for social as well as financial impacts, in managing community assets. In addition, intermediaries are critical to better connect demand and supply but it is important to ensure that the market is not overstimulated creating a shortage of processing capacity among intermediaries (NEF, 2007). Mauksch et al (2017) stress the cultural resistance within the community development sector to using private capital but also identified a lack of skills in putting a business case together and a weak credit history as key obstacles. Moreover, the level of risk, the fact that many loans cannot be secured against property or other assets, means that interest rates are set too high and for smaller organisations, the costs of processing and managing loans are excessive.

The supply of social finance

As Nicholls notes, the supply side has expanded in volume, diversity and fiscal complexity since the 1990s and reflects the way in which grants from the state, often the primary sponsor of the community and voluntary sector, are increasingly displaced by a range of products and intermediaries. Charities have always used blended forms of finance through a mix of grants, gifts, reserves, secured and unsecured loans, mortgages and community shares and so, to some extent, there is nothing particularly new about social finance (Benedikter, 2011). However, as Moore et al (2014) have shown, there has been considerable development in instruments to support larger charities including partnership models with the private sector. These include:

- Social venture funds, which are becoming more prevalent but are small in scale, often do not have a proven track record, making it harder to attract investors, and lack viable opportunities for this type of high-risk environment (ICF GHK, 2013). Some are independent while others are affiliated with larger banks and financial institutions including, for example, the Social Venture Fund based in Germany and Bridges Finance, established in London in 2002.
- Pay-for-success instruments, such as social impact bonds, are public–private partnerships in which commissioners reward independent providers for the achievement of specific outcomes. Pay-for-success models have expanded considerably, especially in the US, Australia, Africa and India (GIIN, 2013). These tend to be at the commercial end of the investment spectrum and have attracted criticisms, not least because they reduce complex social problems, such as recidivism and homelessness, to an economic opportunity for speculation (Margarian, 2017).
- Community development finance institutions (CDFIs) are specialist organisations whose primary mission is to promote social welfare rather than private profit by providing affordable finance that would otherwise be unavailable to social enterprises from high-street banks and loan companies (Nicholls, 2010). Many CDFIs are funded by governments and charitable trusts although they usually do not take savings or deposits as with commercial banks. The New Economics Foundation (NEF, 2007) showed that CDFIs have been effective in getting funding into underinvested areas but that most are small and growing slowly and that there is over-optimism about their longer-term economic impact.

- In the 2014 Budget, the UK government established a new Social Investment Tax Relief (SITR), which gives individual investors in broadly defined 'social sector organisations' a reduction of 30% of the investment on their income tax liabilities for the financial year. This builds on the experience of Community Investment Tax Relief (CITR), which encouraged private investments in specific CDFIs, again with tax relief incentives for the investor.

As noted earlier, part of the challenge in social finance is that it is at a comparatively early stage of development and lacks the structures, systems and security associated with mainstream capital markets (Nicholls, 2010). This includes intermediary services (brokers, technical assistance and regulators) that are important in lowering transaction costs, reducing risk, creating liquidity and keeping the focus on social value. Social stock exchanges enable charities to attract capital but also provide investors with a degree of certainty about liquidity and risk management. The London Social Stock Exchange was established in 2013 and is now authorised and regulated as an investment exchange for trading in securities of social enterprises and social purpose businesses. The Impact Exchange aims to become a social stock market across Africa and Asia for mission-related investments but liquidity and exit still remain significant obstacles to charities and how they manage equity finance (ICF GHK, 2013).

There has also been a strengthening of wholesaler investors, especially linked to an increase in CDFIs. Big Society Capital (BSC) was launched in the UK in 2012 as a social investment bank to provide finance to CDFIs who lend on to social enterprises, charities and voluntary organisations. It was funded from £400 million in dormant bank accounts, in addition to £200 million from the four main British retail banks. The main activity of these wholesalers is to improve the capital levels of CDFIs, provide working capital to support day-to-day operations and provide technical assistance to help skill-up the sector.

Other intermediaries focus less on the supply of finance and more on making the social finance market work effectively. The Global Impact Investing Network (GIIN) was established in 2008 by 40 investors, mainly to address barriers to investment by training, strengthening knowledge and research and improving reporting standards (GIIN, 2013). For example, the Impact Reporting and Investment Standards (IRIS) is a set of metrics that describe the social and environmental performance, as well as the financial health, of social purpose organisations. This is designed to address a lack of transparency in how organisations measure and publicise their performance, particularly to social investors (OECD, 2015). In what follows, two examples are briefly considered that show social finance operating toward the value-driven side of Nicholls continuum as well as the factors that are critical in resisting the drift to market cultures and outcomes. Some of the potential and dynamics of social finance are best explored through case studies and we will now offer two brief examples of what is possible through such activity.

Case studies: Mondragon in the Basque country and BRAC in Bangladesh

The Mondragon Corporation Cooperative (MCC) is one of the largest cooperatives in the world and is the 11th largest business in Spain, employing 84,000 people (Morgan, 2016). The company started in 1956 when a local priest led a worker takeover of a failing factory in the small Basque town. To increase the supply of skilled labour, they later established a technological college which became the Mondragon University and a consumer cooperative that developed as a national retail chain, EROSKI. As the organisation grew and diversified globally, the MCC set up its own bank by pooling profits and creating investment funds to support both existing as well as new cooperatives. There is a particular emphasis on skilled employment sectors, social innovation and training to enable worker-members to participate in the governance of the company and to shape its strategic direction (Morgan, 2016). The corporation is now subdivided into four divisions – finance, industry, retail and knowledge – and these involve 281 companies in 27 countries. The finance division is based on the *Caja Laboral* bank, which works alongside initiatives on mutual benefit credit and insurance and had an equity fund of €4.5 billion in 2011. In the same year, the retail area had gross sales of €8 billion, the university has nearly 3,500 students and the MCC invested €165 million on R&D and innovation (MCC, 2012). The organisation emphasised that 'capital is considered to be an inherent subordinate to labour, which is necessary for business development' (MCC, 2012: 35). In short, capital is deployed to extend and scale up the cooperative ideology and the company's governance council is directed by a social council representing the membership and a monitoring commission ensures compliance with social outcomes as well as financial performance.

Mondragon had a population of around 8,500 people in the 1950s and like many community development projects, responded to a local crisis of the factory closure. It is now a multinational, functionally integrated social business that makes profits for reinvestment, including through its bank, to support its ethical mission (MCC, 2012). The Basque economy is heavily reliant on cooperatives or part-employee-owned manufacturing firms, supported by a permissive legal, fiscal and regulatory regime. It has an exceptionally low Gini coefficient and is one of the most resilient economies in Europe (Morgan, 2016). The SSE does not occupy a marginal space at the edge of state or private markets but is culturally embedded and politically backed as a mainstay of the regional economy. The assemblage of regulations, R&D and the emphasis on innovation linked to self-generated finance are at the heart of scaling up and scaling out strategies. However, the bank was exposed to investment in the property sector and the subsequent economic crash in Spain. The need to refinance the bank, seek out returns and ultimately speculate, emphasises the risks and contradictions involved in social finance institutions working within capital markets.

Like Mondragon, BRAC (Building Resources Across Communities) in Bangladesh developed an integrated approach to finance, training and technical support for social enterprises providing for disadvantaged communities. The organisation also operates at scale, with 111,000 employees, an annual expenditure of $1.1 billion, 48 schools and 117,000 community health workers (BRAC, 2016). BRAC delivers programmes on health, water and hygiene, education, capacity building for NGOs and local economic regeneration. The BRAC model also involves the creation of a connected network of enterprises, development programmes and a standalone financial investment capability. Half of all surpluses from BRAC's social enterprises are reinvested in its own businesses in an attempt to reduce their grant dependence, especially from international aid organisations. BRAC currently operates 16 social enterprises across health, agriculture, green energy and retailing. Aarong was one of the first companies established and developed as a fashion retail chain in Dhaka, initially to provide secure distribution outlets and fair prices for rural craft workers. By 2015, Aarong had served 9 million customers through 15 retail stores and e-commerce sites, generating an annual turnover of $62 million. It employs 3,000 people with 65,000 artisans in the supply chain and these are, in turn, organised into 80 producer groups in 15 craft production centres and 535 hand embroidery centres. This also provides an organisational channel to deliver health care programmes, family support and sanitation education at a community level.

As noted earlier, microfinance is not without critics, not least because it appears to discipline the poor in the ways of the market and uses debt to address poverty. However, in the case of BRAC, the idea of a resource-dependent NGO subjected to and unable to resist intergovernmental agencies transacting neoliberal solutions is simply not borne out by the evidence. Strategic investments, primarily in low-income housing, microfinance and small enterprises, all help to develop reserves in order to cross-subsidise businesses that face short-term liquidity problems or want to scale their operations, open branches or start new product lines. This has helped reduce dependence on international aid which has declined from $191.44 million in 2014 to $100.2 million in 2015. Over the same period, microfinance investment increased from $171.35 million to $195.44 million and education programmes from $64.99 million to $71.40 million and by 2015, BRAC had invested $150.61 million across its social enterprises (BRAC, 2016).

Conclusions

These examples illustrate the various roles that social finance has played in creating a largely self-regulating system of production, consumption and circulation that operates well beyond a local level. Each now operates at scale and neither owes its origins or development to neoliberal politics, government policies or the conditions that often accompany international aid. They have responded to highly localised crises including factory closures, poverty, unemployment and lack of credit. Moreover, they use the technologies of finance, stay close to government and help to create preferential regulatory conditions for cooperative and social enterprise growth. Finance and recycling self-generated surpluses have been critical to their own assemblage tactics and practices. They are, of course, integrated into local, national and even international capital circuits and scaling community development projects to become meaningful alternatives to neoliberal economics requires such entanglements and the skills to operate effectively in the market. Mondragon speculated in the property boom in Spain and BRAC has extended its microfinance products, including to other developing countries. The need to recapitalise social finance institutions draws providers into the same accumulation and risk strategies as for-profit organisations, and mistakes, poor judgements and questionable ethical practice in decision making and strategic planning all arise. The need to build a learning culture around such judgements and to strengthen governance mechanisms to protect organisational ethics are as vital for large enterprises as they are for community groups using social finance for the first time.

The priority for community development is not to dismiss finance as necessarily neoliberal, nor to present a pure, but ultimately unattainable, ethical vision for the sector. The skills, knowledge and learning needed to use social finance are critical foundations to using it responsibly. This means making judgements about its effects, balancing means-driven and value-driven logics and being clear about its impact – socially, environmentally and economically. As Nicholls showed, the market is turning to the SSE for new investment platforms for security, publicity and for *some* ethical purposes. It has stimulated finance structures with a thin connection to the social and with market products such as social impact bonds, in which private sector practices and values dominate. To reassemble social finance in a way that minimises such risks, more explicitly pro-social intermediation, research, impact measures and laws are clearly needed. Mobilising around such a strategy is critical, not just to resist the potentially punitive effects of social finance, but to create more independent and secure access to resources that enable more effective community development.

References

Baker, L. and Goggin, N. (2016) *Small charities and social investment*, London: Institute for Voluntary Action Research (IVAR).

Benedikter, R. (2011) *Social banking and social finance: Answers to economic crises*, New York: Springer.

Block, F. and Somers, M.R. (2014) *The power of market fundamentalism: Karl Polanyi's critique*, Cambridge, MA: Harvard University Press.

BRAC (2016) *BRAC annual report 2015*, Dhaka: BRAC (Building Resources Across Communities).

Defourny, J. and Nyssens, M. (2010) 'Social enterprise in Europe: At the crossroads of market, public policies and third sector', *Policy and Society*, 29(3): 231–42.

Edwards, M. (2010) *Small change: Why business won't save the world*, San Francisco: Berrett-Koehler Publishers.

Ferguson, J. (2015) *Give a man a fish*, Durham, NC: Duke University Press.

GIIN (Global Impact Investing Network) (2013) *Catalytic first-loss capital*, New York: GIIN.

ICF GHK in association with BMG Research (2013) *Growing the social investment market: The landscape and economic impact*, London: HM Government.

Iona, J., de Las Casas, L. and Rickey, B. (2011) *Understanding the demand for and supply of social finance*, London: NESTA.

Maas, K. and Grieco, C. (2017) 'Distinguishing game changers from boastful charlatans: Which social enterprises measure their impact?', *Journal of Social Entrepreneurship*, 8(1): 110–28.

Margarian, A. (2017) 'Tell me your financing and I will tell you who you are: Organizations' strategies and project funds' effectiveness', *Social Enterprise Journal*, 13(1): 53–77.

Mauksch, S., Dey, P., Rowe, M. and Teasdale, S. (2017) 'Ethnographies of social enterprise', *Social Enterprise Journal*, 13(2): 114–127.

MCC (Mondragon Corporation Cooperative) (2012) *Mondragon 1956–2012: A review of the key milestones in the cooperative's group history*, Mondragon: MCC.

McFarlane, C. (2011) 'Assemblage and critical urbanism', *City*, 15(2): 204–24.

Moore, M.-L., Westley, F.R. and Nicholls, A. (2014) 'The social finance and social innovation nexus', *Journal of Social Entrepreneurship*, 3(2): 115–32.

Morgan, K. (2016) 'Collective entrepreneurship: The Basque model of innovation', *European Planning Studies*, 24(8): 1544–60.

NEF (New Economics Foundation) (2007) *Reconsidering UK community development finance*, London: NEF.

Nicholls, A. (2010) 'The institutionalization of social investment: The interplay of investment logics and investor rationalities', *Journal of Social Entrepreneurship*, 1(1): 70–100.

OECD (2015) *Social impact investment: Building the evidence base*, Paris: OECD Publishing.

Peck, J. (2013) 'For Polanyian economic geographies', *Environment and Planning A*, 45(7): 1545–68.

Polanyi, K. (2001) *The great transformation: The political and economic origins of our time*, Boston, MA: Beacon Press.

Roy, A. (2012) 'Ethnographic circulations: Space-time relations in the worlds of poverty management', *Environment and Planning A*, 44(1): 31–41.

SIIT (Social Impact Investment Taskforce) (2014) *Impact investment: The invisible heart of markets*, London: SIIT.

Thorlby, T. (2011) *Finance and business models for supporting community asset ownership and control*, York: Joseph Rowntree Foundation.

Trudeau, D. (2012) 'Constructing citizenship in the shadow state', *Geoforum*, 43(3): 442–52.

UNRISD (United Nations Research Institute for Social Development) (2016) *Inputs to the elements paper in the preparatory process of the 3rd international conference on financing for development*, New York: UNRISD.

Utting, P., van Dijk, M. and Matheï, M.-A. (2014) *Social and solidarity economy: Is there a new economy in the making?* Geneva: United Nations Research Institute for Social Development (UNRISD).

Wheeler, P. (2017) 'Where have all the radicals gone? How normative pressures can blunt the radical edge of a social enterprise', *Social Enterprise Journal*, 13(2): 163–79.

Wilson, K. (2014) *New investment approaches for addressing social and economic challenges*, OECD science, technology and industry policy paper 15, Paris: OECD.

SIX

Corporate funding and local community development: a case from the mining industry in Australia

Robyn Mayes

Introduction

Since the 1990s the role of the private sector in community development has become more overt and widespread (Blowfield, 2005). This has its roots in a 'growing belief that corporations alone have the power to catalyse development' (Welker, 2009: 146), and the parallel decline of the state as a central development actor (Richey and Ponte, 2014; Banks et al, 2016). The involvement of business tends to occur under the banner of corporate social responsibility (CSR), with 'a range of development effects, some intended, some not' (Banks et al, 2016: 246). Business participation, particularly in the mining sector and as framed by pro-business bodies such as the International Council on Mining and Metals,[1] tends to focus on 'the social, economic and institutional development of host countries and *communities*' (ICMM, 2017b, emphasis added). Indeed, the mining industry, widely acknowledged as leading the adoption and refinement of CSR (Kapelus, 2002), is a global exemplar of private sector involvement in the funding of community development. Corporations undertaking mining operations in remote locations 'often assume a state role' in precipitating and, to a lesser extent, subsidising public infrastructure (Welker, 2009: 146). In Australia, mining companies have historically been central actors in the development of local communities, just as the mining sector continues to provide 'services and development opportunities' to remote communities, 'supplementing, and in some cases substituting, the state in providing essential health, education and community facilities' (Cheshire, 2010: 19).

This chapter elucidates the social and political complexities of corporate community development as practised in the mining industry, with attention to implications for meanings of 'community' and 'development'. This is achieved through examination of corporate funding of community initiatives in the rural Shire of Ravensthorpe in Western Australia, the greenfield site of the Ravensthorpe Nickel Operation (RNO), owned by BHP Billiton (hereafter BHPB) until 2010. I draw on substantive empirical data collected during a two-year ethnography in the Shire encompassing 120 semi-structured interviews conducted in 2006 to 2008 with community members, local representatives, business people and corporate staff. Field work spanned the end of the mine's construction phase and its operationalisation, including the official opening in May 2008. During this time, I collected data about the experiences of long-term, pre-mine community members (the presumed beneficiaries of corporate programmes and funding), and corporate and government staff members with responsibilities for community development. This research illuminates the ways in which corporate funding can shape local understandings of community and governance, while failing to advance local development agendas.

The chapter begins with an overview of CSR and the contested concept of development before turning to an examination of the community development practices undertaken by the mining sector in Australia, and in particular as undertaken by BHPB. Having started out in Australia in 1885 as Broken Hill Propriety (BHP) Company Limited, BHP merged in 2001 with the equally long-lived Billiton firm. As an 'advanced global corporation' (O'Neill, 2012: 82), BHPB offers rich insights into the nature of contemporary transnational private sector involvement in local development. I critically analyse the firm's claimed commitment to community development and then explore more specifically its role in 'developing' Ravensthorpe.

CSR, neoliberalism and development

CSR refers to a set of practices that link businesses 'to social and environmental goals through their supply chains, policies, and operations' (Edwards, 2008: 26). It includes corporate philanthropy, volunteering and corporate codes of conduct as well as activities such as ethical trading. The widespread adoption of CSR in the mining sector can be understood as a globalised and programmatic response to mounting, well-organised and transnational criticism of the industry's poor environmental and social track record since the 1980s (Kapelus, 2002; Mayes, 2015). CSR is celebrated in the business literature as a way to disarm criticism and to minimise, if not avoid, regulation (Kapelus, 2002). Not surprisingly, critical perspectives have highlighted CSR as an example par excellence of a neoliberal response to neoliberal failures (Mayes et al, 2014). At the same time, critics question the capacities of private corporations to deliver development, and to do so in ways that meet broader goals of poverty reduction and sustainability (Frynas, 2005). They point to a problematic privileging of the 'business case' and entrenched understandings of development as deeply intertwined with the 'logics of global capital' (Richey and Ponte, 2014: 2; see also Mayes, 2015).

Within CSR, development is normatively conceived through 'business-like' approaches and language (Blowfield, 2005: 521). In this discourse various actors, including communities, find themselves recast as stakeholders (Banerjee, 2008) and at risk of co-optation in the service of advancing business goals (Mayes et al, 2012). While these criticisms might suggest that business involvement is the main problem, development itself, as ideology and practice, both in the past and the present, has significant, if not fatal, flaws. As Corbridge (2007) has amply demonstrated, key premises underpinning 'development' as both practice and scholarly field can 'other' 'developing' countries, positioning them as in need of (colonising forms of) assistance to become 'more like us'. Accordingly, development is best, though rarely, understood as 'sets of social practices, or technologies of rule', the forms of which include 'doctrines such as participation, good governance, sustainability' (Corbridge, 2007: 179). Much mining industry community development discourse uses this sort of rhetoric: for example, BHP Billiton's public documentation foregrounds community participation (if not collaboration), governance mechanisms, and the provision of company 'support designed to improve, in a sustainable way, the social and economic circumstances of the communities in which we operate' (BHPB, 2008: 125).

The mining sector and community development in Australia

Mining in Australia has long been linked to regional development notably in connection to job creation and contributions to infrastructure (Brueckner et al, 2014). In particular, resource extraction in Australia has historically been associated with the construction of 'mining towns' (Roarty, 2010). Prevalent in Western Australia in the 1960s and 1970s, these towns were purpose-built by mining companies to house workers and families near remote mining operations. They have since given way to fly-in, fly-out (FIFO) long-distance commuting arrangements in which workers fly to mine sites and live in camp accommodation for the duration of their shifts before returning to homes elsewhere (Mayes, 2015). This has led to regional concerns around the loss of development opportunities traditionally associated with the arrival of locally based workforces (Storey, 2001). However, other scholars (for example, Cheshire, 2010) have identified development advantages for communities in the vicinity of FIFO operations.

The impact of mines on communities is significant and wide-ranging. A review of 15 recent mining company sustainability reports undertaken by Kemp (2009: 204) shows that community development undertaken by the world's biggest mining companies encompasses activities such as: 'local employment (direct or indirect through the supply of goods and services), training and skills development, provision of infrastructure (such as roads, water and sanitation facilities), service delivery (such as health and education), employee volunteerism, and donations as well as non-mining-related opportunities such as capacity building and empowerment programs'.

In monetary terms, the Australian 'mineral industry's spending on community projects and local businesses' in 2011/12 has been estimated by the sector's representative body, the Minerals Council of Australia (MCA), as exceeding AU\$34 billion (Hooke, 2013: 1). The broad range of 'types of spend' encompasses both hard and soft infrastructure (for example, schools and healthcare), education and training for non-employees, land access related payments, local business development and support (spend on local suppliers and contractors), along with indigenous contracting and 'other community investments' such as donations to charities and 'direct costs associated with community investment and social programs' (Hooke, 2013: 2). The latter included health programmes, and support for local farming and sporting events. As such this corporate investment spans an eclectic array of spending types not all of which might be widely recognised as 'community spending' just as it is unclear to what extent it constitutes community development. Significantly, the MCA argues that this spending, which is claimed to exceed the industry's company tax and royalty payments in 2011/12, demonstrates how 'unnecessary' it is to apply other taxations.

The case of BHP Billiton

BHPB (2017) undertakes a range of activities as part of its global 'social investment framework' implemented in 2015. These activities arise out of 'a longstanding commitment to invest one per cent of our pre-tax profits in programs that aim improve [sic] the quality of life for people around the world' (BHPB, 2017). Further, the Framework is described as aligning 'strongly with the United Nations Sustainable Development Goals which are most relevant to our business and society' (BHPB, 2017). Through its UK-based charity, the BHP Billiton Sustainable Communities Fund, the company, by 2015, had invested 'US$35 million in community health partnerships' (BHPB, 2015). Along with contributions to initiatives in Mozambique, South Africa and Chile, the company has donated to projects in Australia including AU$2.5 million to the refurbishment of a local hospital in Muswellbrook Shire, New South Wales, where BHPB has significant coal mining operations (BHPB, 2015). 'Community Development' spending accounted for 51% of BHPB's overall expenditure on 'community investment' in its 2009 financial year and Australia received the second highest allocation from this investment fund (34%) after South America (47%) (BHPB, 2009: 22).[2] Africa received 14% and North America 3% (BHPB, 2009: 22). In 2016 the company allocated 'US$123.7 million of cash towards community development programs' almost half of which was invested in local communities (BHPB, 2016: 39). In Australia, for example, AU$5.7 million was donated to the Broken Hill City Council 'to fund the Living Museum and Perfect Light Project for the protection and promotion of the Broken Hill Archives' (BHPB, 2016: 39).

Through these varied initiatives, BHPB clearly functions as a 'development tool', but also potentially as a 'development agent'. According to Blowfield and Dolan (2014), business participation as development tool is characterised by contributions to wealth creation and employment, and payment of taxes. Conversely, the criteria that mark the development agent include *intentional* and *accountable* deployment of capital and assets in the service of 'an expected, calculated development benefit' primarily in order to remedy poverty and marginalisation (Blowfield and Dolan, 2014: 25, emphasis added). However, this deployment of capital, as Blowfield and Dolan (2014) argue, is fundamentally different from the use of company surplus for charitable donations – for example, the use of pre-tax profits. While intention is broadly signalled in the use of the term 'community development' to specify spending separate to that on 'education, health, other, arts/culture, sport/recreation, environment' (BHPB, 2017: 22), there is no evidence in the public reports of evaluation of, or accountability for, the outcomes of this spending and the programmes it supports. Further, BHPB's commitment to community development is clearly focused on the 'communities in which we operate' (BHPB, 2008: 125) and thus enacts a geography of spending driven by the emplacements of its mine sites, as opposed to a driving sense of 'development' centred on poverty and social justice especially in the Global South.

Community development in Ravensthorpe

BHPB, the state and uneven regional development

BHPB RNO's public communications repeatedly claim that the presence of a mine in a local community will directly foster local economic and social development. In its 2005 *Sustainability report*, for example, BHPB refers to RNO as 'a significant opportunity to advance regional development in the southeast coastal region of Western Australia'. Similarly, the Department of Industry and Resources in Western Australia (2008: 2) noted that: '[t]he successful opening of this project is as much about the development of regional Western Australian communities as it is about the State's buoyant resources industry.' Relative to urban areas, contemporary Australian rural communities are understood to be under-resourced, particularly in terms of infrastructure, and thus in need of the development opportunities mining is believed to offer (Cheshire, 2010). Provision of infrastructure was meant to be the central benefit to Ravensthorpe communities arising from the arrival of the AU$2.2 billion RNO and its residential workforce. RNO was at the time somewhat unusual in its commitment to a residential workforce: the mine's desirable location by the sea worked as a labour drawcard in the then highly competitive mining labour market. In 2008, 300 employees and families were residing in Hopetoun (Mayes, 2008). In bringing people to the region, RNO precipitated a 'multi-user infrastructure package' (MUIP) funded jointly by the Western Australian state government, BHPB and the federal government (Department of State Development, 2010). A memorandum of understanding (MoU) outlined these financial contributions towards infrastructure to service the anticipated mine workforce (both residential and FIFO) required by the AU$2.2 billion mine:

- Western Australian state government: AU$18.5 million for a new primary school in Hopetoun, waste water treatment services, upgraded state roads;
- BHPB: AU$9.5 million for construction of Ravensthorpe airport and upgraded state roads; and
- federal government: AU$9.8 million for upgraded local roads, co-located emergency services and Rural Transaction Centre

buildings in Hopetoun and the Ravensthorpe Entertainment Centre. (Department of State Development, 2010)

BHPB's unexpected twofold expansion of the RNO workforce, which occurred after these arrangements had been made, meant that the budget for potable water, sewage systems, and access to (affordable) power was insufficient to meet the needs of the rapidly expanded local population. Government reluctance to make up the shortfall was in part due to changing perceptions of government and industry responsibilities. According to a senior government actor, when the MoU was signed in 2004 the prevailing policy of regional development meant that government funding was a straightforward "matter of supporting regional development, like locally based workforces and so on". Just a few years later when the mining boom was in full swing,[3] this was no longer perceived as a role for government because "there's so much money in the resources industry … if the company wants something they've got to pay for it". According to this senior government representative, BHPB was reluctant to contribute beyond what had been agreed in the MoU, arguing that it was "putting money into other areas" including "into the community".

The stalemate around this funding in effect stifled *local* community development: for example, shopkeepers were unable to access or afford connections to the power grid and thus expand their businesses, and not as much land as anticipated was available for development in Hopetoun resulting in a hybrid FIFO and residential operational workforce. A very large part of the local experience of the 'development' of the community was of an ongoing and frustrating lag in the provision of (basic) infrastructure. In the words of a closely involved government actor, Hopetoun was "effectively ringbarked".[4] At the same time, the expansion of RNO meant that the company bought more residential properties in Hopetoun to house the larger workforce. This in turn devalued the Shire's pre-existing arrangements with BHPB in which the company made contributions to Shire maintenance budgets and to a community fund instead of paying rates on company-owned commercial and residential properties in the Shire. BHPB contributed funds to the running of the airport, primarily used to enable the RNO use of FIFO workers, and paid AU\$120,000 annually to a community development fund; however, the local council was forced to enter into an AU\$2.6 million Treasury loan to maintain local roads subjected to increased usage and associated rapid deterioration (Department of State Development, 2010), which led to increased rate levies on local (non-mining) residents.

Furthermore, there were a number of omissions in the MUIP, including provision for a local childcare centre. This omission had a direct impact on women's capacities to take advantage of employment opportunities at RNO. The delayed and highly politicised provision of formal childcare services exemplifies the way in which BHPB's contributions to community development were largely directed at Hopetoun where the bulk of RNO residential employees were housed. One pre-mine local resident involved in trying to establish a childcare centre in the town of Ravensthorpe noted that "BHPB won't fund it; they funded the one in Hopetoun because they've got a lot of mothers [mainly partners of BHPB staff] that work, so they have got one down there. I don't know but I have heard that it's only for the workers." The experience and perception of uneven community development was pronounced and pervasive. Local residents consistently commented on the emphasis on developing Hopetoun to the exclusion of other communities in the Shire, while at the same time describing the development within Hopetoun of a separate and better serviced 'New Hopetoun' where mine workers resided (Mayes, 2008). As a government interviewee commented, "it's fairly deep-seated with the Ravensthorpe people that you know, they feel they got a pretty raw deal out of all this". Overall, local development was very much limited to projects and infrastructure that met the needs of RNO. For example, the gravel access road to the mine was bituminised so that trucks could travel safely to and from the mine but this ended at the mine gate – the short stretch of road continuing to the local primary school was not upgraded.

A telling example of RNO's emphasis on developing infrastructure attractive to its workers, under the banner of community development, was the company's plan to construct a recreation centre and indoor pool in Hopetoun. According to numerous interviewees, the projected cost was in the vicinity of AU$8 million. From the perspective of an informed local government actor, this plan very much reflected BHPB's idea of "what's needed in the area to keep their workers happy. An indoor swimming pool is not so important to the rest of the community". Moreover, at the time the council was in the midst of a strategic review of the recreational facilities in the Shire. This was seen as a necessary step prior to committing to new facilities, especially since, as this local government interviewee pointed out:

> 'the community will end up paying for the maintenance of the facility and indeed many of the workers are not ratepayers, or will not be ratepayers for more than a short

period. The council survey is irrelevant to BHPB who have the attitude "yes well do your survey and in the meantime we'll get on with the indoor pool".'

Local pre-mine residents more generally also questioned the sense of this proposal, pointing to the existence of a "perfectly good" community swimming pool in Ravensthorpe.

Though BHPB's construction of RNO as a residential mine clearly precipitated a range of infrastructure improvements, these can be seen to be of questionable and uncertain local benefit. BHPB's investments in the local community, as enumerated earlier, occurred alongside government contributions three times greater than that of BHPB. In this case at least, corporate contributions to community development are not in place of, but rather are in addition to, government spending on development. Further, BHPB's involvement in community infrastructure development was very clearly undertaken in the interests of creating an environment attractive to its residential workforce. Any benefit to local communities must be understood as collateral to the interests of the corporation.

BHPB and the funding of community projects

In addition to the contributions to infrastructure projects already described, RNO sought to fund local community projects. According to corporate interviewees, BHPB's policy of setting aside 1% of pre-tax profit for community initiatives posed a challenge. In 2007/08, at the highpoint of the Australian mining boom, the value of this 1% 'increased by $37.6 million from the previous year to $141.0 million' (Kloppers, 2008: i). One corporate interviewee with responsibility in this area opined that it was "never believed that it would be so much" and that, as a result, distribution "was a difficult task". This difficulty was understood by corporate interviewees to arise from the "problem" of "community expectations" in that "more money equals higher expectations. Communities want the company to not only fund things but to do them as well". At the heart of the matter, in this interviewee's estimation, was a fundamental tension: "We're a mining company [as opposed to development agent] – we need to keep reminding ourselves." Corporate interviewees presented the company stance as "keen to partner, that is take the lead in initiatives but not the doing". One interviewee explained that, "We're looking for some of those win-win type relationships; that's fairly important" and went on to offer the example of the way that one community was:

'very keen to have us engage with them on fire control issues, and particularly helping them equip their fire services locally, which for us is a win–win because we're part of that community, you know? We're a landowner and … we want to protect our land and we don't want fires to come through it.'

In addition to identifying 'win–win' opportunities,[5] RNO representatives were responsible for disbursing grants directly to local community groups.[6] The availability and manner of distribution of such grants was a matter of contention for many local interviewees. As one such interviewee phrased it: "I think, sometimes RNO's buying the community". At the same time, access to this funding was experienced as unreliable and messy: "there's lots of promises [from company representatives] and then it's like, 'oh no, sorry we didn't say that…'" In the following extended interview excerpt, a local pre-mine community member describes the perception and experience of acquiring such funding. This experience was common and is worth presenting in detail as it neatly captures the tensions and contradictions attending this type of funding:[7]

> *Interviewee*: 'And getting back to the pros and cons of the mine here as well, one thing we have noticed like for our fundraising efforts that we do, oh, they're so generous, just amazingly generous. Rather than us fundraising and selling lamingtons or whatever to raise $750 to get the pipe for a dressage arena [at the local pony club], the company up there just went oh, "750 bucks worth, oh here you are. We'll drop it off as well". And to us it was like … we have never, ever experienced that sort of generosity before … and they just said "any time you want anything, just give us a call".
>
> Well that was in the construction phase but still even with BHPB … they're currently sponsoring a coach to come down from Perth [for our pony club]. Now, she is $400 a day. They're paying for two days' full coaching plus her airfare and we've got … 30 riding members … So, that to us is just amazing because otherwise we'd all be paying probably at least $100 per child … and if you've got three or four kids doing the school, it's a lot of money … And BHP just said, "we're happy to … for coaching purposes". Not to buy equipment, that sort of thing. So we'll trundle off and do fundraising to buy equipment. And they said

they'd like to do this on an ongoing basis so we just went ...
"wow, yeah".'

Interviewer: 'So, how do they find out what you need or
what you want?'

Interviewee: 'We ring X. Going through X is very good.
I don't think we'd get to the stage where we abuse the
situation either and just call X at the drop of a hat and sort
of expect this and want that. But the more you get, the more
you want. We're still in that honeymoon stage where we're
sort of just going "wow, this is so good". Yeah so before
this, before the mine it wasn't available. It was all real hard
yakka to get coaching and things. You know fundraising
and cooking and cleaning.'

This funding appears to have been distributed across the life of the
operation in ways that were at best ad hoc, and at the discretion of
corporate individuals. This low-level funding is important to the local
community and was seen as generous. Significantly, it is not suited to
long-term development; after all, the BHPB funding could not be
used for the purchase of equipment. Further, this approach to funding
means that local groups needed to maintain cordial relationships with
RNO staff and to ask, cap in hand, for corporate sponsorship each and
every time there was something they hoped BHPB would support. In
this way, this system is a means to long-term (paternalistic) corporate
control over what local community projects receive funding. The
interviewee in the preceding paragraphs was careful to point out the
risks of this 'easy' money – namely greed, local dependence on BHPB
and the devaluing of community fundraising activities. Similarly,
other interviewees felt that 'the whole Shire is already looking to
BHP Billiton to do stuff. It's stopping people doing what they would
normally do. They say, "why have a cake stall? Let's just ask BHP
Billiton"' (cited in Mayes et al, 2014: 405).

While the budget for these grants was at the outset very modest,
according to a local government interviewee:

'all of a sudden BHP were saying well we can do $250,000,
so it's just become a "throw money at, keep happy"
thing. Nobody wants to talk about uncomfortable things,
everybody shies away from it, much easier to get money,
much easier to get a cheque ... [P]eople only see that

superficial thing, … look not that I'm saying that the money isn't good, like you know the money is to do community projects, but not this greedy grabbing thing that I'm seeing lately. And then we have people saying, "well if you won't give us this money, we'll go to the Community Liaison Committee [set up by RNO] because X's already promised us that we can have the money".'

These experiences on the part of local community members demonstrate how funding for community development can function as a 'technology of rule' and extend BHPB's power. That is, the manner of funding allocation did not allow for sustained development, or the community co-development of a carefully considered, reliable funding programme. Further, it worked to discipline local community behaviour – keeping on the good side of X – and created a sense of having been 'bought'. Importantly, this corporate disbursement of funding worked to undermine local government control over development in the Shire. This funding, furthermore, was both superficial and *fleeting*. Citing falling nickel prices, BHPB without warning closed RNO in January 2009, at that point honouring only contractual agreements. The substantial local, state-level and national investments documented earlier were thus in support of a short-term project.

Conclusion

This case study illustrates that the funding dispersed through corporate-led community development is largely applied in the service of supporting the corporation's commercial interests. In terms of community benefit, this funding can be characterised, in the words of one local government representative, as an attempt to "control people with one's chequebook", in ways that potentially subvert local government and local residents' control of community development. The power of the chequebook was such that there was little discussion about, and accountability for, the diverse social and political impacts that RNO had on the local community. Corporate funding was allocated in a piecemeal and ad hoc fashion rather than being strategically targeted at inequality or pressing social issues. The vagaries and contingencies of funding community development in this way are illustrated by the difficulty BHPB had in spending an unexpected surplus in its community development fund but also by the sudden withdrawal of the company from the area due to a change in global commodity prices.

BHPB identified primarily as a business entity and it demonstrated, at best, a fundamentally weak commitment to local development. There was a clear sense on the part of the corporation that community expectations needed to be kept in check, and that community groups should actively participate in realising (only) win–win arrangements. Thus, BHPB's contribution to community development in Ravensthorpe was principally as a problematic and short-term development tool. Community development operated in this instance as a technology of rule that increased corporate power by virtue of its position as a fickle, yet welcome, source of funds, and positioned 'community' and 'development' as interlinked support mechanisms for the advancement of business. Local development was also stymied and distorted by the unplanned-for growth in the mine's operational workforce which placed unexpected additional pressure on local infrastructure. Alleviation of these pressures incurred substantial local government debt as the corporation and the state sought to position each other as the responsible party. This was costly to both community and state. The experience of residents in this community highlights some of the limits of corporate funding for community development in terms of accountability, effective goal setting and medium-term planning, and stands as a corrective to the notion of corporations as valid supplements to or substitutes for redistributive, state-driven development.

Notes

[1] The ICMM, founded in 2001, is an international organisation with a membership of 23 mining companies and '33 regional commodities associations'. It is 'dedicated to a safe, fair and sustainable mining industry' and the enhancement of 'mining's contribution to society' (ICMM, 2017a).

[2] These figures do not include the US$60 million donated to the company's UK Sustainable Communities charity already noted (BHPB, 2009).

[3] Many regard late 2004 as marking the beginning of Australia's most recent 'mining boom'. It peaked in mid-2008, before collapsing in late 2008 (Richardson, 2009).

[4] 'Ring-barking' in Australian parlance refers to stripping a circle of bark from a tree's trunk thereby killing it.

[5] See Mayes et al, 2012 for an extended critique of win–win approaches.

[6] In addition to this individual discretionary funding, community project funding was also managed according to RNO wishes through the Community Liaison Committee (Mayes et al, 2014).

[7] A number of firms were contracted to BHPB for the mine construction phase. Some of these made donations to local community groups.

References

Banerjee, S.B. (2008) *Corporate social responsibility: The good, the bad and the ugly*, Cheltenham: Edward Elgar.

Banks, G., Scheyvens, R., McLennan, S. and Bebbington, A. (2016) 'Conceptualising corporate community development', *Third World Quarterly*, 37(2): 245–63.

BHPB (BHP Billiton) (2008) *Resourcing the future: Sustainability report 2008, full report*, www.bhp.com/-/media/bhp/documents/investors/reports/2008/fullsustainabilityreport2008.pdf?la=en.

BHPB (BHP Billiton) (2009) *Summary review 2009*, www.bhp.com/~/media/bhp/documents/investors/reports/2009/summaryreview2009.pdf?la=en.

BHPB (BHP Billiton) (2015) 'Improving health in communities', 23 September, www.bhpbilliton.com/community/case-studies/improving-health-in-communities.

BHPB (BHP Billiton) (2016) *Integrity, resilience, growth: Sustainability report 2016*, www.bhp.com/-/media/bhp/documents/investors/annual-reports/2016/bhpbillitonsustainabilityreport2016.pdf.

BHPB (BHP Billiton) (2017) 'Our social investment framework', www.bhpbilliton.com/community/social-investment.

Blowfield, M. (2005) 'Corporate social responsibility: Reinventing the meaning of development?', *International Affairs*, 81(3): 515–24.

Blowfield, M. and Dolan, C.S. (2014) 'Business as a development agent: Evidence of possibility and improbability', *Third World Quarterly*, 35(1): 22–42.

Brueckner, M., Durey, A., Pforr, C. and Mayes, R. (2014) 'The civic virtue of developmentalism: On the mining industry's political licence to develop Western Australia', *Impact Assessment and Project Appraisal*, 32(4): 315–26.

Cheshire, L. (2010) 'A corporate responsibility? The constitution of fly-in, fly-out mining companies as governance partners in remote, mine-affected localities', *Journal of Rural Studies*, 26(1): 12–20.

Corbridge, S. (2007) 'The (im)possibility of development studies', *Economy and Society*, 36(2): 179–211.

Department of Industry and Resources (2008) 'Ravensthorpe on world stage as nickel project opens', *Prospect, Western Australia's International Resources Development Magazine*, June–August 2008: 2–3.

Department of State Development (2010) 'Submission to public accounts committee: Ravensthorpe Nickel Operation', www.parliament.wa.gov.au/parliament/commit.nsf/(Evidence+Looku p+by+Com+ID)/2438F1000CBC7043482578310042F0D4/$fi le/37516915.pdf.

Edwards, M. (2008) *Small change: Why business won't save the world*, San Francisco: Berrett-Koehler.

Frynas, J.G. (2005) 'The false developmental promise of corporate social responsibility: Evidence from multinational oil companies', *International Affairs*, 81(3): 581–98.

Hooke, M. (2013) 'Minerals industry's community spending exceeds $34 billion', Minerals Council of Australia Media Release, formerly available at: www.minerals.org.au/file_upload/files/media_releases/Banarra_CSR_18_Nov.pdf.

ICMM (International Council of Mining and Metals) (2017a) 'About us', www.icmm.com/en-gb/about-us.

ICMM (International Council of Mining and Metals) (2017b) 'Principle 9', www.icmm.com/en-gb/about-us/member-commitments/icmm-10-principles/icmm-principle-9.

Kapelus, P. (2002) 'Mining, corporate social responsibility and the "community": The case of Rio Tinto, Richards Bay Minerals and the Mbonambi', *Journal of Business Ethics*, 39(3): 275–96.

Kemp, D. (2009) 'Mining and community development: Problems and possibilities of local-level practice', *Community Development Journal*, 45(2): 198–218.

Kloppers, M. (2008) 'Message from the Chief Executive Officer', in *Resourcing the future: Sustainability report 2008, full report*, pp i–ii, www.bhpbilliton.com/-/media/bhp/documents/investors/reports/2008/fullsustainabilityreport2008.pdf?la=en.

Mayes, R. (2008) *Living the resources boom: Towards sustainable rural communities*, Sustaining Gondwana Working Paper Series 11: Curtin University, http://apo.org.au/system/files/98216/apo-nid98216-354641.pdf.

Mayes, R. (2015) 'A social licence to operate: Corporate social responsibility, local communities and the constitution of global production networks', *Global Networks*, 15(s1): s109–s128.

Mayes, R., McDonald, P. and Pini, B. (2014) '"Our" community: Corporate social responsibility, neoliberalisation, and mining industry community engagement in rural Australia', *Environment and Planning A*, 46(2): 398–413.

Mayes, R., Pini, B. and McDonald P. (2012) 'Corporate social responsibility and the parameters of dialogue with vulnerable others', *Organization*, 20(6): 840–59.

O'Neill, P. (2012) 'The industrial corporation and capitalism's time-space fix' in T.J. Barnes, J. Peck and E. Sheppard (eds) *The Wiley-Blackwell companion to economic geography*, Chichester: John Wiley, pp 74–90.

Richardson, D. (2009) *The benefits of the mining boom: Where did they go?*, Technical brief no. 3, May, The Australia Institute, www.tai.org.au/sites/defualt/files/mining_boom_final_7.pdf.

Richey, L.A. and Ponte S. (2014) 'New actors and alliances in development', *Third World Quarterly*, 35(1): 1–21.

Roarty, M. (2010) 'The Australian resources sector: Its contribution to the nation, and a brief review of issues and impacts', Parliamentary Library, Parliament of Australia, Background Note, 23 September, www.aph.gov.au/About_Parliament/Parliamentary_Departments/Parliamentary_Library/pubs/BN/1011/AustResources.

Storey, K. (2001) 'Fly-in/fly-out and fly-over: Mining and regional development in Western Australia', *Australian Geographer*, 32(2): 133–48.

Welker, M.A. (2009) ' "Corporate security begins in the community": Mining, the corporate social responsibility industry, and environmental advocacy in Indonesia', *Cultural Anthropology*, 24(1): 142–79.

PART 2

Questions of state and grassroots democracy

SEVEN

Funding community organising: diversifying sources, democratising civil society

Robert Fisher and Hélène Balazard

Introduction

Throughout the history of community organising in the United States, funding has been a serious and, until recently, neglected issue (Fisher, 1994). This chapter recognises the variety, complexity and contested politics of community organising, a practice that ranges from consensus-based community building to more conflict-oriented grassroots organising confronting oppression. Our main interest is the need for movement-like organising for economic and social justice at the local level and beyond. Since 2008, funding for organising in the US has declined. A 2009 National Organizers Alliance survey of 203 community organisations reported that 65% of respondents had undergone dramatic funding cuts since the recession, 40% had depleted their financial reserves, and 33% survived on a month-to-month basis (Waheed et al, 2010). According to an Urban Institute study, community organising organisations were hit the hardest (Boris et al, 2010). While there has been increasing interest in community organising since the election of Obama in 2008, 'one of the most important questions facing organisers [remains] can we translate this growing public awareness into serious funding that will propel growth and strengthen the field?' (Dorfman and Fine, 2009: 2).

This chapter will make the case that an over-reliance on progressive philanthropic sources has resulted in the underfunding of community organising. It has also contributed to the depoliticisation of 'civil society' (we will scrutinise the use of this term more closely later) and has obscured the potential role the state can play in achieving egalitarian social change. We argue that it is time to diversify funding sources for community organising and to re-evaluate debates in the field about the limits and difficulties associated with state funding.

We foreground a case study from outside the US – the Community Organising Programme (COP) (2011–2015) in England – to illustrate how state funding for community organising can lead to progressive outcomes, even when initiated by a Conservative government that is firmly committed to neoliberal policies. Community organisers in the US have, we believe, much to learn from this programme. We argue that a failure to advocate for greater state support for US community organising unintentionally reinforces the delegitimisation of the state which has occurred under neoliberalism and limits the scope and power of grassroots organising.

The chapter begins by outlining the value of community organising and the variety of funding models currently in operation in the US before turning to a review of critical debates on funding for community organising in which we think the importance of public sector funding is generally underplayed. It then makes the case that highlighting the importance of public sector funding for community organising highlights the existing interconnections between civil society, state and market. This offers a way of challenging depoliticised interpretations of civil society and, ultimately, we argue could serve counterhegemonic purposes. Finally, the COP case is presented in support of these claims. The aim is to contribute to debates on resourcing community organising and democratising state and civil society under neoliberalism (Edwards, 2010; Trudeau, 2012; Fisher and Shragge, 2017).

The importance of community organising

The value of community organising has been widely recognised (Boyte, 1980; Warren, 2001; Staples, 2004). Walker and McCarthy (2012) suggest that grassroots organising contributes to substantial changes in communities, improving employment opportunities, workplace conditions, neighbourhood safety and the quality of public services. These initiatives also empower people and amplify the voices of poor and moderate-income citizens in the public sphere. To pick just one example, Delgado (2009: 268) highlights the success of ACORN, once the largest community organising organisation in the United States, in 'successfully accruing power and benefits for its low-income base.' ACORN blended conflict-oriented labour union strategies and tactics with a social movement culture and sought to organise at the local as well as national and even international level. ACORN's contributions included getting its members, primarily people of colour, to act in their own interest, on issues such as a living wage, better housing and services and predatory financial lending practices. It achieved this by creating strong community organisations, building a multiracial constituency, developing both local and national capacity, experimenting with alternative institutions, engaging in electoral politics, internationalising membership beyond US borders, and using conflictual tactics such as direct action protests.

Clearly community organising is not without its limits or critics. Romanticisation of community and community initiatives is widespread (Joseph, 2002). Major contemporary challenges include sustaining organisations over time, developing and advancing progressive goals in hostile conditions, building beyond local contexts in order to increase power and impact, fending off attacks from the Right if an organisation successfully accrues scale and power and having enough capacity to hire community organisers to provide leadership, training and continuity. As Dodge et al (2013: 2) puts it, 'We are in a moment when it is critical to make investments in learning and experimentation to better understand what support can increase long-term sustainability for social justice organizations.' Before exploring critical issues of resourcing and sustainability, an overview of the predominant forms of funding used in contemporary community organising in the US is in order.

Models of funding for community organising in the US

There are at least nine major funding sources within community development and 'third sector' organisations in the US: campaign victories, which can win funds from corporate or public sources;[1] canvassing, which solicits funds through personal or electronic requests; congregation tithing; institutional support from unions and churches; membership dues; philanthropic foundations; political parties; government contracting for community service delivery, and social entrepreneurialism. Different segments of the not-for-profit sector rely on different sources of funding. For example, arts and culture and environmental organisations get most of their funding from individual, foundation and corporate donations. The human and social service delivery sector overall, including social justice organisations, has a more diverse funding base: 41% from private payments by clients, 36% from government contracts and 16% from other contributions (Boris et al, 2010). Despite the existence of a multiplicity of funding models, social justice community organising is dominated by philanthropic foundation funding sources. A study of 213 grassroots organisations by the Center for Community Change in 2006 concludes that the social change sector received 62% of its funding from foundation grants. Government sources represented only 5% of total funding for these organisations. Current funding is driven by institutionalised practices, network connections, accepted norms and perceived convenient sources (Beckett et al, 2006: 5). Of course this over-reliance on the philanthropic sector has spawned a literature highly critical of philanthropic funding (INCITE! Women of Color Against Violence, 2007; Ashton and DeFilippis, 2014) and has helped to ignite a debate regarding alternative funding sources for progressive social change.

A review of the debates on funding community organising

Despite the funding crisis within community organising and the corresponding need for diversifying funding sources, the debate over funding remains curiously 'stuck' and public sector funding of community organising is rarely mentioned within the US literature on this topic. For example, *Beyond foundation funding: Revenue-generating strategies for sustainable social change* (Dodge et al, 2013), a study which is wary of the anti-democratic dimensions of 'philanthrocapitalist' foundation funding, concludes by encouraging more dialogue between foundations, social change organisations and technical assistance providers.[2] This conclusion is especially intriguing given their critique of foundations as beneficiaries of the state as well as their understanding of the prominent role the public sector plays in funding human service organisations. Similarly, a report of the National Committee for Responsive Philanthropy and the Center for Community Change proposes that this is a good time to fund community organising. They advise developing 'good relations and expanding networks with a wide variety of donors and funders,' but focus almost exclusively on philanthropic sources (Dorfman and Fine, 2009: 2).

INCITE!'s *The revolution will not be funded* (2007) sharply criticises social change organisations' reliance on philanthropic foundations. For the Women of Color Against Violence collective, foundations are part of the problem, supporters of the status quo. But INCITE!'s suggestions regarding alternative models – membership dues and partnerships with other community organisations – also focus heavily on sources within the civil society sector. Most recently, a Center for Popular Democracy report, *Seeding justice* (2015), identifies lessons of revenue generation from the field of mass base-building organisations. While the study recognises the need to diversify funding streams and become less dependent on grants from foundations for their financial health, it excludes public funding as a possible source. This relates in part from an analysis, questioned by others, that an overdependence on federal funding caused ACORN's downfall in 2009 (personal communications, former ACORN employee, 2016).

Another stream in the literature explicitly warns against public sector funding for social change. For example, Piven and Cloward (1978) illustrate how state funding and government involvement lead to the control of labour and movement incorporation, blunting militancy, inhibiting membership growth and weakening membership ties. They contend it shifts the focus from grassroots organising and brings movements into the maze of legislative and bureaucratic politics. More recently, problems of government contracting are examined in Fabricant and Fisher's (2002) study of contemporary settlement houses in New York City where organisations were trying to survive draconian budget cuts, excessive project goals and bureaucratic burdens. These grassroots organisations were under siege due to the highly partisan, unstable and demanding system of government contracting and cutbacks brought about by the right-wing 1994 'Contract with America'.

While critics underscore the problems associated with both current government programming and dominant forms of charitable giving, including movement philanthropy, some do acknowledge the potential of public funding of democratic initiatives. For example, Wolch (1990: 224) argues that the involvement of the state 'could lead to greater state control over everyday life and/or to an extension of participation and democracy.' Fabricant and Fisher (2002: 290) concur and conclude their study with a call to challenge the privatisation of contemporary government contracting, rather than the public sector per se. Organisations must struggle to balance the dynamic of maintaining their core mission and avoiding incorporation and manipulation. Michael Edwards captures these complexities well. He argues that money is both the 'beauty' and 'beast' in community organising, no matter the funding source. 'In market-based societies "money talks", but it rarely speaks the language of democracy and social justice. Recognizing and acting on this fact is vital rather than pretending that money is somehow neutral or separated from the broader processes in which it is accumulated, expended, and exchanged' (2013: 5).

Clearly neoliberal hegemony makes achieving public sector funding more difficult than before. For some, a key task is to render the system of outsourced public governance more effective (Salamon, 2002). In our view, what matters most in the struggle against neoliberal hegemony is the democratisation of the public sector and civil society.

For example, the welfare state, a primary target of neoliberalism, is not simply a tool of capitalist hegemony; it reflects concessions won by popular struggles. Publicly funded community organising can itself be a challenge to the shrinking state under neoliberalism. It has the potential to contribute to counterhegemonic movements with the potential capacity to win crucial concessions. Even in the historically weak and decentralised state form that has predominated in the US, gains secured by publicly funded organising during the 1930s and 1960s are clear examples of this sort of 'democratic realignment', a point which we will return to below.

Relations between state, civil society and market

The argument for diversifying funding for community organising and to seek public sector support for such activity rests on two key claims: we must challenge the idea that civil society can be regarded as independent of either state or market; and we must recognise the role that public funding has historically played in funding social change in the US.

First, it is worth recalling that there are long-standing interconnections between civil society, state and market through the existence of funding partnerships, tax breaks for philanthropy, policy networks and other such phenomena. The erroneous idea that civil society constitutes a sphere separate from the state and the market has been reinforced by developments since the 1980s. Ehrenberg (2011: 23) argues that the revival of the notion of civil society during this period has its origins in the antagonism towards the state of Eastern European dissidents who called for 'a revolt of civil society against the state'. Thus, civil society has become associated with a celebration of the local as the source of democracy (Bellah et al, 1985) while the state became associated with top-down control. But this coincided with the emergence of a neoliberalism in the mid-1970s that also distrusted the 'big state' and has led to the hollowing out of social welfare and the outsourcing of public services to business (DeFilippis et al, 2010; Smith, 2011).

The reality is far more complex than this notion of civil society allows for – the state, market and civil society are highly interrelated and the 'public' and 'private' are not easily disentangled. We believe it is useful to begin with this premise in analysing possible sources of funding for organising. For example, the philanthropic sector uses public sector subsidies in the form of tax breaks and exemptions. While private foundations are said to control their funds for private ends, in reality they 'intervene in public life with no accountability to the public required' (Barkan, 2013). The Gates Foundation's work around charter schools and public school reform is highly political and controversial, as is the conservative lobby group ALEC (American Legislative Exchange Council). Such 'civil society' organisations use 'wealth derived power in the public sphere with minimal democratic controls and civic obligations' (Barkan, 2013). Greater public funding for community organising could arguably serve as something of a counterbalance to the unaccountable political influence of policy-active philanthropies.

Second, despite contemporary historical amnesia about the role of public funding, as we noted briefly before, the US government has a long history of funding social change. There is an authentic and deep, if intermittent, tradition of state action to address inequalities on a significant scale (DeFilippis et al, 2010). Although since 1980 there has been a major thrust, largely successful at the national level, to undermine the federal government, there is a well-established practice of state funding for social change in the US. There are historical examples that should remind both practitioners and academics not to exclude the state as a potential partner in supporting community organising and grassroots social change. In the 1960s, for example, President Johnson's 'Great Society' and, more specifically, the Community Action Program offered a model of federally funded community action as an instrument of social reform grounded in an anti-racist, anti-poverty, participatory view of democratic politics (Korstad and Leloudis, 2010). Since then there have been a series of government programmes that funded organising, including VISTA (Volunteers in Service to America), which trained volunteers as organisers in the late 1970s, and support for organisations challenging bank redlining and predatory lending during the Clinton era (Dreier, 1996).

The interrelationships between state, market and civil society in the here and now and the longer historical record of state initiatives are especially important to bear in mind in a neoliberal era. While acceptance of state funding can, as critics have highlighted, lead to the spread and 'normalisation' of neoliberal values and practices (Larner and Craig, 2005), the narrow focus on civil society as a 'pure' and separate sphere, and the belief that it is more legitimate to secure funding from within civil society rather than from outside it, arguably *reinforces* the neoliberal 'turn to community'. Reclaiming the historical memory of successful state initiatives and using them as a basis for advocating for greater public funding for community organising could help challenge the delegitimisation of the state that has occurred under neoliberalism.

The Community Organisers Programme

In 2011, the British Conservative government under David Cameron initiated the COP in England to hire and train 500 'senior organisers' and educate 4,500 volunteers in the basics of community organising. With government funding of approximately £20 million (Fisher and Dimberg, 2015), its explicit focus on the hiring and training of community organisers on such a grand scale is extraordinary. What is also singular about COP is that it emerged from Cameron's so-called 'Big Society' initiative that fused neoliberal and communitarian goals by arguing for a strong role for the state in strengthening communities and expanding grassroots participation (Balazard and Fisher, 2016). Big Society organisers would, it was argued, 'facilitate local action and give support to groups looking to come together to tackle identified problems' (Cabinet Office, 2013: 1). It was, however, intended primarily to undercut the British welfare state (Fisher and Shragge, 2017). In fact, at the same time of Cameron's unveiling of 'Big Society' policies, Chancellor of the Exchequer George Osborne concurrently announced a five-year austerity plan that included the largest budget cuts since the Second World War and the elimination of almost half a million public sector jobs (O'Hara, 2014). In a period of neoliberal policies and austerity the Big Society plan was not fully implemented. But COP remained and continued to move forward through the end of Cameron's first term in 2015, partly because it was already contracted out to two organisations, Locality and RE:generate, and partly because it attracted so much interest, especially among existing community development professionals and among people wanting paid work as community organisers (Fisher and Dimberg, 2015). That interest and support continues; in March 2017, the COP legacy organisation, the Company of Community Organisers (COLtd), received a £4.2 million contract from the post-Cameron Conservative government's Office of Civil Society for further training of community organisers (Community Organisers Ltd, 2017).

While the value and the impact of the COP remain contested it nevertheless provides an illuminating example through which to explore the limits, but also the potential, of state-funded community organising in a neoliberal era. Drawing on secondary research and on interviews undertaken during the summer of 2014 with COP staff, organisers and external organising professionals, we can state that COP clearly promoted a neoliberal interpretation of community organising that lent support to the retreat from public service delivery. But it also provided, amid draconian budgetary cuts and austerity policies, an alternative opportunity for the development of movement-like community organising inspired by the ideas of US community organiser Saul Alinsky (1972). Alinskyite approaches typically involve the recruitment of trained organisers who build power within poor communities by mobilising its members and forging alliances with organisations with common interests. Tactics range from negotiation to more confrontational modes of protest (Taylor, 2011).

There was some ambivalence in the government's approach to the programme. On the one hand, a preference for a more consensual community organising model can be discerned from the fact that Locality (2010) won the tender to operationalise COP over Citizens UK, an organisation loosely affiliated with the IAF (Industrial Areas Foundation), the direct heir to Alinsky organising in the US. The Locality tender emphasised personal responsibility, entrepreneurialism and assets-based approaches, which are characteristic of more neoliberalised models of community organising. On the other hand, while most observers think that Citizens UK didn't get the contract because its approach was too confrontational (Third Sector, 2011), other experts suggest the Cameron administration was selectively open to collective action on the part of citizens and, where it suited Cameron's political interests, to protest tactics targeted at public authorities. According to one source, the Cameron administration had no problem with citizens marching on local town halls to reform public services, especially in Labour Party strongholds (M. Taylor, personal communication, 12 October 2014). Indeed, at first Cameron had seemed willing to give the bid to Citizens UK. He was quite taken with an impressive Citizens UK meeting where he told the large audience, 'You are the Big Society.' Cameron advisers were sent to the US to meet with the American equivalent of Citizens UK and with President Obama advisers on how Obama used community organising to get elected in 2008.

Evidence of varying discourses, different types of political commitment and diverse modes of engagement are also evident within the programme itself. The capacity for COP to achieve far-reaching social change was stymied by the training model used by the programme which followed traditional forms of government-funded community development in the UK rather than using more radical models (Craig et al, 2011; Scott, 2011). For much of the four years, RE:generate (Action to Regenerate Community Trust), the organisation which provided the training on behalf of Locality, delivered a depoliticised community-building model. Its 'Root Solutions – Listening Matters' (Kearney and Olsen, 2009) educational programme emphasised the basics of listening to local people, letting them decide on key issues and projects. Training sessions held by RE:generate focused more on resolving, rather than creating conflict, and on building relationships with all stakeholders rather than challenging people in positions of power. They were much stronger on process and relationship building than organisation building or social justice outcomes.

Besides these training modules, for a year organisers had to 'listen' to 500 people, recruit and train nine volunteers and help three projects come about, even if they stayed at the level of an idea. The projects mainly depended on a few training sessions offered to residents that focused on the creation of social network bonds, neglecting the importance of creating organised groups and actions. Despite the progressive inclinations of Locality staff and Board members, the choice of this depoliticised model had a huge impact in determining the types of issues selected and results accomplished. For example, much of the community work was about helping improve service delivery and outreach in 'host' social welfare organisations or activities such as creating community gardens, litter picks, an annual music festival for young people, and neighbourhood watches.

However, there were also instances where Alinsky-style community organising did occur. Though a large number of organisers have indeed focused on community-building methods (listening, building relationships, recreating a sense of community and using existing assets), a minority of organisers succeeded in using direct action to help groups to organise and voice demands to improve their living conditions. Among these latter initiatives, one can find the Sheffield group of residents who managed to pressure local authorities to save a bus line and the development of an ACORN branch in Bristol, which took actions for economic and social justice, especially around housing issues (Rathke, 2015).

In fact, interviews conducted in 2014 revealed a great deal of autonomy at the grassroots level. The lack of a political vision for this experimental programme and the loose management in each organisation hosting trainees gave the organisers a significant degree of independence. This 'hands-off' policy was a surprise to almost everyone, including Locality staff, but especially those hired as organisers. Young people who had applied for the job because of their commitment to changing society used their relative independence to implement action-oriented community organising: "Some people got really dispirited by the lack of structure, the lack of training. I just thought great, I can do what I want. This is a great opportunity. Because I come from a politicised background, I do want to change things. This is the first step towards doing that" (organiser A).

Furthermore, as organisers were part of the same cohort, being and reading together enabled them to voice critiques of the programme and to build alternative visions of community organising:

> 'The people on our team were all pretty bright individuals and so we would have our team meetings every week and there were great moments for us to kind of develop our own ideas around what community organising should be and what we didn't like about the programme, ... eventually that what was led us in to building ACORN now.' (Organiser B)

Another positive impact of the COP was noted by this participant: "The great thing about the programme is the idea that, along with your salary in year 1, you were also given matched funding in year two so that you could go out and set up your own organisation" (organiser B).

A critical lesson of hiring and training people to do this work is that they often come with activist politics and, given the chance, pursued more radical forms of community organising and civic engagement. Such outcomes are not unprecedented. As a result of state incorporation of local community organisations, Trudeau (2012: 442) finds that community organisations in the US are increasingly able to 'inflect agendas with other priorities or subtly resist them'.

It is easy to dismiss the Big Society and its associated funding initiatives as neoliberal policies disguised as reforms to strengthen civic life and local participation. But such analyses miss the particular distinctiveness and potential importance of COP. It was the largest and best-funded social change initiative in more than a generation explicitly focused on hiring and training community organisers. Even with the programme's obvious limits in terms of training and outcomes, it did, in places, help to seed a more transformative model of community organising and, not to be underestimated, it further legitimised community organising as an approach to community development in England. Despite the dilemmas and contradictions this form of funding has entailed its effect on community organising cannot be fully predicted.

Conclusion

As Taylor and Wilson (2016) note, all organising, especially among disenfranchised groups, is difficult, complex and challenging work and obviously this valuable activity requires funding. We have argued that there is a strong case that community organising in the US should demand, and seek the legitimation of, more public funding especially from the state. Among community organisers and researchers in community development there is a well-established critique of relying on state funding. However, we think circumstances have changed and we need to reconsider this position. The long-term effects of neoliberal thinking have had an enormous impact and part of the response to this should be, we believe, a struggle to democratise the state and to challenge depoliticised interpretations of civil society.

Moreover, as discussed earlier, we need to bear in mind the realities of funding community organising through sources other than the state. Such sources carry risks similar to those associated with state funding, that is to say, funders setting the agenda, insecurity of funding over the medium term and so forth. At least with the state there is a conception, however notional, of the public good and historically we know this can be built on in significant ways. We also know that even in unpropitious circumstances, such as under a strongly neoliberal government of the British Conservative Party, securing funding for community organising can have important and interesting unintended consequences.

Our aim here is to provoke debate and to engage in dialogue on how we can best rethink funding community development. There is no simple answer on how to approach this. What we have done is provide arguments and models for considering how to broaden funding efforts. The ultimate aim is to support community organising in the belief that it has a vital role in addressing critical societal needs such as the widespread contemporary challenges to democracy. The public sector – at the local, state and/or national levels – should be reconsidered as a potential ally and target, depending on the context, for the public support of grassroots initiatives in social change and democratic practices. In the US, with the Trump administration (in office as at the time of writing), public funding of progressive community organising is most likely to come from state and city levels, certainly not from the federal government. Nearly all funding comes with 'conditions' and it requires careful thought and consideration to maintain core organisational practices and values and to avoid manipulation in securing and sustaining funding. But neither the contemporary turn to the Right, nor evidence of incorporation and 'domestication' of community organising in the past through public funding, should lead us throw up our hands and cede the vital territory of the state to other forces. Accordingly, we propose that diversifying and expanding resources for community organising, while seeking to democratise the state and civil society, are crucial short- and long-term strategies for transformative change.

Notes

1. One significant example of this was ACORN's campaign against H&R Block, a US multinational tax preparation company, which won funds for ACORN and reduced predatory rates for neighbourhood people (see Fisher et al, 2007).
2. Technical assistance providers consult not-for-profit organisations on development and funding matters.

References

Alinsky, S. (1972) *Rules for radicals*, New York: Vintage Books.

Ashton, P. and DeFilippis, J. (2014) 'Now where I'll find comfort, God knows, 'cause you left me just where I needed you most: Non-profits, business cycles and the remaking of the American welfare state' (unpublished manuscript).

Balazard, H. and Fisher, R. (2016) 'Community organizing: Remedy to neoliberal policies or slow revolution?', *Mouvements*, 85: 105–113.

Barkan, J. (2013) 'Plutocrats at work: How big philanthropy undermines democracy', *Dissent*, Fall, www.dissentmagazine.org/article/plutocrats-at-work-how-big-philanthropy-undermines-democracy.

Beckett, J., O'Donnell, S. and Rudd, J. (2006) 'Fundraising practices in community organizing', *Shelterforce Online*, 145, https://web.archive.org/web/20060512153912/http://www.nhi.org/online/issues/145/fundraising.html.

Bellah, R.N., Madsen, R., Sullivan, W.M., Swidler, A. and Tipton, S.M. (1985) *Habits of the heart: Individualism and commitment in American life*, Berkeley, CA: University of California Press.

Boris, E., de Leon, E., Roeger, K. and Nikolova. M. (2010) *Human service nonprofits and government collaboration: Findings from the 2010 national survey of nonprofit government contracting and grants*, Washington, DC: Urban Institute.

Boyte, H.C. (1980) *The backyard revolution: Understanding the new citizen movement*, Philadelphia, PA: Temple University Press.

Cabinet Office (2013) *Big Society: Frequently asked questions*, www.gov.uk/government/uploads/system/uploads/attachment_data/file/85850/Big_Society_FAQs.pdf.

Center for Popular Democracy (2015) *Seeding justice: Revenue-generating membership and fundraising canvasses for community organizing: Lessons from the field*, 21 October, Washington, DC: Center for Popular Democracy, https://populardemocracy.org/news/publications/seeding-justice-revenue-generating-membership-and-fundraising-canvasses-community.

Community Organisers Ltd (2017) *Massive expansion of community organisers programme*, 2 March, www.corganisers.org.uk/news/massive-expansion-community-organisers-programme.

Craig, G., Mayo, M., Popple, K., Shaw, M. and Taylor, M. (2011) *The community development reader*, Bristol: Policy Press.

DeFilippis, J., Fisher, R. and Shragge, E. (2010) *Contesting community: The limits and potential of local organizing*, New Brunswick, NJ: Rutgers University Press.

Delgado, G. (2009) 'Does ACORN's Work Contribute to Movement Building?', in R. Fisher (ed) *The people shall rule: ACORN, community organizing, and the struggle for economic justice*, Nashville, TN: Vanderbilt University Press, pp 251–74.

Dodge, J., Hofmann-Pinilla, A., Beard, A. and Murphy, C. (2013) *Beyond foundation funding: Revenue-generating strategies for sustainable social change*, New York University, https://wagner.nyu.edu/leadership/research/past-projects/sustainable#.

Dorfman, A. and Fine, M. (2009) *Seizing the moment: Frank advice for community organizers who want to raise more money*, Washington, DC: National Committee for Responsive Philanthropy and Center for Community Change, www.ncrp.org/wp-content/uploads/2016/11/seizingthemoment.pdf.

Dreier, P. (1996) 'Community empowerment strategies', *Cityscape*, 2(2): 121–59.

Edwards, M. (2010) *Civil Society* (2nd edn), Cambridge: Polity Press.

Edwards, M. (2013) '"Beauty and the beast" Can money ever foster social transformation?', Hivos Knowledge Programme, June, The Hague: Humanist Institute for Cooperation with Developing Countries, www.hivos.org/sites/default/files/m_edwards_beauty_and_the_beast.pdf.

Ehrenberg, J. (2011) 'The history of civil society ideas', in M. Edwards (ed), *The Oxford handbook of civil society*, Oxford: Oxford University Press, pp 15–28.

Fabricant, M. and Fisher, R. (2002) *Settlement houses under siege: The struggle to sustain community organizations in New York City*, New York: Columbia University Press.

Fisher, R. (1994) *Let the people decide: Neighborhood organizing in America*, Boston, MA: Twayne.

Fisher, R. and Dimberg, K. (2015) 'The community organisers programme in England', *Journal of Community Practice*, 24(1): 94–108.

Fisher, R. and Shragge, E. (2017) 'Funding community organising: Lessons from England and Quebec', *Community Development Journal*, 52(3): 454–69.

Fisher, R., Brooks, F. and Russell, D. (2007) ' "Don't be a blockhead": ACORN, direct action, and refund anticipation loans', *Urban Affairs Review*, 42(4): 553–582.

INCITE! Women of Color Against Violence (eds) (2007) *The revolution will not be funded: Beyond the non-profit industrial complex*, Cambridge, MA: INCITE! and South End Press Collective.

Joseph, M. (2002) *Against the romance of community*, Minneapolis, MN: University of Minnesota Press.

Kearney, S. and Olsen, J. (2009) *A guide to root solutions: Listening matters – engagement that works*, London: Action to Regenerate Community Trust.

Korstad, R.R. and Leloudis, J.L. (2010) *To right these wrongs: The North Carolina Fund and the battle to end poverty and inequality in 1960s America*, Chapel Hill, NC: University of North Carolina Press.

Larner, W. and Craig, D. (2005) 'After neoliberalism? Community activism and local partnerships in Aotearoa New Zealand', *Antipode*, 37(3): 402–24.

Locality (2010) *Tender to provide a national partner for the Community Organisers Programme*, formerly available at: http://locality.org.uk/projects/community-organisers/.

O'Hara, M. (2014). *Austerity bites: A journey to the sharp end of cuts in the UK*, Bristol: Policy Press.

Piven, F.F. and Cloward, R.A. (1978) *Poor people's movements: Why they succeed, how they fail*, New York: Vintage.

Rathke, W. (2015) 'Bristol wins first agreement for improved rental standards', *Chief Organizer Blog*, 15 March, http://chieforganizer.org/2015/03/15/bristol-wins-first-agreement-for-improved-rental-standards/.

Salamon, L.M. (ed) (2002) *The tools of government: A guide to the new governance*, New York: Oxford University Press.

Scott, M. (2011) 'Reflections on the "Big Society"', *Community Development Journal*, 46(1): 132–37.

Smith, S.R. (2011) 'The nonprofit sector', in M. Edwards (ed) *The Oxford handbook of civil society*, Oxford: Oxford University Press, pp 29–41.

Staples, L. (2004) *Roots to power: A manual for grassroots organizing*, Westport, CT: Praeger.

Taylor, M. (2011) 'Community organising and the Big Society: Is Saul Alinsky turning in his grave?' *Voluntary Sector Review*, 2(2): 257–64.

Taylor, M. and Wilson, M. (2016) 'Community organising for social change: The scope for class politics', in M. Shaw and M. Mayo (eds), *Class, inequality and community development*, Bristol: Policy Press, pp 219–34.

Third Sector (2011) 'Analysis: Why Alinsky's supporters lost out', *Third Sector*, 8 March, www.thirdsector.co.uk/analysis-why-Alinsky-supporters-lost/infrastructure/article/1058293.

Trudeau, D. (2012) 'Constructing citizenship in the shadow state', *Geoforum*, 43(3): 442–52.

Waheed, S., Kim, M. and Davis, W. (2010) *Sustaining organizing: A survey of organizations during the economic downturn*, Washington, DC: Data Center and National Organizers Alliance, http://noacentral.org/files/public/docs/SOSReport%202010.pdf.

Walker, E.T. and McCarthy, J.D. (2012) *Continuity and change in community organizing: A report to organizers*, Los Angeles, CA: UCLA.

Warren, M.R. (2001) *Dry bones rattling: Community building to revitalize American democracy*, Princeton, NJ: Princeton University Press.

Wolch, J.R. (1990) *The shadow state: Government and voluntary sector in transition*, New York: Foundation Center.

EIGHT

'It is time to reterritorialise utopian thinking': community, the commons and the funding of autonomous movements in Latin America – an interview with Marcelo Lopes de Souza

In this chapter, the editors interview Marcelo Lopes de Souza, a scholar who cooperates with social movements, and professor in the Department of Geography at the Federal University of Rio de Janeiro, Brazil. Drawing on the experiences of Latin American social movements, Marcelo discusses the implications of a commitment to radical autonomy for the funding of community-based movements and for emancipatory community development more broadly.

You are familiar with the way many English-speaking practitioners and researchers discuss community development. How is this similar or different from the sort of emancipatory community mobilisations that you have researched in Latin America?
First of all, let me say that 'Latin America' is a problematic expression as it was coined as a way to make claims to territory by European colonial and imperial powers, more specifically France under Napoleon III. To what extent are South America, Central America, the Caribbean and Mexico 'Latin'? The vast majority of the population in the Andean countries, in Mexico and in many other countries are *indígenas* or *mestizos* whose mother tongues are in fact Aymara, Quechua, Mayan, Guarani and so on. That is the reason why the indigenous movements speak of *Abya Yala* instead of 'Latin America.' Sure, Latin America or *Abya Yala* is culturally, ethnically and linguistically highly heterogeneous. We have very 'European' countries such as Argentina and Uruguay, as well as complex, almost 'unclassifiable' countries such as Brazil. Having said that, despite this heterogeneity, two centuries of more or less common history and struggle at the 'periphery' of the capitalist world order has created a certain sense of 'unity in diversity'.

This has led to a fascinating exchange of ideas and experiences between communities, states and regions.

In the continent 'community development' is an expression that has historically been linked with politically and ideologically problematic phenomena, from an emancipatory point of view. In the 1950s, 1960s and 1970s it was widely used by governments and international institutions to foster, or impose, a view of 'development' that led to material and cultural dispossession and disempowerment. In general, it has been linked to a form of 'socio-spatial engineering' aimed at social control by the nation state. But there have also been some interesting attempts to give 'community development' a truly emancipatory meaning, using as sources of inspiration 'Latin' American thinkers such as Brazilian educator Paulo Freire (1972). Nonetheless, *desenvolvimento comunitário* and *desarrollo comunitario* are expressions that are not part of the typical vocabulary of emancipatory movements here.

However, 'community' is a word that is very important in 'Latin' America, and for good reasons – not only because of a long tradition of communitarian organisation but also because of the ongoing relevance of the 'commons' for many people in the face of threats represented by economic 'integration' (read: dissipation and subalternisation of traditional economic and sociocultural structures) and cultural homogenisation in the wake of globalisation and the neoliberal agenda. As Maria Mies recently wrote, there is 'no commons without a community' (Mies, 2014: i106).

Can you say a little more about what you have in mind when you say 'the commons' are important in the life of communities?
In terms of economic activities, we are speaking about a whole set of heterogeneous realities and strategies when we speak about the commons and community. Let me mention just a few examples: (1) the persistent relevance of common lands for many groups, such as the *faxinalenses* (peasants who use shared pasture land in the state of Paraná, Brazil) as well as *indígenas* and *quilombolas* (descendants of African slaves who managed to escape from plantations in the 17th, 18th and 19th centuries); (2) the 'recovered factories' or 'recovered enterprises' [*fábricas recuperadas, empresas recuperadas*] in Argentina, which became famous after the 2001 economic crisis, when many thousands of workers (15,000 in 2005) took over their own factories and other companies after bankruptcy and began to run them cooperatively; (3) cooperatives developed from inside social movement organisations whose identity and origin is not primarily related to the production sphere, for instance the cooperative for the production of sandals

founded by activists of the *sem-teto* (poor and politicised squatters) movement in Rio de Janeiro's harbour area, in the last decade. There are many other examples across the continent.

Of course, in order to defend the 'commons', it is necessary to be willing to take part in resistance. Moreover, alternative economic, cultural and, ultimately, also political projects, such as the defence of the 'commons', need an adequate social basis to develop. Through social struggles a certain web of alternative social relations – based on horizontal decision-making, reciprocity and cooperation, rather than on competition and hierarchy, – can be consolidated. This is how *dignidad* [dignity] has become a key term for 'Latin' American movements and led to new or renewed notions of the 'good life' [*el buen vivir* or *Sumac Kawsay* in Quechua]. We see 'community' not in a romanticised way but as a political-cultural concept that fosters opposition to the dilution of place-based ties and their replacement by 'functional' relations that conform to the capitalist and neoliberal order. It is crucially relevant both for everyday life and political struggles. It allows for the preservation of the fabric of communities, culturally, politically and economically.

For example, in Bolivia during the 'Water Wars' in El Alto and Cochabamba communities mobilised to fight against the commodification of water. A certain sense of community has been a precondition for many struggles across the continent; struggles not only against economic crisis and political oppression, but more generally against the meaninglessness and emptiness of life in a neoliberal world. It is crucial from my perspective to link questions of community empowerment to the activity of social movements. These movements, especially those that are termed 'autonomous' have sustained and modified the meaning of community in very significant ways.

Can you explain how you see the role of 'autonomous' movements in community empowerment?

In terms of theory, I have been heavily influenced by the political philosophy of Cornelius Castoriadis, a Graeco-French thinker who brilliantly renewed radical political thinking in the second half of the 20th century (see, for example, Castoriadis, 1987). 'Autonomy' is rooted in two Greek words (*autos* and *nomos*), meaning 'to give oneself one's own laws'. Among ancient Greeks, the *nomos* did not mean formal, government-imposed laws, on the contrary: *nomos* (plural *nomoi*) refers to the rules and norms that orientate collective life in general. Our experience of *nomos* or *nomoi* is usually imposed from above or from the outside (heteronomy), but decision-making processes and the establishment of *nomoi* cannot follow this model if we want to build emancipation.

It is important to stress that Castoriadis's 'project of autonomy' is not restricted to the individual level, as in Kantian and liberal philosophies; autonomy for Castoriadis possesses two interrelated and interdependent aspects, *individual* and *collective* autonomy. To a large extent, we can see what Castoriadis called the 'project of autonomy' as a *radicalisation of democracy*, aimed at surpassing *both* representative 'democracy' (which in his words is a kind of 'liberal oligarchy') *and* the project of building a socialist state on the basis of vertical organisations such as communist parties, a core proposition of Marxism–Leninism. However, autonomy also encompasses other, more subtle dimensions, related to the domain of culture or 'imaginary' and the complex relationships between individuals and institutions in economic and political systems.

So how have Latin American movements contributed to this 'project of autonomy'?

Since the early 1990s, 'Latin' American movements such as the Mexican Zapatistas and a part of the Argentine *piqueteros* (a movement of unemployed workers, so named because of its tactic of picketing on main roads) have actually reinvented the project of autonomy according to local, regional and 'national' particularities and possibilities. Without these attempts to make autonomy possible under concrete circumstances, this project would be nothing but a further contribution to philosophical thinking.

Perhaps the most important and interesting characteristics of many, though certainly not all, 'Latin' American movements - characteristics that occur in various degrees and forms - are, first, the 'reinvention' of horizontal practices (self-management, radical critique of the state apparatus and political parties, and so on) informed by local and regional particularities. In the wake of this process, the traditional left (above all, Marxism–Leninism) has come under suspicion. On the other hand, it is not just a matter of '(re)discovering' European anarchism: Zapatistas and other movements are certainly left-libertarian, but they are not 'anarchists' in a strict sense, despite all the affinities with European anarchism. In other words, 'Latin' American movements have been often characterised by an agenda which is clearly committed to *autonomía* as a goal *and* means and they have developed this path in a very complex way in terms of sources of inspiration: from a creative dialogue with academic culture to the 'rediscovery' and recontextualisation of local and regional traditions in terms of organising and cultural values.

A second characteristic is the fact that most of these movements possess a very clear and 'holistic' territorial sensibility. Access to land, adequate housing and so forth is not just a question of economic survival, but a matter of *dignity* in its deepest sense. This holistic approach includes a focus on the spheres of production and consumption; economic exploitation and cultural oppression; power relations and the 'politics of identity'; class, ethnicity and gender; workplace and neighbourhoods. All these aspects were very often disconnected in past movements, or some of them were clearly treated as of secondary importance, but a new sense of relatedness between these struggles has emerged. For instance, Argentina's *piqueteros* developed the notion of '*trabajo territorial*' [territorial work]. By this they mean practices related to economic microcircuits as well as bottom-up decision-making processes in the *barrio* [neighbourhood]. This is not just a parochial approach, however, we must also build forms of cooperation beyond the local level.

Another interesting characteristic is how these autonomous ideas and practices are circulating across the continent and beyond. We can see some exchange of ideas and experiences, and even some cooperation between the movements, despite the huge geographic distances between them and their different languages and cultures.

The influence of European emancipatory ideas and projects in South and Central America, Mexico and the Caribbean has always been enormous, from Enlightenment ideals and liberalism, which influenced the independence movements at the end of the 18th and beginning of the 19th century, to anarchism, which was very influential in several countries at the beginning of the 20th century. On 'Latin' American soil, ideas were adapted, and flourished in a specific manner. However, in recent decades, Latin American movements began to inspire other movements across the globe, and it has now been Europe's turn to look for sources of inspiration elsewhere. Sure, things have by no means evolved in a linear way: after all, 'Latin' American activists and thinkers keep discussing European authors and paying attention to European and North American experiences; in fact, we have witnessed a complex web of exchanges and reciprocal influences between Mexican Zapatistas, Argentine *piqueteros*, the *Occupy* movement, European *Autonomen* (Germany) and *Indignados* (Spain). But the fact is that 'Latin' America is clearly no longer seen as just a 'recipient' of influences in a (neo)colonial way.

So if autonomous communities and movements are committed to horizontal decision-making and democracy as well as independence from the state and market, this raises all sorts of questions about how they resource themselves. Can you tell us a little bit about how questions of funding and resources are approached?

Curiously, the subject of funding has remained underdeveloped in the academic literature on social movements. There are some relevant works, but other subjects have attracted more attention. As I jokingly say, it is as if the topic of funding was not 'sexy' enough. That is surely an intellectual and, from a scholar-activist perspective, strategic mistake: few themes could be as important as funding, as one does not need to be a 'historical materialist' to admit that it is difficult to develop alternative ideals on an empty stomach; what is more, all sorts of activities – from popular libraries to *comedores populares* [community kitchens and restaurants] to human rights campaigns to educational activities – need to be adequately financed to be successful or simply viable.

I have in mind the use of the commons that I already mentioned. But let me emphasise that funding is about more than sustaining an organisation or movement, important as that is. Funding can serve as part of what have been termed 'prefigurative politics', that is, the forms of organisation and tactics we employ and the social relations we cultivate here and now, which serve as steps towards the creation of a better society.

It can't be easy trying to sustain autonomous forms of economic activity. What dilemmas or compromises have ensued?

Let us take the example of Argentina's self-managed workplaces. These are a good example of funding as prefigurative politics but they also illustrate some problems: as I could see personally in Buenos Aires ten years ago, some *empresas recuperadas* broke with the principle of equality of wages and even introduced salary work. They evolved into cooperatives where the cooperative's members act as 'microlevel capitalists' and exploit other workers very much in a capitalist way. Moreover, I also observed that their marketing methods were often very conventional: products such as breadsticks and biscuits were marketed and sold without any concern with what have been termed 'awareness-raising', a concept very important in 'fair trade' marketing. So, an emblematic social movement, which walked hand-in-hand with the *piquetero* movement for a few years, gradually became, to some degree, part of the new economic establishment. The original, huge politico-pedagogic potential of the movement partly vanished or was forgotten. This kind of situation tells us a further lesson: 'co-optation' is not just the co-optation of an individual;

co-optation is also 'structural co-option' sometimes and the enormous seduction exerted by capitalism and the state.

In relation to cooperatives, as I could see as someone who has collaborated with the *sem-teto* (homeless workers) movement in Rio de Janeiro and sporadically in São Paulo, the experience of founding and managing a cooperative is by no means a trivial enterprise. The workers who are the backbone of the *sem-teto* movement have difficulties in finding time to organise themselves, and they have often little or no experience in this sense; not to mention the problem represented by scarce resources to buy even a small amount of raw material to produce things that can be successfully commercialised outside the *ocupação*. Of course, the prejudices against the *sem-teto*, who are often seen as dangerous or even criminals by the middle-classes and mainstream media, have also played a role in this.

The fact that the commons are still alive in many places demonstrates that it is possible to have other ways of organising the economy outside the capitalist market. In the countryside, agriculture can generate income. We might, therefore, think that rural movements are less vulnerable to co-optation than urban movements, but the reality is a little more complex. MST [*Movimento dos Trabalhadores Rurais Sem Terra*: the Landless Workers' Movement] which is a more or less vertical organisation, influenced by Marxism and Liberation Theology, managed approximately 1,500 schools in the *assentamentos* [peasants' settlements or encampments] it controlled in 2005. At the same time, the organisation has been partly dependent on public funding in various ways: for instance, funding for the settlements, and this has haunted MST almost from the beginning.

Another challenge relates to the fact that institutions linked with the traditional, Marxist–Leninist or populist left (above all political parties) have tried to co-opt social movements organisations. Funding and subsidies have been one of the strategies (such as the *planes* [unemployment subsidies] in Argentina); the promise of 'participation' in the government is a further strategy, even by means of recreating and co-opting institutions such as popular assemblies (for example the government-sponsored *cabildos abiertos* in the Andean countries). In Chile, for instance, the *pobladores* movement (a poor people's movement rooted in neighbourhoods responsible for, among other things, mass land seizures) explicitly cultivates *autonomía* as a core principle, but at the same time self-management [*autogestión*] is often reduced in *pobladores*' discourse to the movement's management of fiscal funds obtained from the state! It becomes evident that the meaning of *autonomía* cannot be as radical in this context as one might hope.

To make things even more problematic, while 'autonomy' should be understood as antithetical to party politics and statecraft, the *pobladores* movement was deeply involved itself in the founding of a new political party, *Partido Igualdad* (Equality Party). 'Autonomy' is a fragile plant and the threats come from all sides.

Things are different, of course, if you really try to remain as independent as possible from the state apparatus and capitalist market. The Zapatista territory in the south of Mexico offers an example of this. It is a remarkable experiment built from the bottom up in indigenous towns and villages. For over 20 years they have 'controlled' a whole region (five provinces in the state of Chiapas) which encompasses a thousand communities and around 200,000 people. It is completely independent of the Mexican state and is basically self-funded apart from some funding from sympathisers across Mexico and through the international solidarity movement. They have sponsored and developed a whole set of initiatives, from occupation of land and the fostering of less or non-coercive social relations of production, to the creation of anti-hierarchical and anti-colonial schools (*escuelitas*) to build an 'alternative life' in 'little islands' which are nevertheless highly networked with national and international movements. This relies primarily on ecological, collective agricultural production but is supported by complex political structures at local and regional levels, which also cooperate with, and to an extent offer services to, people in the territory who are not Zapatistas. They have cooperatives that engage in international trade, and they sustain their own institutions of culture, education and health, an army and even their own autonomous banks. The economic conditions are very basic, though, and also the situation is quite specific in many respects as they have access to resources and opportunities that are not easily available in other contexts, especially in big cities.

In sum, we shall not forget that we are dealing with a multiplicity of sometimes even contradictory approaches to funding autonomy; that is probably a characteristic of praxis whenever a project is pursued by a plurality of social actors who live in different places and have to struggle under different conditions in terms of political culture, institutional challenges and so on.

Latin American civil society has been particularly prone to so-called 'NGOisation'. To what extent has this phenomenon been a feature of the movements with which you are familiar and what effects did it have? What role did funding play in this?

Popular movements in 'Latin' America have increasingly raised reservations and made criticisms of NGOs in recent decades. There are both conceptual and political differences between NGOs and emancipatory popular movements. Conceptually, an NGO is, as the name itself suggests, an organisation, while a social movement is something that can be adequately understood only at a very different level of scale: it refers to a larger or smaller part of an entire society, a part which does not accept its 'place' in the existing social order and sometimes does not accept the social order at all. Sometimes, the public visibility and importance of a social movement organisation is so great that many people even make the mistake of confounding the part (that is, the organisation) with the whole (the movement). That has happened in Brazil with MST.

There was a definite 'NGOisation' observable in parts of the continent from the early 1990s onwards; a good example are some federations of neighbourhood associations (*associações de moradores*) in Rio de Janeiro. NGOs were then at the peak of their prestige and popularity; the fact that they could obtain funds from international donors has undoubtedly exerted a seduction over low-income activists and many young, middle-class academics looking for jobs in a period of limited career opportunities. Moreover, the 'professionalisation' represented by NGOs seemed very attractive in the context of apparently rising opportunities for 'participation' in a post-dictatorship era - provided you are able to take part in the political process and public debates in a 'well-informed' way. Debates on public policies and 'alternative urban planning' apparently became more important than marches, pickets, sit-ins and other forms of protest in Brazilian cities during the 1990s.

This was a time of euphoria about 'participatory budgeting' (an interesting but also limited and limiting experience that became famous in Porto Alegre under the Workers Party local government, and which was then 'exported' to other cities and even to other countries) as well as about the prospects of a government-sponsored 'urban reform' (which similarly to a true 'land reform' has never happened). NGOs have often supported precisely the least radical aspects of the economic initiatives known as '*economía solidaria*'/'*economia solidária*' [solidarity economy] or '*economia/economía popular*' [popular economy] that emerged during this period. Many people seem to ignore the fact that despite its relative potential for popular creativity, the solidarity economy can be and has been useful for the capitalist system, as late capitalism has expelled legions of workers from the formal economy and condemned them to unemployment and precariousness. I do acknowledge that self-help organisations and even cooperatives can play a relevant role in preventing a further deterioration of the social fabric. But it would be delusional to believe that microcredit or 'fair trade' organisations can 'change the world'.

Social movement organisations have tried to avoid becoming part of a bigger strategy of socio-spatial stabilisation and control, even if it is difficult sometimes: in Argentina, for instance, many *piquetero* organisations supported the governments of Néstor and Cristina Kirchner. That shows that in spite of all conceptual and political differences, social movement organisations and NGOs are not always that different in terms of their political roles.

For social movement organisations, funding obtained from some foundations and state sources (especially or basically in the case of so-called progressive governments, as conservative governments and big business are understandably not prone to finance radical popular movements) can be a short-term solution and a long-term problem. Although foundations and governments can provide resources that can be very useful for financing several types of activities, it is crucial to see that foundations and governments have their own agendas and interests, and these interests can gradually influence social movement organisations in various forms: increasing bureaucratisation, less emphasis on contentious politics, more 'adaptive behaviour' within the framework of the capitalist status quo in general. This can be the beginning of the end of a social movement organisation.

As far as NGOs are concerned, it is important to say that I do not think that *all* NGOs are *necessarily* damaging or useless for the purposes of popular organising and emancipation. First of all, there are many different types of NGOs: they perform different roles and obviously there are those that are constituted by competent and honest people doing a serious job. NGOs can sometimes help social movement organisations, for instance, working as technical supporters in various fields - from environmental protection to legal assistance. For various reasons, however, NGOs have become much closer to the state apparatus and even big business than to social movements, both ideologically and materially, and their proliferation has to be understood within the context of the rise of neoliberalism worldwide. There has also been some confusion between NGOs and actual social movement organisations, and NGOs are not totally innocent in this regard – a kind of 'discursive mimicry' between them and social movements can provide additional legitimacy for many of them.

Communities' relationship to the state has long been a vexed question within community development – and this relationship is often mediated by funding. The need to work both 'in and against the state' (London Edinburgh Weekend Return Group, 1980) was and continues to be a key tension within community development practice. Could you elaborate a little on what relationship autonomous movements have – or should have – with the state?

At least among true social movements, feelings such as suspicion and hostility towards the capitalist state have been understandably strong. But concrete politico-philosophical backgrounds range from 'state-phobia' (when activists try or claim to have nothing to do with the state apparatus, regardless of the circumstances) to a much more ambiguous Marxist–Leninist position which is 'state-centrist' in the sense that its opposition to the capitalist state does not mean that the institution of the state *itself* is critically assessed in a truly profound way.

Now, a radical rejection of statecraft in the name of autonomous, horizontal, prefigurative politics does not necessarily mean that one simply ignores the state apparatus for the sake of an assumed 'purity'. Even if we try to live in a galaxy far, far away by means of, say, founding an eco-anarchist community somewhere in the countryside, we can hardly escape the tentacles of the capitalist state entirely. Otherwise we risk total isolation or we miss the opportunity to dialectically use some 'cracks' offered by the contradictions of the state itself (certain potentialities offered by specific legislation and regulations, for instance).

I am convinced that it is necessary to combine two pieces of wisdom, respectively inspired by Spinoza and Nietzsche, in order to avoid both sterile dogmatism and demoralising opportunism. From Nietzsche's *Thus Spoke Zarathustra*, we should borrow his, or actually Zarathustra's, words: 'and he who would keep clean among men, must know how to wash himself even with dirty water' (1909: 153); from Spinoza we should borrow the Proposition 65 of his *Ethics*: 'A good that prevents us from enjoying a greater good is really an evil' (2017: n.p.). It is necessary to assess costs and benefits on a case-by-case basis, while not forgetting that the state apparatus ultimately remains a structurally heteronomous institution, and therefore a threat. That is to say that even in the context of 'progressive' governments, emancipatory social movements must keep a 'safe' distance, as party politics and statecraft in general are by no means a soil where the seeds of self-management, horizontality and autonomy can adequately grow. I developed this approach particularly in my book *The Prison and the Agora*, published in 2006 in Brazil (Souza, 2006).

Even allowing for the dangers of what you call 'structural co-optation' do you feel there is a role for social movements in defending the state in order to democratise it and reclaim it 'as a shared resource' (Shaw, 2014: i18)?

I do not think that we should 'defend the state'. This position is grounded, among other things, on two false assumptions: (1) the capitalist state is a kind of 'common resource' that needs to be defended against capitalists' greed and power; (2) the best way to oppose neoliberalism is 'defending the state'. Well, the capitalist state is not a 'common resource' or the potential defender of the 'common good': it has been from the very beginning a heteronomous, class-biased institution that serves the self-reproduction of heteronomy and capitalism.

Now, to which extent is it necessary to 'defend' the state, as many progressive people say, in order to defend the interests of the oppressed? I would like to reframe the problem. It is necessary to defend *rights*; this usually means to oppose privatisation and deregulation, and in some cases that also means to defend specific laws, for instance. Not because state enterprises are 'in the hands of the people', but because privatisation commonly has a negative impact on the poor; and not because regulation of the relationship between labour and capital by the capitalist state is 'good', but because neoliberal deregulation is an even greater evil; and not because formal laws are necessarily 'good', but because they can be sometimes used to consolidate some gains for the subaltern, for the workers. But it is crucial to see clearly the dangers and challenges we have to face, in order to avoid underestimating them. The *ultimate* goal does not lie in improving state legislation or public policies, otherwise the movements will just contribute to stabilise status quo.

Our ideas - from 'alternative master plans' to innovative proposals regarding environmental protection - can always be partly captured and assimilated by the state (or even big business, sometimes with help of NGOs). If we fail to show how the potentialities of state politics are limited, and sometimes a trap, then that means we are not persuasive enough and that we need to refine our arguments. The theme of funding offers a wonderful instance in this regard, as one of our strategic priorities, not only for obvious material reasons, must be the development of innovative forms of self-funding combined with efforts in terms of 'awareness-raising', counterhegemonic struggles including creating a radical and politicised culture. It is time to reterritorialise utopian thinking, not least on a community level, in the sense of rehabilitating, reinventing and reclaiming it on a renewed basis - and this is not contradictory to a non-opportunist, ethically grounded pragmatism.

Could we also understand autonomy as a Trojan horse sometimes? There is a long tradition of 'self-help' within community development, a tendency that has proven fruitful for neoliberal restructuring as responsibility for public services is shifted onto the community sector. Is this a risk within a 'project of autonomy'?

'Autonomy' is a word that has been used by many people with different purposes - it is no different from terms such as 'freedom', 'equality', 'justice', 'development' or 'sustainability', which have been used in a disparate manner. If we think of 'autonomy' as a component of the neoliberal agenda - alongside decentralisation, privatisation and deregulation - this 'autonomy' does not have anything to do with the 'project of autonomy' in a radically emancipatory sense. In terms of capturing and domesticating key political terms, there is nothing new under the sun: conservative forces have always tried to do this, in the wake of attempts to 'tame' potentially disruptive and subversive social forces and redirect social energies for stabilising purposes. Look at what has been done with Henri Lefebvre's 'right to the city' motto, now used by all sorts of institutions from UN-Habitat to the Brazilian Ministry of Cities.

On the other hand, I can understand if Marxists do not try to defend 'autonomy' as a key political term, or even when they reduce it to its conventional and conservative modes of appropriation. After all, they have been politically committed to vertical modes of organising ('socialist state', Leninist-style parties, and so on) that do not have anything in common with the 'project of autonomy', to use Castoriadis's expression.

Do you think similar movements and tendencies can be identified beyond Latin America?

Sure. Not only similar experiences and discussions, but of course similar threats and problems as well. In South Africa, for instance, the shack dwellers organisation *Abahlali baseMjondolo*, very active is some cities, has faced similar problems under the ANC government as 'Latin' American autonomous movements, though criminalisation and police repression have been even more brutal in South Africa than here.

In Europe, several social movements have developed agendas and a repertoire of spatial practices that are convergent with concerns, debates and experiences we have found in countries such as Argentina, Brazil or Mexico, even if the social basis of the movements is different: in Amsterdam or Berlin, squatters are often people with a middle-class background, while in cities such as Rio de Janeiro and São Paulo the *sem-teto* are basically (hyper)precarious, informal workers, who in many cases are former *favela* residents (very often drug-trafficking related violence drove them out of the *favela*) or homeless people – even if middle-class people, usually students, are often active supporters of the *sem-teto*. From Reclaim the Streets to the critical social centres, there have been movements and experiences in Europe that can be understood as convergent in terms of a basic *ethos* with movements such as the autonomous *piqueteros*, for instance. Not to mention the fact that there have been a lot of exchange and some good examples of transnational activism.

However, the dilemmas and problems are very similar, too. And they repeat themselves generation after generation, in spite of the many warnings expressed by history itself. The seduction exerted by political parties seems to be a perpetual challenge, even if the aftermath of taking power (or even before) is frustration and disappointment. Recent cases have been the Coalition of the Radical Left or Syriza in Greece, the 'pirate parties' in several countries and *Podemos* in Spain.

Have you any final reflections on autonomous movements, funding and community emancipation?
I cannot offer a recipe, and no one could. Finding solutions in terms of funding is not a matter of theoretical reasoning or of individual reflection alone; it is a *praxis* question, and as such it is a matter of *collective experimentation* – and even of historical creation or invention. What I can do is offer some suggestions – suggestions that are not new, as they are based on generations of collective debates and struggles.

First warning – and forgive me for repeating myself: the state apparatus is ultimately not a partner for freedom, but a 'liberticidal' institution. Social movement organisations must demand, for tactical reasons, that the state redistribute government revenues in a less class-biased way but social movement organisations cannot transform themselves into 'managers' of public funds. That is the reason why movements cannot simply ignore participative schemes such as 'participatory budgeting', but they cannot allow that the state apparatus alone conditions the timing and spaces of popular organisation.

A second warning, which is a provocative suggestion at the same time: even if the 'solidarity economy' has been domesticated and institutionalised, giving rise to the creation of a ministry-like Secretaria Nacional de Economia Solidária in Brazil under the Workers Party, this does not mean that some debates, tools and experiences developed under the banner 'solidarity economy' and the like are not useful for radical purposes. Crowd-funding and fundraising campaigns can be used in some circumstances, but social movement organisations must develop their own, innovative forms of self-financing activities. Many organisations have already developed important experiences, for instance by means of creating cooperatives. But other tools and methods are also interesting; social or community currencies, for example, were crucially important in Argentina especially at the peak of the economic crisis at the beginning of the last decade, but it remains relevant there - and this kind of thing should not be seen as relevant only in the context of acute crises. That means that we must always be aware of the necessity to constantly reinject critical intentions and energies into our alternative economic practices, otherwise they will cease to be alternative and will be gradually assimilated by the status quo. Is this awareness a totally safe immunisation against structural co-optation? Of course not. Life itself is a risky business.

If we are really radical, in the sense of grasping the root of the matter, 'autonomy' is not just about trying to be autonomous in the face of the capitalist state and market. Autonomy in its strongest sense is about a sociopolitical *project*, a deep alternative *both* to political liberalism (and capitalist thinking in general) *and* bureaucratic 'socialism' and its sources of inspiration. Autonomy must be about trying to build a tomorrow that is substantially different from today and yesterday in all respects.

References

Castoriadis, C. (1987) *The imaginary institution of society: Creativity and autonomy in the social-historical world*, Cambridge, MA: MIT Press.

Freire, P. (1972) *Pedagogy of the oppressed*, Harmondsworth: Penguin.

London Edinburgh Weekend Return Group (1980) *In and against the state* (2nd edn), London: Pluto Press.

Mies, M. (2014) 'No commons without a community', *Community Development Journal*, 49(S1): i106–i117.

Nietzsche, F. (1909 [1891]) *Thus spake Zarathustra* (translated by T. Common), New York: the Modern Library. [This book has also been translated as *Thus spoke Zarathustra*.]

Shaw, M. (2014) 'Learning from *The Wealth of the Commons*: A review essay', *Community Development Journal*, 49(S1): i12–i20.

Souza, M.L. de (2006) *A prisão e a ágora: Reflexões em torno da democratização do planejamento e da gestão das cidades*, Rio de Janeiro: Bertrand Brasil.

Spinoza, B. de (2017 [1677]): *The ethics* (translated by R.H.M. Elwes), available at: www.gutenberg.org/files/3800/3800-h/3800-h.htm.

PART 3

Modes of agency and horizons of possibility

NINE

Keeping the show on the road: a reflective dialogue between a community worker and a funder

Lin Bender and Japhet Makongo

Introduction

This chapter consists of a dialogue between Japhet Makongo, a community development worker based in Tanzania, and Lin Bender, CEO of the philanthropic organisation, the Helen Macpherson Smith Trust in Victoria, Australia. Lin and Japhet have each worked on both 'sides' of the funding relationship and through their discussion they offer insights into the day-to-day realities of managing funding relationships. They analyse the risks and challenges involved, but also the possibilities for effective funding for community empowerment. Their discussion of funding speaks to perennially important themes within community development such as power, agency, community ownership, process versus outcome, and the meaning of 'success'.

Introducing ourselves, the work that we do and why we are drawn to it

Lin: I am a first generation Australian, daughter of Polish, Jewish migrant parents. My circuitous career started as a photographer and graphic designer, and I transitioned to starting a number of social enterprises, which provided invaluable learning that continues to inform my practice. A series of senior management roles in the not-for-profit sector followed, across operations and marketing to strategic business development, as well as CEO positions.

My appointment in 2013 as CEO of the Helen Macpherson Smith Trust has provided me with the opportunity to draw on my experiences. I understand how the not-for-profit sector works from the inside, and I know what it's like to work tirelessly to realise a seemingly impossible dream. I know that systemic change needs to be inclusive, respectful and collaborative. And I know that finding, securing and maintaining the right funding partner requires a combination of skills including strategic planning, research, negotiation and the art of managing stakeholder expectations. The right partner will not only share the dream, but will understand that long-term impact requires patience and flexibility, an appetite for risk, and a preparedness to view failure as an opportunity for learning.

I have never worked harder nor felt the weight of responsibility as heavily as I do in my current role, and I have never been more content.

Japhet: I was born and raised up in a rural community on the shores of Lake Victoria in Musoma, Tanzania. During my teenage years I experienced the beauty of rural communal life in fishing, farming, livestock keeping and wildlife hunting. My professional career started as a field extension officer in the Ministry of Agriculture and Livestock at district level. For more than 15 years, I enjoyed the privilege of learning from rural communities on how they perceive development, a period that shaped my understanding of community development.

Over the last 30 years, I have changed jobs, but kept my role as a development facilitator. Between 1990 and 1993 I worked on flood and irrigation projects, funded by the International Labour Organization (ILO), as a mentor and facilitator of the Farmers and Water Users Associations,[1] then becoming a part-time trainer in community development in the Arusha region, Tanzania. Working with International NGOs and donor agencies has exposed me to various grant-making strategies and the dynamics of the grant-making world. Moving to the other side as a grantee, working with HakiElimu (a national advocacy organisation promoting equitable and quality education for all children) in 2002, I realised the importance of strengthening internal capacity for handling negotiations and relationships with funders.

My current work as a development consultant has exposed me to the challenges of the relationship between communities (beneficiaries), aid recipient organisations (local grantees) and donors. Learning the dynamics and lessons of partnership in development is a complex process.

Perspectives on community development

Lin: We represent different sides of the funding fence, different countries, different economic and political climates, and different needs. We share the same principles, objectives and aspirations, but does community development mean the same thing to each of us? I think it would be useful to 'negotiate' a mutual statement summing up what we each mean by 'community development'. I have drafted a sentence for you to edit:

> To enable disadvantaged communities to empower themselves to achieve sustainable social, economic, environmental, cultural and political conditions, which have been identified by the community as essential for them to flourish and fulfil their potential.

Japhet: The statement you have made is good, but it will make more sense if we take a holistic community definition to include everyone and not only disadvantaged groups. I would therefore propose the following:

> Self-empowered communities realise their needs and achieve sustainable socioeconomic, environmental and democratic political conditions for their well-being.

I think it changes the focus of self-empowerment when we use 'enabling' or 'to enable'. My understanding is that enabling is a process of ensuring communities are self-empowered.

Lin: It's interesting that your statement focuses on an aspirational outcome of community development, whereas I am including the role of the funder in providing the means to deliver the outcome. One is reliant on the other and I think it's important that this statement represents both sides. I agree that we should include all communities, and I like that you have included that the community should 'realise their needs'.

This small exercise has highlighted the importance of taking the time to understand each other, and the importance of words. The seemingly small differences in our perspectives of the same aspiration must be negotiated from the outset to ensure that we have the same expectations of each other and the outcomes. So here is a third draft:

> Self-empowered communities, enabled to realise their needs and achieve sustainable socioeconomic, environmental and democratic political conditions for their well-being.

Japhet: I can see that the statement you have made captures and improves on what I initially proposed. So, let's keep this.

How do we find the right partner?

Lin: How do you find your funders?

Japhet: It has been a long process, which is changing. Previously, communities were guided by leaders, consultants or advisers. So, they sent applications to embassies, to international NGOs, to different philanthropic groups. And the funders would say 'this seems like a good idea so can you put up a proposal which we can discuss'. That process went on until they agreed either to take on the collaboration or not. But the practice has changed now, where funders have taken a lead to invite grantees, to seek collaboration through calls for proposals through adverts on websites and other media outlets. You find which funders are there, then you try to see how you can fit into that programme. There is little room for dialogue at this stage, and most grantees may be tempted to adjust their goals to fit the call for proposals.

Lin: We call for proposals, but we have an open-door policy where we talk to potential grant seekers before they submit an application. Because the needs are so big and funding is limited, we narrow the focus so that we attract enquiries from a smaller pool. It means we can spend more time with grant seekers to understand what they need, what we can do, how we can help pull together other resources, other partnerships, and help them beyond the grant itself.

But I completely agree with you, I'm now reading through 32 applications, of which we can only fund maybe 14 and, it's obvious which ones are trying to push a square peg into a round hole, they are the ones who did not speak to us first. It's also frustrating when we see a good project, but whoever has written the application hasn't expressed themselves properly. It's why we encourage applicants to talk to us first, and when we need more clarity we try to visit them. We understand that it's hard for grant seekers, because they're desperate for funding. Their challenge is to align what they want with the funding source without compromising the integrity of their work.

Funding is very competitive. So how does a disadvantaged group have the expertise to identify who they should be talking to? Does the funder find you or do you find them?

Japhet: I am experiencing approaches where funders are putting forward what they can support and asking people to join them in partnership in projects. I was wondering about the other way around, what if the communities were the ones who were putting up calls for proposals? Saying we want to do something towards mental health, among the youth or our targeted group, this is how we are doing it and is there a funder who is interested to work with us? Has this ever happened in your experience?

Lin: Yes, it does. Generally, community organisations come to us with projects they believe are a good fit with our areas of interest.

Securing major funding requires a level of expertise, and we're seeing that organisations are becoming more professional in how they look at funding options and the funding mix. This is a challenge for smaller organisations and communities, where there isn't that level of sophistication.

Japhet: I am aware that most well-established and professional organisations may have an advantage over good community-based organisations. I am not sure that I have a good answer, apart from emphasising the need to create space and time for dialogue at the outset of the relationship as part of the process of building their capacity. Language and differences in the culture of expression are among the barriers.

Lin: Perhaps a funding opportunity is to build the leadership skills of small not-for-profits to better understand the funding landscape. Another opportunity is for a number of small not-for-profits to collaborate on a project and pool their resources to engage an independent business development manager.

'Whoever has the gold makes the rules.' True or false?

Japhet: It can be both, depending on the level of ownership. In small-scale mining, the gold miner is the first custodian and owner of the gold. Apparently s/he has no powers in making rules! The buyer makes the rules and keeps the miner at the digging level.

This can be translated in the context of funding for community development. Gold can be the 'information about the changes' the community aspires to see, but also what the funder wishes to support or buy. So, the interesting discussion is when and how these changes/needs fall into the hands of a funder, who may now dictate the rules of the game.

What we experience in this part of the world is that the funder often takes the lead to negotiate with the community regarding how to state the needs, the outcomes, the evidence of success, the investment needed, the approach and capacity. For example, currently, most funders use pre-prepared formats for grant applications that are filled electronically and do not provide room for pre-dialogue. For most communities, it requires strong negotiation capacity and resilience through their representatives (usually a community-based organisation or NGO) to ensure equality in negotiations. However, in most cases the funders may find themselves wearing two hats. One is of the sympathy with the local beneficiaries and the second is maintaining power in the process of investing.

Lin: It depends on your definition of the gold. Is the gold the money, or is it the skills, culture and wisdom of the community?

Japhet: The community has to have a common vision and understanding of what they want. The funding opportunity will help the community come together to see how they can use the different resources they have, including this funding opportunity. But I think often the funding opportunity is seen as the superior resource and people tend to forget there are other community resources.

Lin: So what happens at that point? Does a level of resentment start coming in? Are there mixed messages in terms of the agenda? Are the expectations not the same?

Japhet: I think when you have the community on one side and the funder on the other, it goes back to each group's values and expectations of each other. I think these expectations are sometimes not given enough time for discussion. It is important we know our differences and our similarities, so maybe we can take the risk of moving forward together.

Lin: It's an interesting challenge to balance different agendas. You have the needs of the community, government with its agenda, then the funder with their own agenda. So how do you see this partnership working in harmony?

Japhet: I think this requires patience, so each group is given time to understand the other, so it's about time frame. I wonder when we sign an agreement, are we all satisfied that we have all the information we want and are we comfortable with each other? Especially agreeing on how long it takes to see results.

Lin: Is it because we are impatient? There's a need and we want to address that need. You have a potential funder and there's an impatience to make things happen, so we don't lose the opportunity. There is a need for balance.

Japhet: Yes, and this balance is at different levels. On the community side you have the beneficiaries' expectations of their leaders who have identified the donors, and they are saying we have the donor, now we want to see the result. Then you have the expectation on the community leaders, who also want to see this process moving fast enough so they can show they have been able to deliver on the expectations of the community and the funders.

And you have expectations from the funders who are always pushed by time frames. The proposal includes a schedule of activities that results in rushing to save time but also save money.

Governance and reporting

Lin: As funders we must be careful not to impose our expectations, but allow the community and its leaders to guide the project. We must also be careful not to create a whole new infrastructure with new people who don't have the same passion, knowledge and level of commitment as the community.

Japhet: We have projects where the donors have been the initiator, either through their own research or an extension of a project. The funder may have interest in a certain community or working with a certain team. Normally, they will hire experts and even though they may come from the local area, they may not be linked to the community and the community sees them as aliens, as people who come in and create new project management structures. In many cases they run parallel to the existing structures already in place. Effectiveness of the newly introduced structures tend to end with the project.

Lin: There is a fine balance between developing a community-led collective impact model that strengthens all participants and delivers the best holistic outcomes to the community, and imposing a new governance structure and expecting they will comply with expectations. I was interested to read in your case study on HakiElimu that they have negotiated one report to all stakeholders.

Japhet: That is one of the core negotiation points and it is clear in the partnership agreement. We had a case in 2002, when the Department of International Development, UK came to us with an offer to fund more than 75% of our programme budget, together with a condition to follow their budget requirements. We insisted on our approach and refused the funding offer. However, they came back and we negotiated to include additional reporting requirements into our comprehensive report that goes to all stakeholders.

Lin: I am impressed you insist on developing one standard report. We have ongoing discussions with our funder colleagues on this issue. Unfortunately, it becomes complicated because we all have very different legal and policy requirements. In Australia, there is a growing awareness of the need for transparency, which will make it easier for us to collaborate as funder and for grant seekers to identify who is doing what.

Investing in a fence at the top of the cliff, not just an ambulance at the bottom. Community development requires long-term vision, commitment and patience

Lin: These are questions we ask ourselves all the time: as a funder do we just invest in the fence at the top of the cliff, because sometimes you have to be an ambulance first? The needs are so big and the resources are limited.

Japhet: I would also add that it requires a combination of innovation and flexibility. The patience to spend enough time to understand the behaviour at the hilltop and the way it connects the ambulance needed at the base.

Lin: Some funders have the luxury of working holistically on one long-term goal. However, most of us fund across multiple areas. If I was to personally choose one goal, it is equity in education, which I see as the key to self-determination and self-empowerment. We could start by identifying potential community leaders and invest in building their capabilities. I know that community development is complex, and I believe that equity in education can help communities navigate solutions for themselves.

Japhet: I think it's important to recognise that knowledge and skills are dynamic and keep changing. Knowledge needs to be embedded in dynamic leaders both in communities and in funders, so that there is agreement on the level of knowledge and skills required. But having the knowledge and skills may not be enough. It has to be applied so people themselves can determine whether the skills are relevant to the context and that there is an enabling environment.

Lin: I agree. The success of a complex community project is dependent on the knowledge, skills, vision and track record of project leaders who are embedded, accepted and respected by the community. We need to be careful that funding doesn't take precedence over the knowledge and resources within the community and the need for quick results. Our learning has been that initiatives have to come from within communities, to grow organically, and the community needs to be responsible for its own decisions.

Japhet: We have a pastoral community here called the Masai who have lived harmoniously with wildlife in national parks and conservation areas. They've been living in an amicable way with the wilderness, but now the government is inviting in foreign investors with the stated aim of benefiting the community and protecting wildlife and conservation areas. Unfortunately, this has resulted in misunderstanding and tensions between pastoralists and political powers. Pastoralists perceive foreign investors as interference in their traditional life, leadership and power relations and feel that the poor and vulnerable community members may risk losing their survival threshold. This tension has escalated to violence, and sometimes loss of property and life.

Lin: Yes, but it's also a lack of respect for values and a way of life that is not your way of life. A funder should not impose their agenda and time frame over a community. When we see an alarming increase in young people on drugs, it is important to understand the reason why they have come to this point. So much funding targets the ambulance at the bottom of the cliff, not the fence at the top of the cliff. We need to understand the drivers of a particular issue, as opposed to applying another band-aid.

What does success look like?

Japhet: Success can be measured at different levels. At a basic input/output level, it can be measured in terms of products being delivered or services being provided such as infrastructure or knowledge/skills imparted. It can also be measured at outcome level where the product or service is willingly used by the beneficiaries without additional efforts from the supporting funder. My experience is that changes or successes at outcome level are usually not fixed or linear and rely on both internal and external factors such as state intervention. For example, in Tanzania, civil society organisations have for many decades advocated for government to facilitate all school-age children to be in schools. But the successes have been sporadic. School enrolments had dropped from about 98% in 2010–12 to below 70% in 2015. Then the new 2015 government decided to remove all compulsory fees and contributions and the enrolment went up to almost 100% within one year.

You also have to bear in mind time frames. In another case, I am evaluating a project aimed at preventing violence and abusive killings of older women (mainly widows) in some Lake Victoria regions. Findings show that the two-year project was successful in reducing killings and violence. However, the community is posing a challenge that the project time frame was too short. They observed that:

> 'we were not consulted on how long this project should last. We think we are just starting to see the benefits, but our big aim is that we would like to look at how to use the peace that the project has created to make a better life for us economically'.

The proposal clearly indicates that, at the end, local government and community leadership will take over. But how would they take over? The 'how' was not discussed at the beginning and so it is difficult to sustain the results.

For this project, the bottom line is ensuring equitable livelihood and positive economic change in the community. Currently youth are unable to gain employment, which goes back to education. Some young people who are linked with the violence and killings have experienced problems with education, which does not augur well in influencing cultural changes in an economic and social context. I'm now trying to ensure that any funding investment is locked into a holistic, longer-term perspective.

Lin: One of the key things we always look for in a proposal is the project sustainability beyond our funding period. Too often you see a good initiative stop just when it is gaining momentum because the funding runs out and the community is left disappointed. If we believe a project is worthwhile, we will consider extending our funding and be active in helping the organisation leverage our funding.

One thing we do is ensure the project budget includes an independent evaluation, so the organisation has a credible evidence-based report they can take either to government or to another funder to show proof of concept.

Japhet: So, are you saying you have room for continuation or interventions at the end of most of the projects?

Lin: Yes, we do. If we have a partner with strong leadership, a strong board, the project is a strong match to our focus areas and objectives and is going well, why would we not want to continue the relationship? Especially if we can build the capacity of the organisation to enable long-term sustainability. We often fund pilot projects and if we can see the pilot has value, we will help the organisation develop a sustainable business model.

Keeping the show on the road

Japhet: There was an established funder in the community who was funding early childhood development for a long time, and then suddenly the funder, with less than three months' notice, said: "we have changed our priorities and we want to focus on child labour and unemployment among youth".

Most of the previous grantees who were delivering early childhood programmes were caught off guard and struggled to write calls for proposals that fit the funder's new priority focus. This is a case of the donor changing abruptly and thus dictating a change of direction and thinking of local organisations.

We seem to be experiencing this more and more. There is a commitment with a signed agreement but there is also an addendum with an 'out' clause that enables the funder to exit but does not allow grantees to demand extension.

Lin: I have been on your side of the fence as a grantee and for us a key priority was to find a way to personally involve the funder at the highest level. A direct connection with the community, seeing and hearing the difference their funds are making to people's lives, is very powerful and very different from just reading a report. It is easier for us, because we work in one state, but digital technology makes it possible to make personal connections.

The grantee needs to be as creative in managing the relationship with their funders and key stakeholders as they are in delivering the project.

It requires specific skills and strong networks that are not always covered by directors and staff, but there are ways of bringing these skills into an organisation by establishing a subcommittee of skilled people to build strategic relationships with your supporters and potential funders.

Japhet: I think you have mentioned something very important in having a strong board beyond the project manager, with directors who can help build relationships. The point here is how much time should the funder spend on building relationships before actually committing to a project? You never solve problems in two years – the problems facing the communities have been there for many, many years, so taking an extra three to six months to understand the project can help to define difficulties and expectations.

Lin: This is one of the many challenges we are grappling with. We want to spend more time and resources in understanding our areas of interest and potential projects, however, we are required to work within a designated expense ratio in terms of the cost in managing an average annual distribution of $4 million. Our Trust can only generate income from growth on investment and our operational budget is limited. The way we have been able to increase the amount of time we can spend with potential grantees has been by narrowing our areas of interest.

Our open call for applications isn't the end point, but it's an effective way to start the filter process within our specific areas of interest. It provides us with an opportunity to meet new organisations, to identify potential collaborations and to alert organisations that they may be reinventing the wheel. This comes back to organisations needing to be proactive, to do their research, identify a potentially good match, write a strong application and negotiate a mutually beneficial partnership. Securing philanthropic funding is a competitive process. There are far more worthy projects and causes than there is funding, and it is an unfortunate reality that a good project can be passed over because of a poor application. It is harder for small grassroots organisations, because they often do not have access to skilled staff who can navigate the funding process. We try to counter this handicap by talking to all applicants.

Japhet: I think this is why, in Tanzania, the Foundation for Civil Society was established to help smaller community-based organisations identify their potential and capacity, and help them grow so that over time they would be in a position to negotiate with donors.

Lin: Yes, there have been some similar initiatives here, where organisations have been established to help build capacity and capabilities of indigenous community groups, so they can operate more effectively and efficiently.

Japhet: We need to go beyond educating. So much money has been spent on training and building the capacity of leaders here. I think education of leaders needs to be broadened beyond training on technical matters to practical self-organising skills.

The training and workshops are just pushing people to finish things quickly. And then success is counted on the number of courses, the number of people trained and the few actions that they have done. But before we even start talking about training: how do we help the organisation find its potential leaders?

Most organisations are founded by people who have seen something they want to change, they volunteer their time and they continue to be in the organisation without the capacity to recruit or get extra knowledge or capacity. It is important not to overstay as a founder, because when you are a founder you tend to hear more and more of your own voice. But it is also risky bringing in new professionals, as some may not have the original passion of the founders!

Lin: Yes, we call it founder's syndrome. But it all comes down to the governance and board. Unfortunately, some founders pull together the board that will support them. One of the things that is really important for a not-for-profit is governance education, because compliance and due diligence rests on the shoulders of the board. Is there training for board directors in Tanzania?

Japhet: Yes, there is an attempt to do that, but then the question is, who is on the board?

Lin: This is a common challenge: how do we bring diversity of skills and lived experience into our organisations? One way is to establish an informal reference group of people with lived experience across our five programmes who can provide strategic advice.

There is a fine line between benevolence and strategic philanthropy. If our aim is to enable communities to help themselves, we need diverse voices around the table and we need to listen to the communities we want to support. We often talk about risk, but is it not the role of philanthropy to back innovation? We need the courage to back good people with good ideas, and we need to reframe 'failure' as 'learning'.

This is why we insist that the cost of evaluation is included in the overall project budget. A trial project that may not deliver expected outcomes will provide valuable learnings for the organisation, the funder and the wider sector. I call that success.

Japhet: To which I would say that success looks like results from many failures and learnings. But we don't have that luxury of having the funder staying and trying many things for many years. Our funders are generally there for two years with a maximum of five years, but the community is there forever.

Lin: Two years is far too short.

Japhet: And unfortunately, the call for proposal approach is becoming too restrictive within the time frame, because they are always saying this project will run for only one year. And then people are rushing to apply and before they even start getting the proposal on the ground, one year is gone.

Lin: When we're approached by organisations who have a good idea but it's not ready, we suggest they first apply for one of our smaller one-off grants to fully scope the project. Once they have acquitted that grant and have a detailed budget, partners in place and an implementation plan, they can apply for a multiyear grant.

The conversation between grant seeker and funder needs to be open and transparent. As a grant seeker, you're in a position to show us what is needed, not the other way round. You know your community, you understand the complexities and you are the implementers. Of course we want projects we fund to succeed, but then knowing what doesn't work is also success as long as we share the learnings.

Japhet: For many organisations here, the relationships with a funder tends to end with the project time frame. This is not a healthy relationship.

Lin: That's such a shame. We try to keep our dialogue going with our grantees after the actual grant has finished. It is rare that the full impact of a grant is realised at the end of the funding period. Our grantees let us know about any developments, and trustees and senior staff are often invited to participate when there is an opportunity to showcase the project. If we see there was an interesting learning from the project, we will organise a presentation for other funders. We also post case studies on our website.

Our funding strategy supports our vision for a strong, just and sustainable Victoria. The grantee is simply the conduit to supporting our target beneficiaries, the people of Victoria. We fund the organisation that can best serve those that we want to benefit. That's what success looks like for me.

Japhet: Our vision is not towards the organisation; the organisation is the means for taking us there. So we assess our successes on the long-term changes we wished to see or on the reduction in the issues which were giving us sleepless nights.

Lin: Our aspirations are the same.

Japhet: Success will be if the same issues you have been pushing for are still being pursued even in your absence. When you have brought them to a point that the community start taking up actions independently, not necessarily following what you have been doing.

Lin: Precisely, it's about independent, resilient, sustainable communities living a good life. It's about equity. So, you know, success looks the same for both of us.

Japhet: So, the question still remains, who controls the 'gold'?

Note

[1] The Irrigation Water Users Associations were formed during the Flood Control and Irrigation Project supported by the ILO in the Mto wa Mbu and Gichameda Irrigation schemes between 1988 and 1993. Eleven associations have been registered as Irrigation and Water Users Committees.

TEN

Local philanthropy and women's empowerment: the case of Tewa, the Nepal Women's Fund

Rita Thapa

Introduction

'Community development' is a contested term. It can mean one thing to development aid workers and international NGOs, another to local NGOs and something else to local community groups themselves. It has often been associated with large infrastructure development, access to water, sanitation, education, health services and so forth. But especially since the early 1990s, a rights-based approach with an emphasis on local-level ownership and participation, equity and justice has gathered momentum. Development, from this perspective, is about changing people's quality of life for the better, as is felt, and expressed, by the people involved *themselves*. It is an approach that also requires that attention be given to the inequalities associated with gender, age, class, caste, ethnicity, disability and sexual orientations that exist within any given community. Unless one is explicit about this, there is a risk that when, for example, we say 'women' we may obscure the diversity within that 'category' and involve only the privileged segment of that population. This sort of community development is not easy to achieve since it calls for an analysis of power, politics and especially agency. Also, inclusive development work is intensely time consuming and demands a great deal of energy.

This understanding of community development has informed my life's work, mostly with women at the community level in Nepal. In this chapter, I reflect on how a commitment to these development principles has been applied to funding. I share my experiences at Tewa, the Nepal Women's Fund, a feminist organisation that I founded right after the UN World Conference on Women in Beijing in 1995, with the explicit aim of fostering local philanthropy as a means to empowering women. Over the past 21 years, Tewa has successfully raised 3.6 corer, equivalent to US$355,600, from approximately 5,000 Nepali donors and made 573 grants to over 454 community groups of women in 69 of the 75 districts of Nepal. Tewa has trained and mobilised over 680 fundraising volunteers. It has been a forerunner among the women's funds in the Global South, and a model for women's groups and others in Nepal.

The chapter will begin by placing this work in its social and political context. It then describes the establishment of Tewa and analyses its values, and the approaches Tewa has taken to fundraising and grant making based on local philanthropy.

Setting the scene: politics and funding in Nepal

Nepal opened to the outer world in 1951 when 104 years of autocratic rule by the Rana dynasty came to an end and the monarchy was reinstated. Under King Mahendra, a one-party system of *Panchayat* – a system under which there are elected representatives but real power remains in the hands of the monarch – took root. Nepal became a Shangri-La for development aid from 1954 onwards. Five-year plans were drafted and implemented by the government, supported by bilateral and multilateral donors. International and local NGOs also played a significant role in development. By 1990, over 40,000 local NGOs were registered, primarily with the aim of accessing donor funding and/or building political constituencies. A people's movement in 1990 began to destabilise the monarchy and led to growth of political parties. Today in Nepal, most formal organisations are now aligned with one or other of the political parties.

In 1996, a Maoist group took up arms. Over the course of a ten-year civil war more than 16,000 people lost their lives, thousands were disappeared and thousands more internally displaced. With the signing of a peace accord in November 2006, Nepal entered a peace process but the transition has been difficult and political struggles for power related to a range of social, economic and cultural divisions are ongoing. This, among other factors, has meant the state has been highly ineffective. As a consequence, Nepal has poorly developed infrastructure, negligible social welfare and an absence of local-level governing bodies for 20 years (this is changing as I write).

The loss of life and internal displacement, high outward and seasonal migration among men during the armed conflict and after, escalating inflation and unemployment, and political corruption at all levels have left Nepal's peace process and its new democracy volatile and precarious. Women and children are particularly vulnerable. There has been an increase in violence against women (both domestic and public), including rape and incest – leading to a high rate of infanticide and suicide among women – and attacks on 'witches' among the weak and disenfranchised. Violations of human rights, especially of women human-rights defenders are commonplace. These political upheavals, allied with the effects of modernisation, urbanisation and globalisation of communications and media, and the impact of the 2012 earthquake, have taken a heavy toll on the communal safety nets which were until recently woven intricately into family and community life.

Tewa: the Nepal Women's Fund

This was the environment into which Tewa was born in September 1995. Tewa means 'support' in Nepali, the kind of support used to prop up leaning walls and buildings.

There were two main reasons why I founded Tewa. First, traditional forms of philanthropy based on religious and cultural norms were dying out rapidly as individualism and consumerism have spread. Second, and most importantly, although Nepal received a comparatively high level of foreign aid, women had little access to funding. Despite the fact that donor aid was being increasingly directed towards women, following the UN's 'decade for women' and particularly after the UN Global Women's Conference in Beijing, the lack of structures at grassroots level and restrictions on women's mobility and voice meant these resources hardly ever reached them. I felt that the best way to increase women's political visibility and participation was by making small grants to groups of rural women all over Nepal, who were beginning to get organised yet had almost no access to external funding. There was no funding available from the Nepali state for the development initiatives of these emergent NGOs.

In founding Tewa, we sought to assert that we could run sustainable structures in 'aid-ridden' Nepal, and get away from 'donor dependency'. We believed that our model of raising funds locally, primarily from individual Nepali donors, and making grants to registered women's groups all over Nepal would help build communities, make philanthropy more relevant to present times and need, and in the process help restore human dignity to some extent. If it was successful, we hoped it would provide an inspirational model for similar feminist initiatives as well as for other development practitioners including external funders and international NGOs.

Owing to my past involvement in donor agencies and as an applicant to other agencies in Nepal, I had extensive networks throughout the development world globally. At the time I founded Tewa, I was working with UNIFEM and had a New Zealand government ministerial scholarship (both of which I let go in order to work for Tewa in a voluntary capacity). For Tewa's operational costs we sought support from the international women's funds such as the Global Fund for Women (GFW) and Mama Cash, as well as from feminist philanthropists and the Ford Foundation. Targeting the international women's funds for operational finance was intentional. We wanted credit for the establishment of Tewa to be primarily given to feminist funders, and we did not want to be slowed down or curtailed by the bureaucracies of external aid agencies working in Nepal. We have found these feminist funders supportive and reliable partners for over 20 years and they have never imposed their agenda in making funds available to us.

In order to establish Tewa, I spoke with women from all walks of life to put together a membership base. I again had a very clear idea that this needed to be a diverse women-only group. Only women, because few women in Nepal at the time had the experience and the capacity to negotiate on development and on feminist issues. It was also important to cut across class, caste, ethnicity and age to gather strength from our diversity rather than being isolated or limited by it. Less than two weeks after I initially had the idea in Beijing, a group of about nine women attended the 'talk' on the importance and experience of women's funds given in my living room by colleagues from two US-based women's funds, who had been travelling in Nepal. At the end of the afternoon all of them said that this sounded like a good idea. The women's understanding and experience of women's organisations or NGOs in Nepal was very different from what we were going to be doing in Tewa. Membership grew by the day. Some of the members were young activists, some were development professionals I knew already and a few others were affluent housewives from upper-class families.

I was convinced we had to create a new culture of doing development work. In Nepal an estimated 70% of the government budget is subsidised by foreign grants or loans, and development had become synonymous with jobs for the 'qualified'. Besides which, traditional feudal and patriarchal approaches were the norm in development organisations, so not only did we need to do things in a new way, some 'un-learning' had to be done, including things I and other members had been socialised to accept as normal. Both I and Meera Jyoti, who took over the coordination of the board from me two years after we founded Tewa, come from privileged backgrounds of caste and class (although I had encountered discrimination as a Hindu widow). We grew up in feudal and authoritarian environments, but thank heavens – we changed along the way! We sought to build the organisation on feminist values of transparent and non-hierarchical structures, shared power and a just and equitable approach. But 'feminism' in Nepal is perceived by many people as negative and as something imported from the West. Therefore, though the language that defined the work we did in Tewa was in tune with the more 'acceptable' development discourse, our work was entirely feminist. More and more of our team today understand, to varying degrees, our feminist principles and culture, but there has not yet been an explicit statement at the organisational level. But our work spoke for itself. The way we did our work in Tewa remained true to feminist principles and values.

By way of example, in our office, we decided to create our physical space in a way that would be comfortable for everyone. Because our grantee groups would be women from rural Nepal, it was important to ensure that our physical space allowed all to sit on the floor. We always ate together, a simple meal cooked in Tewa and often extended this hospitality to volunteers, grantees and other visitors who happened to walk in. We made sure that our cleaning woman, Maiya, who came from an 'untouchable' caste in Nepal, would not feel inhibited. She was given the responsibility to clean our office space and bathrooms, as well as the kitchen – this would be unheard of in most other places in Nepal. Whenever we had Tewa events – and these were frequent – we invited Maiya to share a meal with us. She never turned up, so we kept food for her and her young husband who always accompanied her to help. This went on for four years. Then one day she and her family actually came to an event and lined up for food with us. We were ecstatic! I felt that we had succeeded in not only being non-hierarchical, but in actually challenging the age-old practice of caste discrimination. It took us four years to heal the pain of systemic discrimination lodged in Maiya's psyche as well as ours. But we were rewarded for our efforts.

Tewa's approach to philanthropy

Empowering women through education or income-generating activities is not mainstream and, if considered, is seen as the responsibility of the donor agencies or the government. Tewa has taken a very different approach based on local philanthropy. This means Tewa raises all the money it needs for its grant-making purposes from local communities. Many people felt that institutionalising this approach to philanthropy in a Nepalese context was an impossible thing to do. Nepal has an ancient traditional culture of giving which is deeply ingrained in the fabric of Nepali life whatever one's religious or cultural background. But philanthropy as is now understood in the modern world, and as is practised in North America and Europe, is not prevalent and neither is it well understood. There are no government incentives for philanthropy, such as tax-deductible policies for donations. Another problem is that NGOs are also perceived as a 'dollar-farming' industry, and there is little trust for them among the general public. These various factors, and the political and cultural context discussed earlier, mean that while it is easy to raise funds for building a temple or a rest house, or even to build a home for abandoned women, the elderly or orphans, it is very difficult to obtain money to support the empowerment of women. In Nepal generally, women are regarded as 'well looked after' or 'provided for', so there is not a lot of understanding when we say that they are disempowered.

We knew that local philanthropy could only be achieved through approaching people directly. Owing to my experience with the GFW, I knew about so-called 'money workshops' which was a tool on fundraising that the GFW conducted for their grantees. So, with some tools and insights from this, I designed a two-day fundraising training targeting mainly 'educated and resourceful' housewives who were tied into very traditional roles in Kathmandu. This training focused on three things: motivation, the position of women in development, and practical tools on fundraising suitable for this category of fundraisers. The volunteers would be supported through a mentoring programme for a three-month period, at the end of which the volunteer could choose to remain in the Tewa network or not. During this three-month period the volunteers would meet at regular occasions and would interact with and learn from resource persons. They were supported both practically and emotionally in the work they were doing. This support and recognition is maintained after training and keeps people highly motivated. The women who participate in our volunteer programme also gained a huge overall understanding of women's issues. It also became apparent early on to the volunteers that out of every 100 rupees that a volunteer might raise for Tewa, 93% went directly to the grantee groups and only 7% was retained for direct programme support work. This was another very significant source of motivation.

This approach of fundraising through volunteers has allowed us to reach thousands of Nepalis beyond the capability of the core team. It also helped to spread our philosophy. The programme expanded and was holding two or three training events each year. As word of the training spread, aspiring development practitioners, NGO staff or students began to ask to be our volunteers. The challenge for us was to maintain a balance where we could continue to bring in non-professional women who we wanted to work with alongside those with professional experience. Those shackled into their traditional roles had no avenues for personal or professional growth so integrating them into Tewa was a way of changing this.

The important thing we learned was that however hard it was to do this work, we *could* raise money locally in Nepal. The money mostly came from individual donors, both women and men (though money is usually in the control of men, our volunteers were more comfortable in approaching the women in their circle of family and friends), who mainly gave the equivalent of between US$5 and $15. By 2001 when I handed over leadership, we were raising 12 million to 15 million Nepali rupees, equivalent to US$15,000 on average annually, and making approximately 20 to 30 grants every year. This was unimaginable and unheard of in Nepal until then. This was because our donors saw for themselves the way we worked in an accountable and a transparent manner, and we were keeping them well informed through thank-you notes and periodic reports. We have learned over the years that building on community trust and ownership helps us to raise money from the communities in an ongoing way.

Grant making at Tewa

During the very first year of Tewa's establishment we began to look for potential grantees. In that year we gave a grant of over US$3,000 to nine women's groups in rural Nepal. In the early years, Nepal's limited infrastructure meant that informing women's groups was a challenge. We used local development journals produced by donor agencies, our own membership and anyone we could find who would take the word out. However, from the fourth year onwards this was no longer a problem. Word spread and Tewa received many inquiries from far-flung villages, through people travelling to Kathmandu, letters or, when it was possible, telephone. Each year the proposals grew in number. Yet the success of our fundraising enabled us to cope. This was good news, for it meant that rural women were getting organised, but many lacked organisational development skills and there were only so many proposals that qualified, though our proposal process was simple and non-bureaucratic. We were clear that the rural women's organisations we chose would be those who were 'moving towards their own empowerment' and had already made some political assessment of the work that they were doing. This was because there were a great deal of development interventions for savings and credit programmes, or adult literacy initiatives as an entry point for other interventions, but when these women wanted to federate and/or organise independently there was no support to be found. It would also mean that we were pitching scarce resources where it had the most potential to bear fruit in terms of women's advancement.

At Tewa, the grant-making process is respectful and transparent. Grantees fill a simple proposal format in the Nepali language. They are rigorously screened and consulted with during this period by the Tewa staff if further clarifications are needed. The sizes of the grants are not very big, but in rural Nepal, financial resources are scarce. Our grants went a long way in providing some critical support for women's voices. These grants went to support their offices, capacity-building trainings or income-generating activities according to the needs identified. But in the process of doing these activities, the women acquire more visibility and recognition at the local level as well.

In the early days people wondered how money could be just given out to grantee groups all over Nepal. Since there was an environment of mistrust of the development 'scene', it was felt that the monies given would be misappropriated and abused. In Tewa's history this has hardly ever been the case. In a rural environment it is more difficult for a group of women to be corrupt for the fear of losing face, for social recognition and acceptance is often their only security. So even if a few people mess up, it is less likely for this behaviour to be perpetuated. Moreover, everyone knew how painstakingly the money was raised. Most importantly, Tewa is not just a donor to the grantees. They own Tewa and see in them a true development partner. Over the years, as Tewa developed its residential centre, more women's groups who come into this space see it as a model, a possibility. This has helped raise the bar for women's groups who are thinking of building their own office space or training halls.

Tewa in action: two case studies

To cite a recent example of our approach, here is a little story. After the earthquake of 25 April 2015 all of us had to go into relief work. Following the earthquake, Tewa launched a programme entitled *Hamro Tewa Gaon-gharma*, literally meaning 'our support in village households'. In this pilot initiative Tewa called on grantees who had not been affected by the earthquake to help by shadowing the work of grantees directly impacted by the disaster. Although this was new for many of us, we used our common sense and a sense of urgency, recognising how most of the affected people had suffered multiple major losses. I suggested that if anyone was willing and interested, they could contribute a small amount from the cash we gave them as relief for temporary roofing materials to a community fund that we could match many times over and take to other communities or bring back to them. There was an overwhelming response. Over more than two years they have worked tirelessly for their sisters and their communities in many diverse work areas. They have helped to build schools, community buildings and rehabilitation centres, dismantle houses, cleared rubble sites, built shelters and provided informal psychosocial counselling and livelihood training, among other activities.

Another example of our work is the Nepal Rural Self-Reliance Development Centre. This group had come together initially as a saving and credit group. They were acutely aware of the lack of access to health services. When they approached us they were thinking of establishing a local pharmacy. During our conversations they saw the need to go back to do a more in-depth needs assessment in the area of women's health. It did not take them long to identify their priority need in the area. Though they were very close to Kathmandu, they needed to walk for half an hour to two hours to reach a bus or taxi. In an emergency, a pregnant woman had little chance to make it to the hospitals in Kathmandu. They also had only one woman who was a traditional birth attendant (TBA) and she was getting very old. Therefore, the group decided that they would train two women from each of the nine wards in the village development committee as TBAs. The women could benefit in receiving some payment in cash or kind, and in an emergency they could save lives by making advanced referral to the nearest hospitals. They received a grant of 36,000 rupees or approximately US$500 from Tewa. Fifteen women received an intensive 15-day training as TBAs. They were carefully chosen and priority was given to economically and socially disadvantaged women. The group also received a second grant from Tewa two years later for income-generation activity to support their excellent work.

Building networks between the local and global

I learned from international visitors that before the founding of Tewa, the GFW had tried so hard to encourage other women's funds to happen, with little success. Other than Mama Cash and GFW in the 'developed' world, and Semillias in Mexico and Tewa, no other fund had been really successful. Pitseng and Wheat in Africa, Nirnaya in India, Angela Borba in Brazil and the emerging African Women's Development Fund, were all in some ways hesitant or had met with difficulties in developing their work. But once the network of women's funds was established women's funds emerged, particularly in countries where women's human rights or women's advancement were challenged. When the third International Network of Women's Funds (INWFs) meeting was hosted by Nirnaya in Hyderabad, India in 2001 there were over 15 active women's funds – today (2017) there are over 40! So I feel that hosting these meetings in Nepal in many ways catalysed the growing movement of the INWF, and therefore, the growth of the women's movement as a whole.

In retrospect, my work would not have been possible without the support of the feminist donors and the international women's funds. Likewise their giving was informed and shaped by the work many of us did on the ground. This two-way relationship enabled the work, informed our politics and gave us solidarity and strength.

Conclusion

There is no pension package, no gratuity, no social security and very little recognition for the sort of work we do in Tewa. My work is better known and valued internationally in the women's funding world, than in Nepal. So, if we make a commitment to do this kind of work, not only must we go into it in full recognition of this reality, but anyone else who believes in this kind of work and can support these social entrepreneurs, as they have often come to be called, must lend them all the physical, emotional and the moral backing that they can. So yes, the costs are always there, and we must be in full recognition of this so that we can be better prepared for it, mentally and emotionally. When funds slacken off we just work harder. But we have proved you do not need to rely on international funders. It was obvious that we had to demonstrate a model where we could do this sort organisation in a truly sustainable way and hand over the leadership to a younger woman. The important thing here was to demonstrate a model and extend the possibility to everyone, and not to think of doing everything by myself, for no one person in this world really can. This model in Nepal is triggering a whole different reality whereby women's funds and work are growing, a reality that can be transformative and feminist and where men and women can walk together in solidarity and strength, being empowered by the knowledge that we are building a more balanced and better world.

ELEVEN

Communities of hope? Gendered re-signification of microcredit in rural India

Debarati Sen and Sarasij Majumder

Introduction

The international development establishment is currently preoccupied with discussions of resilience – trying to measure what the world's poor are doing in concrete ways to make life habitable under conditions of intense precarity (Khapung, 2016). The discussion of resilience dovetails quite well with the celebratory narratives of market-based community development initiatives which seek to tap into women's creativity and embolden such efforts (Karim, 2011; Sen, 2017). In the 1990s, Western donor agencies in conjunction with the Consultative Group to Assist the Poorest (C-GAP) identified microfinance, the practice of lending small amounts of money to poor households without collaterals, as 'a major donor plank for poverty alleviation and gender strategies' (Karim, 2011: xiv). The first Microcredit Summit at Washington, DC in 1997 presented research in favour of microcredit, identifying it almost as a silver bullet – both profitable and sustainable – unleashing the entrepreneurial power of poor women in the Global South and, in the process, empowering them. In India about 13 million (Morris, 2012) people have taken microcredit-based loans. However, critiques of microcredit as a solution to poverty have been growing, and more recently microcredit has been blamed for rural suicides among loan takers (Associated Press, 2012).

In this context, this chapter presents a picture of what gendered resilience looks like at the ground level in eastern India's Darjeeling district in the state of West Bengal. Our particular focus is how women interpret and react to popular market-based development alternatives like microcredit and the consequences this has had for community development. We contend that:

1. women in Darjeeling's poorest villages have developed a very different understanding of risk – what they term *riks* – than the more narrowly focused 'risky economic behaviour' discussed by microcredit and development NGOs;
2. these different interpretations of credit and risk reveal the situated nature of economic practices and highlight the deep connection between inter- and intra-household power inequalities; and
3. that the women have responded to this situation by demonstrating creative collective social agency that in turn has had noteworthy unintended consequences on them and their community. In other words, the practice of microcredit is deeply embedded in the social and cultural context in which the women were living.

For many women, the experience of negotiating the tensions and difficulties thrown up by taking loans led them to abandon banks in favour of inter-lending among their own self-help groups. We contend that taking note of gendered structures and discourses around microcredit reveals the vital work that women perform daily to sustain their families and develop their communities, while simultaneously deflecting and absorbing the excesses of financial globalisation channelled through microcredit.

While the invisibility of women's work in calculating gross national product has been well-documented (Baksh and Harcourt, 2015), much less discussed is women's invisible work promoting the economic resilience of poor communities. Feminist political economists thus call on the policy and academic world to document how women's labour, especially household-level affective work of social reproduction, is devalued (Rai et al, 2013). These are noteworthy oversights as much effort in the world of international development after Beijing 1995 was supposed to focus on women's empowerment, entrepreneurship and leadership. We emphasise that the existing systems used to account for women's contribution to economic and social development in communities often ignore the complex relationships between women in the Global South (especially in rural areas) and the development processes which seek to 'empower' them. In the case of loan-based development, success cannot just be measured by women's successful loan return; rather, in-depth, longitudinal research is required to shed light on the hidden household labour involved in sustaining this 'success' (Karim, 2011). A feminist intersectional lens (Cho et al, 2013) is crucial to understand these complexities and to account for women's everyday work in maintaining community and household relationships in the context of loan return and use. These cultural and social activities are as important as economic practices in building a resilient future for a village in the context of changing development regimes.

To clearly understand how women engage in this form of community building, we think it is important to emphasise a dynamic, processual view of rural communities. While anthropologists of development have emphasised such a perspective for some time, a static view of community dominates the policy world (Agrawal, 2005). In fact, a community is continuously being formed in response to both internal and external influences. Once we take this view of community as emergent, we begin to understand how crucial micro-negotiations and everyday politics are in forging community on an ongoing basis. From this perspective, research on community development can greatly benefit from exploring how everyday choices, actions and interactions are impacted on by development policies such as microcredit. Relatedly, this chapter positions itself against dichotomous understandings of globally dominant processes, on the one hand, and indigenous alternatives, on the other. We argue that women strategically combine elements from disparate discourses to formulate their own ideas of agency, subjectivity and embodiment which present a counterhegemonic critique, albeit in a fragmentary and embryonic form, of microcredit-based development. We contend that the local knowledge systems, epistemologies, and social organisations from which the women critique microcredit initiatives (Gershon, 2011) are not radically different from Western ideas. Rather, they draw on entrepreneurial logic – a hybrid formation born out of their marginalised position and their urge to overcome such marginality through trade.

Understanding community as a process also underpins this chapter's conception of community development: here community development is seen as a contested process which is shaped by sociohistorical trends, economic and political structures and by the agency of communities themselves. By looking at the market- and finance-based solutions designed to encourage entrepreneurialism in communities of tea farmers, we show how communities cope with changing economic circumstances, a historical legacy of tea plantations, and their politically and geographically marginal locations in the nation state. The poor rural women in our ethnography bear the brunt of this; they are resilient but maintaining this resilience is a struggle in the midst of global forces affecting their livelihoods, and NGO policies that perfunctorily seek to address their plights. Our critique suggests that the microcredit activities implemented by NGOs do not take into consideration the emergent and contested character of communities and the hierarchies within them.

We have divided this chapter into three sections and a conclusion. Drawing from our ethnographic research there since 2004, the first section charts the history and dynamics of microcredit's unfolding in Darjeeling and highlights the practices and discourses through which women demonstrate resilience. The second section lays out how and why women re-signify risk in the context of microcredit to make visible non-financial forms of risk that affect their families and, in turn, their communities. The third section explores how, after encountering the social and economic difficulties that came with the microcredit loans, many of the women set up their own groups for lending.

Everyday resilience and women's economic roles in Darjeeling

In Darjeeling, rural women contribute to the production of both agricultural cash-crops in tea plantations and the rural agricultural economy. The plantation sector formally employs approximately 60,000 workers, but women comprise 60% of the workforce and also dominate the demographics of the seasonal labour recruitment whose numbers are kept secret by plantation authorities (Sen, 2014). Women are also present in the rural areas outside of plantations where the feminisation of agriculture and informal work is on the rise with increasing male out-migration to other areas in India that offer better economic opportunities. Here women engage in a variety of subsistence activities in the informal sector that spans rural and urban locations. The cultural politics which accompanies all economic activities in the Darjeeling district are shaped by the relations between various ethnic groups like Nepalis (the dominant group), Bhutias, Lepchas, Bengalis, Marwaris and Biharis. Although Nepalis are numerically dominant in Darjeeling, they may not occupy the most lucrative positions in business and white-collar work because of colonial and postcolonial dynamics (Sen, 2017). All minority ethnic groups within India are struggling to make a living in the face of dwindling economic opportunities, particularly those in politically and economically fragile border districts like Darjeeling.

Between 2004 and 2011, we observed a core group of 30 women and undertook numerous interviews with community members. The women all belonged to poor Nepali Hindu households located in rural Darjeeling and practised a combination of petty trade and agriculture on their small, family-owned plots of hilly land (Sen, 2014). They were mostly illiterate and did not enjoy the benefits of salaried plantation work. These demographic details are important for two reasons. First, plantations are so ubiquitous in Darjeeling that the lives of those who work in the vast informal agricultural sectors off the plantations are rarely documented. Second, drawing on the local politics of gender, the women in this study distinguished themselves from plantation workers because of the stigma attached to plantation work. As Hindus, all of these informants also distinguished themselves from Tibetan women (Bhoteni) who traded in the urban markets. Their self-identification as respectable Hindu housewives working on their family-owned farms while engaging in petty trade influenced how they assessed the social risk of taking microcredit loans since it harmed their respectability within villages where women's dealings with non-kin/kith-based men were looked down on. Thus, these women loan takers from these rural areas did not want their reputations affected like women plantation workers of Darjeeling who were often described as hardworking but whimsical and promiscuous based on colonial and postcolonial sexualised stereotypes about Nepali women (Sen, 2017). Their frustration with microcredit and their development of alternatives needs to be understood in relation to these social dynamics.

Before the advent of microcredit, women combined agriculture with various forms of petty trade that were not distinguishable from their activities as housewives. The world of small trade and entrepreneurialism was, therefore, not new to women in rural Darjeeling, nor was borrowing money; before microcredit, they dealt with village moneylenders, often their kith and kin. They sold surplus food from household agriculture and sought loans from local middlemen for this business. This form of diversified household procurement is quite common in Darjeeling's non-plantation rural areas. In the villages surrounding Darjeeling town, women entrepreneurs grew crops and regularly sold staples such as alcohol, sweets, vegetables, hand-rolled tea, ramen noodles, *khaini* (chewing tobacco), washing powder and other sundry items that they acquired from town. But none of the village women regularly sold goods in the market or had permanent shops in town, which would have countered their primary self-identification as housewives. It is important to understand that women perceived their economic pursuits as an extension of their role of procurement – *sakaunu* – for household needs. *Sakaunu* was central to the economic and social reproduction of households and to the social norms that governed women's household labour. It concealed the fact that women's entrepreneurialism helped to build their communities' economic resilience. These small ventures enabled women borrowers to stretch the family's cash income without upsetting the gendered moral universe of their villages. These low-key and flexible entrepreneurial activities did not require large investments or NGO support. They occurred through personal kin and kith networks connected to informal trading circuits that sustained rural communities in the face of massive unemployment.

The watershed moment in these women's economic activities occurred in the 1990s when NGOs, as part of the state-initiated microcredit scheme, approached rural women with loan offers. In the 1990s a regional NGO started organising women into self-help groups to familiarise them with microcredit, which they could obtain using the women's group as collateral. However, the social relationships that sustained their earlier economic activities came under severe strain as their engagement with microcredit increased in the mid-1990s. In the next section, we discuss how these changes impacted on the women and their relationships with others in the community. In particular, we analyse how the women engaged with microcredit and interpreted and recalibrated dominant understandings of risk and financial discipline, highlighting how acceptance of loans exacerbated pre-existing inequalities and created new forms of *riks* in their lives.

Rural women re-signifying risk

The type of risk most commonly associated with microcredit relates to women's lack (or perceived lack) of financial know-how and discipline. Concern over the lack of financial literacy among the loan-taking women was a common theme in interviews with NGO workers or bank clerks in Darjeeling. According to one NGO member helping the women borrowers with loan accounting:

> 'These women have never been exposed to how a bank works and that the bank employees are not like their village moneylender who would give them time to return loans. It takes time for them to understand the risk culture where defaults are not appreciated and it also harms the relationship of our NGO with this bank. They also do not follow that the entire group's credibility will be questioned based on one person's loan-taking behaviour.'

However, women borrowers were learning about the nuances of risk in different but important ways. *Riks* is a word frequently mentioned by women in the villages of rural Darjeeling whose use of the term highlights that 'risk' was a lot more complex, multifaceted and systemic than mere financial indiscipline. The women used *riks* creatively to draw attention to the inequities they faced, some of which have escalated alongside the new economic opportunities, and as a way of coping with and displacing the blame that accrued to them if they missed a loan payment deadline or meeting. For instance, they complained about the *riks* created by the barriers to women's economic freedom, as Nita explains:

> 'You know how these NGO brothers talk about *riks* to us, they tell us we should pay up on time and not being able to do so will harm our future loan-taking ability. I say we are the ones who really understand *riks*, we have to return the money, it is us women; we have always taken *riks* for our community.'

The local iterations of the word *riks* help women to link their grievances against patriarchal limits placed on women's entrepreneurship with their dissatisfactions with the narrowly defined empowerment rationale of microcredit, which is blind to the gender politics of social reproduction in the village (see also Katz, 1991). Its use indicates both the necessity for women to engage in businesses as an important component of social reproduction but also a growing aversion towards NGO-based microcredit loans.

Two interrelated issues affected women and informed why they felt microcredit loans placed them at risk. First, spatial restrictions imposed by local cultural norms of gendered respectability were key structural limitations that blocked women's path to economic success. Second, the women had to negotiate relationships within the household on a daily basis in order to repay the loans on time, constantly jockeying to maintain good relations with elder male and female members of their household. Women's positioning in the class order also impacted on how these relations were negotiated and the degree of *riks* that they experienced.

Emerging negotiations around credit and community

Apprehensive at first, loan-taking women eventually began to like being able to access more money without the permission of spouses or other family members and even being able to spend small amounts on themselves. However, the women's monthly meetings, occasional overnight visits to other villages, and increased interaction with male

NGO members disrupted the regular cadence of village life because the women now spent comparatively more time outside the spatial confines of the home and village. So long as the women's activities were individual and small scale they were tolerated, but once women gained the potential to scale up their entrepreneurship, this caused great furore in the community. In particular, the hostilities women faced from male family members, who knew local moneylenders or middlemen, grew because of the women's increased interaction with outside loan-giving agencies and with outside menfolk. As the scale and scope of their petty trade increased with bank loans, women began critically scrutinising their roles as housewives, which limited them to the household and facilitated the devaluation of their entrepreneurial labour. They came to realise that their traditionally defined role restricted their income-earning capacity. The following comment from a woman loan taker demonstrates these tensions:

> 'After I joined the training programmes I realised I was already doing business but we just called it *sakaunu*. That is when I also realised that [women's] work inside the home is rarely recognised. It is nice to know that someone is actually coming to our village to give us money to do what we already did; we do not have to coax our husbands and brothers to appease the middlemen.'

Shanta's reconceptualisation of her labour for household procurement – *sakaunu* – as a business exemplifies how loans provided women with opportunities to reimagine their role in social reproduction. Women realised that with loan money they could transform their household work into a small business. These individual and collective cultural self-understandings of loan-taking women may seem to indicate agency and empowerment that proponents of this microcredit-based development practice had envisioned. But such easy conclusions need to be avoided. As we have stressed, the meaning of credit needs to be understood in its social context. The participants understanding of risk, debt, obligation and respectability are bound to community and wider social structures. Also, as we shall discuss later, in time the women began to develop their own credit system, which differs both from the vision of advocates of microcredit as well as traditional credit systems.

Introduction of microcredit made women question the structures of gendered respectability informing their self-worth. What changed was their attitude towards the politics of respectability that we have already described. They now looked at market-savvy Bhoteni with envy instead of seeing them as less respectable market women, the way men, older women, or wives of powerful men did. These women also realised their comparative disadvantage vis-à-vis the Bhoteni who could sell goods in the market in actual shops. Manju, a woman farmer who borrowed money, explained:

> 'If we take all that we produce and sell to the middleman and display it in a shop in the bazaar I am sure we will be as successful as the bazaar ladies. We are just like them; it's just that we cannot have shops. If we had shops like them then we could have probably returned the micro money faster just like the NGO *dajus* [big brothers] want us to.'

However, the women's entrepreneurialism faced significant obstacles. The advent of microcredit introduced a new way of engaging with existing economic roles and structures of dependence. Before microcredit, women's economic activities were sufficiently covert that male ire was minimal. Rita explained that when middlemen were the only source of loans, in a case of default elder male family members would try to appease the middleman and ask for an extension. Frequently the middleman would be a distant relative or friend of the family patriarch. A woman could also send her family members to the middleman's house as *khetala* (day labourers) – in order to return a portion of the loan in kind. Such informal arrangements were not available with the bank loans. Once women started taking out bank loans their family members no longer supported them in the same way, even though the women still spent their proceeds on family needs. Family members refused to help women financially; because loan officers and NGO workers were not from their villages, they knew that their family's reputation was not endangered in case of a loan default. Certain patriarchs now viewed microcredit as individual loans, not family loans. Other family members believed that the lower interest rates on NGO loans would enable women to repay them easily without their assistance. Along with these emerging reactions, the deep-seated suspicion of women's economic activities caused envy among male kin. The decision to scale up through *thulo yojana* [larger businesses] was an added cause of annoyance. Therefore, while women began enjoying certain aspects of their economic importance in the community, it quickly became obvious how the criticism by NGO members, village middlemen and family elders were related and symptomatic of a web of patriarchal social structures, and so in time women began to tire of taking microcredit loans.

Microcredit, household relations and social class

The introduction of microcredit required women to constantly negotiate complex and unequal family relations, in particular with elder male and female members of their household. For example, Binu, a very active advocate of scaling up loan taking to create larger business ventures, described how microcredit and her associated activities resulted in property battles within her household (consisting of her mother-in-law and her brother-in-law's family as well as her own). Binu's mother-in-law had decided to give Binu's husband a lesser share of the land she owned, claiming that Binu was very *bathi* [street-smart] and could access money from outside, whereas the younger son and his wife needed her support. Binu's mother-in-law's assessment of her resourcefulness placed Binu at a disadvantage. Binu's husband did not have a regular job, so she had used microcredit to bring money into the household, which benefited everyone, not just her husband and children. The smaller plot of land granted to her husband could not produce enough to repay the loans. Binu therefore decided not to contribute any money to the household as a whole. This further escalated family tensions, which Binu described as a *riks* she had to undergo because of the loans.

Economic differences affected how men and women were socially evaluated in their communities, which in turn affected their household relations. For instance, in one wealthy household, the matriarch banned her daughters-in-law, Poonam and Rajni, from becoming members of the women's groups. In conversations with the first author, the mother-in-law, who was never a member of a women's group herself, exclaimed, "Our family's daughters-in-law do not need loans. There is much to do at home." After some time, however, the younger daughter-in-law, Poonam, decided to join a women's group. Her husband did not have regular employment, and she decided she needed to build some savings for the future. Poonam's decision was not welcomed in the household; even her husband was indifferent. There were arguments over her impudence. Poonam's father-in-law, like many other wealthy villagers, had a material interest in defaming the women's groups because he had close ties with the village middlemen who sold produce from his household. Jokes about the women's business ventures were common in wealthy families. Sometimes, even women who had previously benefited from microcredit schemes and now had more stable income sources denigrated the women participants of microcredit-enabled self-help groups, implying that active group members had transgressed the village norms of gendered respectability. Such slander undermined the confidence of women group members and their families, who were already dubious of their daughters' or wives' new activities. Some women blamed microcredit for escalating the severity of these conflicts, which had material consequences for them.

Riks from loans was aggravated to a significant extent by emerging class inequalities among the women. Cash flow into the household was an important factor in determining who chose to take out a loan, whereby both poor and wealthy women were attracted to loans, but for different purposes. Women from wealthy households were much less subject to the cultural and economic risks for two reasons: they did not participate in meetings and they mostly invested in their husbands' successful businesses, meaning that they could repay the money faster. The generational dynamics between current and previously participating women led to more cultural risk for poorer women. Women from wealthier households often pulled out of the self-help groups, and thereafter defaulted on their loans and denigrated the reputations of the remaining women.

Socioeconomic status was the main determinant of who participated in the women's groups, although age was a secondary factor. The active group members were not as wealthy as those women who were interested in loans but never attended meetings. Their homes were also on the margins of the village, and their husbands typically worked as wage labourers in town or farmed at home. Women whose husbands had gainful employment, large landholdings or successful business ventures were more apprehensive of participating in the meetings and were not ashamed to default on their microcredit loans. Women borrowers considered such wealthy women as a *riks* for their group since they were not reliable. These relatively wealthy women also spread the most problematic rumours about poor village women seeking loans and practising inter-lending, which affected their respectability.

Sceptical subjectivities and microcredit

In 2003 some hundred women from the Sanjukta Vikas Sanstha rural cooperative area in Darjeeling participated in microcredit. By 2009 the number had dropped to 25, as women chose to practice inter-lending among their own self-help groups instead of taking out bank loans. They withdrew their microcredit-enabled individual savings from the bank and began circulating it among group members on a monthly basis. These poor, mostly illiterate rural borrowers also started planning new business ventures to increase the monetary value of their labour for household procurement and entrepreneurship (Sen and Majumder,

2011). For example, using their savings they formed an informal women's group in the villages that was independent of the loan-based credit/self-help groups. This meant they could avoid contact with moneylenders. What is most striking is that these groups of women have an entirely new perspective on development ventures, especially those aimed at women. From 2009 onwards they have refused to participate in new development interventions that make demands on their time because they perceive the financial arrangements in these new ventures as posing gendered everyday *riks* for them.

Recent field visits by the first author in 2015 also confirm that women's entrepreneurial practices have only intensified in scale over the years. Their critique of microcredit derived from the practicalities of minimising their own risk while playing according to the rules of microcredit. Attempting to follow NGO-imposed rules in order to repay their loans in a timely fashion, they became aware of a host of economic, social and cultural risks to their status in their villages, costs they had to bear themselves with little support from either their families or the NGOs. Women realised that the practices they were being asked to engage in, in order to reduce the risk of loan default, could not lessen the economic and cultural risks accruing to them at the community, family and personal levels, such as constant conflicts with local middlemen or with elder men and women in their families. Engagement with microcredit made them realise how the terms of trade were stacked against women. Therefore, the daily labour of social reproduction, *sakaunu*, or procuring for the family was increasingly interpreted as becoming a more onerous task because of its constant devaluing (see also Mies, 1982; Rai et al, 2013). Their counterdiscourse of *riks* contested NGO-led propaganda which pathologised women's lack of financial literacy as the only way risk accrued to the bank.

Conclusion

A well-rounded understanding of resilience of rural informal-sector women against the onslaught of corporate capital (Sanyal, 2007) must recognise not only the mutual interdependence of non-corporate capital (the informal sector) and corporate capital, but also their productive friction, where the 'non-corporate' navigates the ravages of corporate capital. It also entails an understanding of rural women borrowers' place-based desires around development, which are complex and might not always coincide with accepted ideas of risk minimisation prevalent in the literature on international development (Klenk, 2004; Moodie, 2008; Sharma, 2008).

Darjeeling women's efforts to navigate the harmful effects of microcredit have centred around strategic engagement with some of its ideas. This aspect is rarely examined in the growing literature that critiques microcredit as another instance of accumulation through dispossession (Mayoux, 2001). Therefore, we move the existing literature on microcredit in a new direction by demonstrating that poor women practise creative agency and are not passive victims of this situation (Sharma, 2008) and by tracking how new, potentially harmful, economic policies engender social subjectivities, affective states and new practices that follow a different kind of logic that is embedded – but not entirely determined by – the culture and existing social relations within a specific community (Moodie, 2008; Sanyal, 2007).

In analysing the background and circumstances of this struggle and negotiation around loans, we have illuminated the circumstances under which women's economic resilience is articulated through a demonstration of creative collective social agency (Purkayastha and Subramaniam, 2004) which emerged within a market-based production system – but not quite in the way the capitalist development project had envisioned. Our study also upholds the need to 'engage with resilience and innovative practices towards a different development model as they move away from an economistic-centred vision to one based on sufficiency, mutual responsibility, equity, care and justice' (Baksh and Harcourt, 2015: 59). Rural women borrowers in Darjeeling did not perceive entering trade and the market as their primary difficulty; rather, they regarded the gendered barriers within their community, which devalued their household labour, and the depoliticising stance of microcredit as the major impediments to their ability to earn cash and supplement their family income – leading to *riks*.

References

Agrawal, A. (2005) 'Environmentality: Community, intimate government, and the making of environmental subjects in Kumaon, India', *Current Anthropology*, 46(2): 161–90.

Associated Press (2012) 'Hundreds of suicides in India linked to microfinance organizations', *BusinessInsider.com*, 24 February, www. businessinsider.com/hundreds-of-suicides-in-india-linked-to-microfinance-organizations-2012-2?IR=T.

Baksh, R. and Harcourt W. (2015) *The Oxford handbook of transnational feminist movements*, New York: Oxford University Press.

Cho, S., Crenshaw, K. and McCall, L. (2013) 'Toward a field theory of intersectionality: Theory, applications, praxis', *Signs*, 38(4): 785–810.

Gershon, I. (2011) 'Neoliberal agency', *Current Anthropology*, 52(4): 537–55.

Karim, L. (2011) *Microfinance and its discontents: Women and debt in Bangladesh*, Minneapolis, MN: University of Minnesota Press.

Katz, C. (1991) 'Sow what you know: The struggle for social reproduction in rural Sudan', *Annals of the Association for American Geographers*, 81(3): 488–514.

Khapung, S. (2016) 'Transnational feminism and women's activism: Building resilience to climate change impact through women's empowerment in climate smart agriculture', *Asian Journal of Women's Studies*, 22(4): 497–506.

Klenk, R.M. (2004) '"Who is the developed woman?": Women as category of development discourse, Kumaon, India', *Development and Change*, 35(1): 57–78.

Mayoux, L. (2001) 'Tackling the down side: Social capital, women's empowerment and micro-finance in Cameroon', *Development and Change*, 32(3): 435–64.

Mies, M. (1982) *The lace makers of Narsapur: Indian housewives produce for the world market*, London: Zed Books.

Moodie, M. (2008) 'Enter microcredit: A new culture of women's empowerment in Rajasthan?' *American Ethnologist*, 35(3): 454–65.

Morris, M. (2012) 'India's microfinance meltdown', *BBC Newsnight*, YouTube, posted 26 June, https://youtu.be/JzF6thf5GqA.

Purkayastha, B. and Subramaniam, M. (eds) (2004) *The power of women's informal networks: Lessons in social change from South Asia and West Africa*, Lanham, MD: Lexington Books.

Rai, S.M., Hoskyns, C. and Thomas, D. (2013) 'Depletion: The cost of social reproduction', *International Feminist Journal of Politics*, 16(1): 86–105.

Sanyal, K. (2007) *Rethinking capitalist development: Primitive accumulation, governmentality and post-colonial capitalism*, New Delhi: Routledge.

Sen, D. (2014) 'Fair trade vs. *swaccha vyāpār*: Women's activism and transnational justice regimes in Darjeeling, India', *Feminist Studies*, 40(2): 444–72.

Sen, D. (2017) *Everyday sustainability: Gender justice and fair trade tea in Darjeeling*, Albany, NY: State University of New York Press.

Sen, D. and Majumder, S. (2011) 'Fair trade and fair trade certification of agro-food products: Promises, pitfalls and possibilities', *Environment and Society: Advances in Research*, 2: 29–47.

Sharma, A. (2008) *Logics of empowerment: Development, gender and governance in Neoliberal India*, Minneapolis, MN: University of Minnesota Press.

TWELVE

Building alternative communities within the state: the Kurdish Movement, local municipalities and democratic autonomy

Ulrike Flader and Çetin Gürer

Introduction

Since the mid-2000s, the Kurdish Movement has put increased focus on the development of alternative communities in the Kurdistan region in Turkey as part of an effort to establish 'democratic autonomy'.[1] This new political paradigm aims at developing an egalitarian, grassroots, democratic and ecological society within the Turkish state, and as such has been suggested as a peaceful solution to the Kurdish Question. Rather than calling for secession,[2] it aims at solving the conflict as well as tackling economic exploitation, gender inequality and ecological destruction by empowering communities through participatory direct democracy. This model, the theoretical basis for which was developed by the imprisoned leader of the Kurdistan Workers' Party (PKK), Abdullah Öcalan, redefines the goal of self-determination as the deepening of democracy and abandons the previous goal of national independence. It aims at empowering society vis-à-vis the hostile centralist Turkish state. Hence, it has opened up space for the development of a range of non-violent political practices and led to a proliferation of formal and informal associations, institutions and assemblies in broader civil society, which we understand as emancipatory community development. Even though the Kurdish Movement does not officially use this term, it chooses a variety of different practices of community development to strengthen communities at a local level in tackling issues which result from discriminatory and assimilative politics of the central state. In this case, community development provides a way out of the binary between submission and secession. These enable communities to exercise more control over issues relevant to them. In this sense, they are challenging a centralist state through grassroots democratic practices within the law.

In the context of democratic autonomy, the Kurdish Movement speaks of establishing a *confederal union of communities*. The term 'community' used here is neither reducible to an ethnic group nor to territorial proximity, but is meant in a pluralistic sense that includes the representation of all sorts of social groups such as youth, women, different professions, as well as language and faith groups. At the same time, the concept of the union of communities is also a way to address the dispersion of the Kurds over four different nation states – Turkey, Iran, Iraq and Syria – as well as in the diaspora. Hence, the term 'communities' addresses the national cause, while acknowledging the diversity of the population and people's multiple identifications. Communities can intersect and overlap; they are both local and transcend borders.

Similar efforts are therefore being made within the Kurdish Movement in Europe as well as in Rojava, the Kurdistan region in Northern Syria, renowned for its resistance against ISIS (Küçük and Özselçuk, 2016). The weakening of the Syrian state has facilitated the rapid development of institutions and practices of democratic autonomy in Rojava, while in Turkey the same institutions have had to develop *despite and within* the state, and have therefore been under severe threat from the state for some years. At the same time, however, the Kurdish Movement in Turkey has managed to make use of the resources and opportunities of state structures to promote democratic autonomy, namely those of the municipal administrations. After years of emergency rule in the Kurdistan region, the Kurdish party[3] has continuously succeeded in winning an increasing number of village, town and city municipalities in the Kurdistan region since 1999.

Several scholars have noted that the municipalities have become key actors within the Kurdish Movement and have emphasised their potential to challenge state politics from their position 'in between' state and society (Scalbert-Yücel, 2009; Gambetti, 2010). Watts (2009: 10) stresses that the municipalities play a particularly important role in 'blurring the boundary between state and society'. This ambiguous position of the municipalities being part of state structures, and simultaneously opposing them, has opened up new opportunities to put democratic autonomy into practice. The municipalities are not only crucial actors in fostering community development, but also provide other actors with necessary tangible and intangible resources. They provide financial means, infrastructure, professional skills and a certain – albeit precarious – degree of protection through their institutionalisation, and they help in the generation of positive discourses regarding participatory democracy, equality and ecology (Gürer, 2015b).

Drawing on ethnographic fieldwork in Diyarbakir from 2011 to 2012 and on documentary analysis, this chapter discusses the different forms of community development that the Kurdish Movement creatively makes use of and how funding is sourced in support of these practices. Academic work on the funding of the Kurdish Movement has been strongly dominated by scholars who are preoccupied with 'proving' the connection between Kurdish Movement and organised crime, especially drug trafficking and money laundering (for example, Pek and Ekici, 2007; Roth and Sever, 2007). In contrast, this chapter provides a sociological perspective on how the practices of democratic autonomy rely on legal community development activities, which are officially funded through a combination of municipal budgets, EU grants and formal private donations.

The chapter is structured in three parts. The first section explains the historical and theoretical background of the paradigmatic shift within the Kurdish Movement from armed struggle for independence towards a movement for democratic autonomy. This is followed by a discussion of the central role of the municipalities in this model and an analysis of three exemplary forms of funding. In doing so, this chapter not only contributes crucial insights into the challenges of egalitarian community development within an oppressive state, but also reveals the limits, contradictions and dangers that lie at the heart of trying to achieve such transformation within the structures, practices and discourses of the state.

Empowering society against the state

Since the early 2000s, the previously Marxist–Leninist PKK has gone through a radical paradigmatic shift. It moved away from armed struggle for independence towards a model of democratic autonomy that questions the need for a nation state altogether. This was triggered by the collapse of the Soviet Union as a socialist role model and an increasing awareness within the Kurdish Movement that the war with the Turkish state could not be won by either side. Although internal debates had already begun in the 1990s, they only gained decisive influence after clearly manifesting themselves in Öcalan's writings and statements in court after his capture in 1999 (Gunes, 2012; Gürer, 2015b). To many people's astonishment, in his prison writings Öcalan abandoned the demand for secession and proposed peaceful mutual cohabitation of Kurds and Turks promoting the concept of democratic autonomy.[4]

In this sense, democratic autonomy was proposed as a solution to the Kurdish Question that has existed since the founding of the Turkish Republic in 1923 and which arose due to the unwillingness of the state to formally acknowledge the Kurds' existence, and due to the violent oppression of Kurds by successive Turkish governments. Drawing on a critique of the nation state and its exclusionary principles of citizenship, the model suggests decentralising state power in a threefold manner: first, by claiming a status of autonomy for the Kurdistan region in Turkey, second, by the recognition of the Kurds as an ethnic group, and third, by realising bottom-up democracy. In this sense, the model can be described as a hybrid form of cultural and territorial autonomy, on the one hand, and an attempt to establish grassroots democracy, on the other (Gürer, 2015a).

The last element of grassroots democracy derives from Öcalan's more general critique of the state. According to this, he argues that states historically brought about hierarchical relations, the domination of women and the beginning of the exploitation of nature, that is, the oppression of *society* through the *state*. Hence, for him liberation cannot come through the state (Öcalan, 2004: 124). Instead, history has been traced by the society rebelling *against* the state. In this sense, he sees the antagonism between the state and society, rather than the antagonism between classes, as the driver of social change. Drawing on this, Öcalan frames democratic autonomy as a way of 'defending society against the state' (Gürer, 2015b: 213–15). The aim is to decentralise the state by organising society and placing decision making back into the hands of the citizens in the hope of making it redundant in the future.

Instead of waiting until after independence, democratic autonomy has therefore opened the path for the Kurdish Movement towards constitutive politics, with the aim of creatively changing and shaping community life in the present by establishing a range of new practices, activities and institutions as well as influencing already existing ones. Most centrally, these activities lie in the field of tackling gender inequality and ecological destruction, and establishing an alternative communal economy as well as fostering grassroots decision-making processes. In doing so, it involves various formally registered NGOs in the field of human rights, women's rights and ecology, as well as trade unions, professional organisations, political parties and the municipalities. The model is based on setting up an independent network of village, neighbourhood and district communes and assemblies inspired by Murray Bookchin's concept of confederalism

(Bookchin, 2015). Instead of making demands for reforms to the state, this model emphasises establishing the necessary instruments and mechanisms from 'below'. Hence, what the Movement is attempting can be described as *prefigurative* (Akkaya and Jongerden, 2014). In establishing such practices in a region of over 120,000 square kilometres with three metropolitan cities and approximately 6.7 million inhabitants, the scale obviously goes beyond many other existing examples of autonomous grassroots democratic movements.

Communalism and the role of municipalities

This crucial role of the municipalities in putting this model into practice in the Kurdistan region of Turkey derives from Bookchin's concept of *libertarian municipalism*. For Bookchin (1992), the specific importance of the municipality lies, on the one hand, in the historic significance of the city as the cradle of participatory citizenship, which he wants to reinvigorate. On the other, he argues that rapid urbanisation and the destruction of nature makes the municipality – rather than the factory – 'the venue for revolution' (Biehl, 2012). The aim of libertarian municipalism is to create non-hierarchical structured communities in which citizens govern themselves through grassroots, face-to-face assemblies and live in harmony with nature. The neighbourhood assemblies would be linked in confederation with one another through recallable deputies of the assemblies who would only have administrative and coordinating functions. In this sense, the aim is not to take over city councils and make them more environmentally friendly, but rather to radically transform and democratise the city governments by tying them into a network of popular assemblies, to challenge state centralism in this way, and even municipalise economic resources (Bookchin, 1992). Nevertheless, Bookchin acknowledges that this process can begin with electing town and city councillors who can promote the cause, or with a left/green movement establishing neighbourhood assemblies. Similarly, he suggests forming civic banks to fund municipal enterprises and land purchases to foster new ecological activities. In this sense, the municipalities are envisaged as motors of this development towards a communitarian society.

In February 2008, this model of libertarian municipalism was officially written into the statute of the Kurdish party (Akkaya and Jongerden, 2014). Although still practically barred from the national parliament due to the legal requirement that parties exceed a 10% threshold to take seats, the Kurdish party had successfully won its first 37 local municipalities in 1999, which steadily rose to a total of 101 municipalities in 2014, which equate to a large part of what is generally associated with Northern Kurdistan. Carrying out a wide range of activities in the field of infrastructure, health, culture and economics, the newly elected municipalities began to play an increasing role in shaping new forms of politics in the Kurdistan region. They also used their local power to challenge the state politics of assimilation by promoting activities that emphasised the ethnic and religious diversity of the region. In exemplary manner, the municipality of Diyarbakir, for instance, implemented a policy of multilingual municipal services, which involved sign-posting in Kurdish, Armenian and Syriac as well as Turkish, fundamentally challenging the law prescribing Turkish as the only official language in Turkey (Casier, 2010). It made strong efforts for the historic city centre of Diyarbakir to become acknowledged as a world heritage site as a step in enhancing activities to reappropriate Kurdish culture and language as well as that of other minorities, which the Turkish state had systematically tried to eliminate. Among others, the municipality restored the historic city walls and the Armenian St George Church, built a place of worship for Alevis, and renamed streets, parks and squares with leftist, anti-colonial or Kurdish connotations. These activities play a vital role in 'decolonising' space (Jongerden, 2009; Gambetti, 2010). Similarly, an increasing range of events, such as art festivals, theatre, film and music events were initiated by the municipality to promote critical art production and 'revitalise' Kurdish (traditional) culture (Scalbert-Yücel, 2009). The metropolitan and district municipalities also conduct activities that are directly linked to community development, such as the inauguration of various communal laundry centres and clay ovens (*tandir*), women's centres, condolence houses, communal gardens, alternative schooling facilities and healthcare centres for mothers and children (Öztürk, 2013; Gürer, 2015b). Moreover, they carried out awareness-raising activities including courses on gender equality and violence against women as well as fostering cooperatives, especially for women. All these activities have managed to reach many who did not fully support the PKK and lowered the level of risk of engaging in politics, even though imprisonment rates remain high. Hence, they have also had an overwhelming importance in 'de-illegalising' the movement and generating a broader acceptance among the population.

Funding the development of alternative communities

The costs of such activities conducted under the auspices of the municipality are covered by the municipal budget. The municipalities pay for the salaries of personnel, the provision of facilities, maintenance costs and equipment. Municipalities are funded by standard taxes, which are collected directly, and through additional funding distributed to the municipalities by the central government according to the size of the population. The budgets of economically weak municipalities are often very strained and the municipalities run by the Kurdish party have limited powers as they are constantly hampered by the governor, a non-elected representative of the central government in every province (Tatort Kurdistan, 2012). In an effort to democratise municipal decision making, Diyarbakir even made an attempt to introduce participatory budgeting in 2009 by including various NGOs and associations in the process. However, the governor vetoed the budget several times in that year alone. For these reasons, the municipalities are forced to find other sources of funding, such as external funds including grants from the EU and other European foundations.

Assemblies, cooperatives and the top-down logic of the state

Assemblies and cooperatives are two key institutions for building democratic autonomy. Officially registered as NGOs called 'free citizens' initiatives', the number of neighbourhood assemblies has steadily increased since the mid-2000s; in Diyarbakir alone their numbers are in the hundreds, with one existing in nearly every neighbourhood. Besides this, there are a small number of 'sample' village communes, for instance in the province of Gewer (Yüksekova), which alone has 28 communes with 140–850 inhabitants per village.

The assemblies solve everyday local problems, from neighbourhood disputes to individual financial crises, and function as a mediator between the municipality and the population. Their relation to the municipalities is not formalised and they do not carry out projects themselves, nor do they receive funding from the municipalities. However, they often hold meetings in venues run by the municipalities for various activities, such as the so-called 'neighbourhood houses' and can make non-binding suggestions to the municipalities. Besides the neighbourhood assemblies, intensified efforts have been made to establish assemblies for women, youth and various faith and language groups. All these assemblies send recallable delegates to an overarching congress for the Kurdistan region in

Turkey, called the Democratic Society Congress (Demokratik Toplum Kongresi, DTK). Founded in 2007 and with a permanent office in Diyarbakir, the DTK has congregated twice a year with approximately 650 delegates.

While the municipalities' support for these assemblies is limited to the provision of infrastructure, the support of cooperatives – especially those of women – has been more integrated into municipal activities. The assumption behind these cooperatives is the hope to be able to 'tame' capitalism in a Habermasian sense, which in time will lead to its end. Cooperatives under the direction of self-ruling communes, which build on principles of self-sustainability, sharing and solidarity, are regarded as crucial to democratise decision making in the realm of production, distribution and consumption, to tackle the high unemployment and poverty in the Kurdistan region, and to challenge the profit-making logic of capitalism (DTK, 2012). In particular, they have been used as a strategy in the effort to empower women and are therefore part of more general efforts to promote gender equality. They include awareness-raising workshops on women's rights, discrimination and violence against women, consultancy, and capacity-building classes on literacy and reproductive health, which have also been funded by national and international NGOs, such as Local Agenda 21, UNICEF, Women for Women's Human Rights, Amnesty International and other European foundations (Ozsoy et al, 2007).

Diyarbakir's largest district of Bağlar – home to thousands of people displaced during the fighting in the 1990s – was chosen as a pilot area for the development of women's cooperatives in 2005. Today, in the late 2010s, Bağlar still struggles with high unemployment rates, poverty, poor housing quality and inadequate infrastructure (Ozsoy et al, 2007). In response, the local municipality helped found the Bağlar Women's Cooperative, which today produces clothing and accessories from scrap leather. All decisions are made collectively and the income is evenly shared among the women, who in this way manage to contribute to their household income (Tatort Kurdistan, 2012). Since 2005, the number of cooperatives has increased and the ranges of products diversified. While some endeavours have been unsuccessful, others have been sustained and have adapted to the challenges. Today, the municipality is even encouraging village cooperatives to sell their own non-industrial produce in the city. Specific women's neighbourhood markets and special shops have been established to address the challenging question of how to make these efforts sustainable. However, this is still an ongoing process. Municipality staff are involved in the establishment and support of cooperatives, but are not paid specifically for any work in connection with them, and these cooperatives work without microcredit loans.

While using the municipalities as mechanisms to support the implementation of the Movement's objectives has many advantages, scholars such as Watts (2009) and Gambetti (2010) have also pointed to the danger of diluting the egalitarian project by what Watts calls the 'institutionalization of resistance'. She argues that the central role given to the municipality reinforces the authority attached to 'state' institutions. She even maintains that the practices reveal a danger of a top-down style of governing 'along lines of the civilizing mission' (Watts, 2009: 11). Although we do not fully agree with this argument, it is true that as the municipalities remain institutions of the state, the ownership of its own activities remains to an important degree with the municipality instead of placing it into the hands of the local population. Such forms of governmentality are not easily overcome. It bears the danger of losing the most central element of democratic autonomy: what Bookchin (1992) called the 'face-to-face-ness' of participatory democracy.

Working within the given structures of the state to realise the Movement's (temporary) goals also means tactically using its given rhetoric, discourses and logics, and constant reflection on these issues is therefore necessary to impede these rationalities from unwittingly shaping and dominating the actual practices. Many of the points that Gambetti (2010) discusses, for instance the lack of vision for certain aspects of sustainability, were discussed very openly and intensely in recent years. However, as democratic autonomy is a prefigurative endeavour, meaning that unfinished, imperfect alternative structures and practices are created in non-ideal circumstances, such issues have to be continuously readdressed.

Developing an eco-society on EU grants

In order to deal with budgetary constraints imposed by the state, external funding from international bodies has become important, especially for large-scale activities. Among such international funding bodies are the European Union itself and various European foundations and embassies. Once again, the municipalities provide the necessary institutional support for accessing such funds. In this way, various municipal activities regarding culture and diversity, ecology and sustainability, as well as violence against women, are made possible despite being at odds with the interests of the central government, precisely because they meet funding criteria of the EU.

One project funded through an EU grant was the *Sümerpark Commons*, which was constructed as a regeneration project of a state-owned carpet factory shut down in 1998. The 80,000 square metre area is located in the city centre and is home to a large social centre, a park, a solar-energy house, library and exhibition hall. After its opening in 2005, *Sümerpark* quickly became a lively centre offering activities, such as vocational courses for youth, afterschool childcare, a centre for people with disabilities, and a venue for conferences and workshops.

Although tensions between the Kurdistan region and the central government were comparatively low at the time, the central government tried to impede the project by refusing financial support and even filing several legal complaints. While the municipality successfully applied for a €7 million EU grant, it had to found a municipality-owned 'subsidiary company' in construction and pipe production whose profits were to cover the outstanding sum (Kuyucu and Danış, 2018). Without such tactical manoeuvring, carrying out the project would have been impossible.

Despite this success, international funding remains a precarious source. As Kuyucu and Danış (2018) also point out, in 2009 the central government established a new EU ministry to channel funds in their effort to centralise the distribution of EU monies. This has made it more difficult for the municipalities to directly apply for grants themselves. Furthermore, various EU foundations have regularly been accused of supporting terrorism by state officials and mainstream media for funding projects in the Kurdistan region.

On the other hand, similar to the difficulties in using the institutional means of the municipalities, these EU funds also bear the danger of imposing their discursive 'frames', as Watts (2009) argues, which subtly limit the activities of the Movement. This is exemplified by the EU-funded municipal 'cultural heritage' project (Scalbert-Yücel, 2009), in which Kurdish *dengbêj* singers are represented as 'innocent relics' and part of the 'Anatolian mosaic', a discourse promoted by the government in the 2000s. In the light of the Kurdish conflict, the project – which was also supported by the Turkish Ministry of Culture and Tourism – makes an important contribution to the recognition of long-denied Kurdish culture, but it makes use of and thereby reproduces a depoliticised understanding of multiculturalism and EU discourses on heritage, which stand in stark contrast to the egalitarian concept of society advanced by the Kurdish Movement.

Networking solidarity through private donations

The last form of funding we discuss here are private donations, which have been used to finance the association for the struggle against poverty, Sarmaşık. Founded in 2006 under the presidency of then-mayor of Diyarbakir, Osman Baydemir, Sarmaşık aimed at supporting those heavily affected by poverty, who are mostly victims of the notorious village evacuations that occurred in the 1990s. The association was specifically founded as a cross-party endeavour, including local members of the governing Justice and Development Party (AKP), the Kemalist Republican People's Party (CHP) and the Kurdish party as well as business people, representatives of trade unions and professional organisations. This collaboration was an attempt to break the existing logic of political patronage in the charity 'sector', through which large parties, such as the AKP, secure their votes by distributing basic foods or heating materials to the poor (Sarmaşık Derneği, 2012). Despite these efforts, Sarmaşık came under scrutiny by state institutions and was finally shut down in November 2016, along with hundreds of other organisations, through one of the emergency decrees frequently issued to crack down on all opposition since the attempted coup in June 2016 (Bozarslan, 2016).

Prior to its closure, Sarmaşık was supporting around 5,000 families through its food bank, reaching a total of 30,000 people in need. It had over 7,000 donors who made regular contributions and relied heavily on volunteers. The aid Sarmaşık provided was obviously more professionalised than previously existing informal neighbourhood solidarity; the financial weight was shared by more people, while distribution itself had become centralised and less face-to-face than before. Insisting on solving the poverty crises locally, the organisation deliberately rejected grants by international foundations. Instead of regarding solidarity as an act of pity or charity, the association saw poverty aid as a claimable *right* and itself a form of solidary network or even – as the general secretary expressed it – as a city-commune (Özgür Gündem, 2015).

Despite the essential service Sarmaşık provided to families suffering from poverty, its work was constantly hampered by the governor of the city, whether through blocking the association's accounts, ordering extra monitoring, issuing fines or confiscating their funds. This was followed by legal investigations in 2011 in the context of the so-called 'KCK trial',[5] a mass-trial against hundreds of people including mayors, municipality staff, activists and members of the press. Hence, with its closure, the government seems to have finally chosen to finish off what the judiciary had not been able to accomplish: the eradication of all community organisations independent of the state.

Conclusions and the crackdown on alternative communities

The discussion of these three different types of community development and their funding has revealed how the Kurdish Movement has creatively tried to find ways to handle the challenges it faces. It has shown the crucial position of the municipality within the state in enabling the various activities, providing essential infrastructure, financial support and the necessary institutional status to apply for external funding. The examples, however, have also highlighted that trying to establish such egalitarian forms of community development within the given conditions, carries the danger of these activities being corrupted by the rationalities and discourses that they are tactically working with but which are different from those of the Movement. The tools and resources associated with government practices have left their imprint on the activities carried out under the auspices of the municipalities. Ceaseless critical reflection on such tendencies is necessary. Despite the intention to enhance direct democracy, the important role assigned to the municipalities also tends to reinstate the top-down logic of state structures. Many international funding bodies also impose their specific agendas, which can contradict the goals set out in democratic autonomy. Nevertheless, the municipalities have clearly managed to push the boundaries of institutional politics by integrating norms and practices of the Movement into municipal policies and have thereby challenged the state on its own terrain.

Currently, of much greater danger to the whole endeavour has been the increasing crackdown on the municipalities which began with thousands of legal investigations, gaining speed with the KCK trials in 2009. This culminated in the fundamental destruction of physical and cultural life and of the political structures of the Kurdish communities after the AKP lost its majority in the national elections in June 2015. Whole districts have been erased during months-long 24-hour curfews declared in 35 districts of nine towns and cities. One million people were forced to leave their homes, more than 338 civilians were killed, 30 of them over 60 years old, 78 of them under 18 (HRFT, 2016). By March 2017, the democratically elected co-mayors of 83 municipalities had been ousted from power and replaced with non-elected state 'trustees', as they are euphemistically called. Thousands of municipal employees have been fired and community organisations shut down either by emergency decree or by the decision of the trustee. By taking over the local administrations and shutting down the community organisations, this crackdown has radically destroyed the achievements in respect to democratic autonomy.

Unfortunately, the focus on community development through the municipalities and legally registered NGOs has now left the organisational structures of the Movement severely weakened. It has shown that such tactics of working within established structures require a minimum of democracy and some form of legally acknowledged status of the new structures and practices. Hence, the violent reaction of the state leads to the conclusion that even more autonomous structures of community development, detached from the municipal activities, may have been more immune to the state's crackdown.

Notes

1. We use the term Kurdish Movement in a broad sense, ranging from the Kurdistan Workers' Party (PKK), political parties promoting the rights of Kurds, and various associations in the field of culture, language, media, ecology and religion. By 'Kurdistan region', we are referring to the region predominantly inhabited by Kurds, often euphemistically termed the 'South-East'.
2. For a concise introduction, see Gunes and Zeydanlıoğlu, 2014.
3. Due to the numerous party closures, the Kurdish parties had to regularly reform under other names, but with similar statutes. We therefore refer to these successive parties as the 'Kurdish party'.
4. Öcalan's defence writings have been published in numerous books. Together with democratic autonomy, he has also developed the concepts of democratic republic and democratic nation. He has attempted to reappropriate these concepts by ridding them of the homogeneity and structural inequality they entail, and by reinventing them in a way that opens the ground for radical social change.
5. KCK stands for *Koma Civaken Kurdistan*, the Union of Communities of Kurdistan, the name given to the overall confederal union of communities mentioned in this chapter. The Turkish government and state prosecutors, however, regard KCK as just another name of the PKK, and therefore used the mass trials as an attempt to eradicate all legal activities for democratic autonomy.

References

Akkaya, A.H. and Jongerden, J. (2014) 'Conferderalism and autonomy in Turkey: The Kurdistan Workers' Party and the reinvention of democracy', in C. Gunes and W. Zeydanlıoğlu (eds) *The Kurdish Question in Turkey: New perspectives on violence, representation and reconciliation*, New York: Routledge, pp 186–204.

Biehl, J. (2012) 'Bookchin, Öcalan, and the dialectics of democracy', *New Compass*, 16 February, http://new-compass.net/articles/bookchin-öcalan-and-dialectics-democracy.

Bookchin, M. (1992) 'Libertarian municipalism: An overview', *Society and Nature*, 1(1): 93–104.

Bookchin, M. (2015) *The next revolution: Popular assemblies and the promise of direct democracy*, London: Verso.

Bozarslan, M. (2016) 'Turkey's emergency rule hits thousands of destitute Kurds', *Al Monitor*, 6 December, https://web.archive.org/web/20161207160944/http://www.al-monitor.com/pulse/originals/2016/12/turkey-emergency-rule-hits-thousands-destitute-kurds.html.

Casier, M. (2010) 'Turkey's Kurds and the quest for recognition: Transnational politics and the EU–Turkey accession negotiations', *Ethnicities*, 10(1): 3–25.

DTK (2012) *Kürt sorunun çözümü için Demokratik Özerklik*, Diyarbakir: Aram Yay.

Gambetti, Z. (2010) 'Decolonizing Diyarbakır: Culture, identity and the struggle to appropriate urban space.', in K.A. Ali, and M. Rieker (eds) *Comparing cities: The Middle East and South Asia*, Oxford: Oxford University Press, pp 95–127.

Gunes, C. (2012) *The Kurdish national movement in Turkey: From protest to resistance*, New York: Routledge.

Gunes, C. and Zeydanlıoğlu, W. (2014) 'Introduction: Turkey and the Kurds', in C. Gunes and W. Zeydanlıoğlu (eds) *The Kurdish Question in Turkey: New perspectives on violence, representation and reconciliation*, New York: Routledge, pp 1–20.

Gürer, Ç. (2015a) 'Aktörün Perspektifinden Demokratik Özerkliğe Bakmak: Kürt Siyasal Hareketinin Demokratik Özerklik Yaklaşımı', *Mülkiye Dergisi*, 39(1): 57–91.

Gürer, Ç. (2015b) *Demokratik Özerklik: Bir yurttaşlık heterotopyası*, Ankara: Notabene.

HRFT (2016) *Curfews between August 16, 2015 – August 16, 2016 and civilians who lost their lives*, *Türkiye İnsan Hakları Vakfı*, 21 August, http://en.tihv.org.tr/curfews-between-august-16-2015-august-16-2016-and-civilians-who-lost-their-lives/.

Jongerden, J. (2009) 'Crafting space, making people: The spatial design of nation in modern Turkey', *European Journal of Turkish Studies*, 10, https://journals.openedition.org/ejts/4014.

Küçük, B. and Özselçuk, C. (2016) 'The Rojava experience: Possibilities and challenges of building a democratic life', *The South Atlantic Quarterly*, 115(1): 184–96.

Kuyucu, T. and Danış, D. (2018) 'Politics of urban regeneration in Turkey: Possibilities and limits of municipal regeneration initiatives in a highly centralized country', *Urban Geography*, https://doi.org/1 0.1080/02723638.2018.1440125 ahead of print.

Öcalan, A. (2004) *Bir halkı savunmak*, Istanbul: Çetin Yayın.

Özgür Gündem (2015) 'Sarmaşık bir kent komünüdür', *Özgür Gündem*, 14 January.

Ozsoy, H., Coşkun, H. and Yasak, Ö. (2007) *Social inclusion at the margins of the city: Diyarbakir public laundries and education support house*, Inclusive Cities Observatory, www.uclg-cisdp.org/sites/default/files/Diyarbakir_2010_en_final.pdf.

Öztürk, D.C. (2013) 'Socio-spatial practices of the pro-Kurdish municipalities: The case of Diyarbakir', MA thesis, Middle East Technical University: Ankara.

Pek, A. and Ekici, B. (2007) 'Narcoterrorism in Turkey: The financing of PKK-KONGRA GEL from illicit drug business', in O. Nikbay and S. Hancerli (eds) *Understanding and responding to the terrorism phenomenon: A multi-dimensional perspective*, NATO Science for Peace and Security Series Vol. 21, Amsterdam: IOS Press, pp 140–52.

Roth, M.P. and Sever, M. (2007) 'The Kurdish Workers Party (PKK) as criminal syndicate: Funding terrorism through organized crime: A case study', *Studies in Conflict & Terrorism*, 30(10): 901–20.

Sarmaşık Derneği (2012) *Sarmaşık yoksulluk mücadele ve sürdürülebilir kalkınma derneği tanıtım broşür*, Diyarbakir: Sarmaşık Derneği.

Scalbert-Yücel, C. (2009) 'The invention of a tradition: Diyarbakır's Dengbêj Project', *European Journal of Turkish Studies*, 10, https://journals.openedition.org/ejts/4055.

Tatort Kurdistan (2012) *Demokratische Autonomie in Nordkurdistan. Rätebewegung, Geschlechterbefreiung und Ökologie in der Praxis. Eine Erkundungsreise in den Südosten der Türkei*, Neuss: Mesopotamien Verlag.

Watts, N.F. (2009) 'Re-considering state-society dynamics in Turkey's Kurdish southeast', *European Journal of Turkish Studies*, 10, https://journals.openedition.org/ejts/4196.1.

Index

References to figures and tables are in *italics*